T0144512

Police Reserves and Volunteers

Enhancing Organizational Effectiveness and Public Trust

Police Reserves and Volunteers

Enhancing Organizational Effectiveness and Public Trust

Edited by
James F. Albrecht

CRC Press
Taylor & Francis Group
Boca Raton London New York

CRC Press is an imprint of the
Taylor & Francis Group, an **informa** business

CRC Press
Taylor & Francis Group
6000 Broken Sound Parkway NW, Suite 300
Boca Raton, FL 33487-2742

First issued in paperback 2019

© 2017 by Taylor & Francis Group, LLC
CRC Press is an imprint of Taylor & Francis Group, an Informa business

No claim to original U.S. Government works

ISBN-13: 978-1-4987-6453-7 (hbk)
ISBN-13: 978-0-367-47266-5 (pbk)

This book contains information obtained from authentic and highly regarded sources. Reasonable efforts have been made to publish reliable data and information, but the author and publisher cannot assume responsibility for the validity of all materials or the consequences of their use. The authors and publishers have attempted to trace the copyright holders of all material reproduced in this publication and apologize to copyright holders if permission to publish in this form has not been obtained. If any copyright material has not been acknowledged please write and let us know so we may rectify in any future reprint.

Except as permitted under U.S. Copyright Law, no part of this book may be reprinted, reproduced, transmitted, or utilized in any form by any electronic, mechanical, or other means, now known or hereafter invented, including photocopying, microfilming, and recording, or in any information storage or retrieval system, without written permission from the publishers.

For permission to photocopy or use material electronically from this work, please access www.copyright .com (http://www.copyright.com/) or contact the Copyright Clearance Center, Inc. (CCC), 222 Rosewood Drive, Danvers, MA 01923, 978-750-8400. CCC is a not-for-profit organization that provides licenses and registration for a variety of users. For organizations that have been granted a photocopy license by the CCC, a separate system of payment has been arranged.

Trademark Notice: Product or corporate names may be trademarks or registered trademarks, and are used only for identification and explanation without intent to infringe.

Library of Congress Cataloging-in-Publication Data

Names: Albrecht, James F., editor.
Title: Police reserves and volunteers : enhancing organizational
effectiveness and public trust / edited by James F. Albrecht.
Description: 1 Edition. | Boca Raton : CRC Press, [2017] | Includes bibliographical
references and index.
Identifiers: LCCN 2016049575| ISBN 9781498764537 (hardback : alk. paper) |
ISBN 9781315367460 (ebook)
Subjects: LCSH: Volunteer workers in law enforcement. | Police administration. |
Auxiliary police.
Classification: LCC HV7935 .P666 2017 | DDC 363.2/2--dc23
LC record available at https://lccn.loc.gov/2016049575

Visit the Taylor & Francis Web site at
http://www.taylorandfrancis.com

and the CRC Press Web site at
http://www.crcpress.com

This book is dedicated to those community members who support the quest for public safety and security by unselfishly volunteering for their local police department.

"Many are called, but few are chosen…

… and even fewer make this sacrifice for the good of their community

… and for humanity at large."

And may those men and women who have made the ultimate sacrifice while pursuing this very special calling rest in peace.

"Blessed are the peacemakers: for they shall be called the children of God."

Matthew 5:9, King James Bible

Contents

Section III

POLICE VOLUNTEER PROGRAMS: GLOBAL PERSPECTIVES

Section IV

POLICE VOLUNTEERS AND OTHER DEPLOYMENT OPTIONS

Section V

PERSONAL REFLECTION AND INSIGHT

Section VI

USING VOLUNTEERS IN OTHER GOVERNMENT ORGANIZATIONS

Preface

Nearly 200 years ago, Sir Robert Peel famously postulated that

> The police are the public and the public are the police; the police being only members of the public who are paid to give full time attention to duties which are incumbent on every citizen in the interests of community welfare and existence.

He made his statement at a time when formal, paid, full-time police were first being established in metropolitan London. Prior to that, of course, what we now call policing was totally the responsibility of volunteers, part-timers, private detectives, and various other informal and ad hoc arrangements.

Historically, then, the concept of volunteer police is nothing new, whether in England, the United States, or elsewhere. But as police institutions worldwide have become more formalized, bureaucratized, specialized, and professionalized over the last century, there has been some tendency to squeeze out amateurs and volunteers. Thus the great value of this book: It reminds us of roles that ordinary citizens can play, of contributions that they can make to public safety, and it provides a wide array of examples from all over the globe.

My take on volunteers is personal. Way back in the 1980s, when I became police chief in the small town of St. Michaels, Maryland (United States), I inherited a rather loosely organized police department—nothing unusual in that. The agency's police officers were capable and well trained, but there was little administrative infrastructure. As a new chief, I had big plans to fix that in short order, but I also had to investigate crimes, look for drunk drivers, direct traffic—I worked shifts and had all the same operational duties as the other officers in the department, which left little extra time for administration. That is when I ran across Bob Seymour.

Mr. Seymour was a retired telephone company engineer. He agreed to come down to the police station a couple days a week to do odd jobs. He was nothing if not organized. First, he tackled the property and evidence room (honestly, it was just a big closet). It took a few months, but he got it all inventoried; figured out what could be returned to owners, sold, or destroyed; and put what was left back in a way that we could actually find it. Similarly, he inventoried all our own department equipment and other property. Then he tackled our outdated directory of contact persons for businesses and properties. People really hate it when you call them at 3:00 a.m. to report that their store's window is broken only to find out they sold the store three years earlier.

None of this may sound very exciting or significant, but without Bob Seymour's volunteerism, it would not have gotten done. We did not have any paid clerical or administrative staff, and we were too busy being police to do these jobs or at least that is how we thought. Moreover, the volunteer work that Bob did (and continued to do for several years) actually provided a service to the town and its residents. Property crime victims and business owners started getting better service from their police department, and it was due to Bob's work—not anything that we full-time police officers were doing.

As Jimmy Albrecht points out in his introductory chapter, there are some particularly important reasons to support and promote policing volunteers today. Three seem especially relevant to me: (1) In the age of tight budgets and "doing more with less," cost-free employees are hard to argue against; (2) in an era in which police departments are challenged to embrace and engage their communities more tightly, bringing a diverse throng of volunteers into the organization makes good sense; and (3) at a time when technology changes so fast, some volunteers can offer highly specialized skills and expertise that police staff just do not have. Or maybe, like Bob Seymour, they are just more focused and organized than the scatterbrained police chief who really needed his help.

Gary Cordner

Acknowledgments

Many people have influenced me across my life from my childhood, through my adolescence, and throughout my dual careers as police professional and academic. First and foremost is my family. My parents laid the foundation and taught me the need for a comprehensive education to better prepare for the challenges that would lie ahead. And the clearest sacrifices have been made by my family, particularly my children, Jimmy and Kristiana, who would rather play with me at the park than see me working at my computer.

Of course, success in life is never guaranteed, and I have been fortunate to have received the support and kindness of many friends, mentors, and colleagues that continue to point me in the right direction. I know that I will fail to name them all, but here is a partial list of those who have positively impacted my life and my career:

Dr. Richard Ward (RIP)
Dr. Robert Trojanowicz (RIP)
Dr. James O'Keefe
Dr. David Bailey
Dr. Gary Cordner
Dr. William Tafoya
Dr. Maria Tcherni
Dr. Hakan Can
Dr. Francis G. Olive III
Dr. Mario Gaboury
Ms. Maureen Aceto
NYPD Inspector/Professor Arthur Storch
NYPD Police Commissioner William J. Bratton
NYPD Chief James McShane
NYPD Chief/Dr. Theresa C. Tobin
NYPD Captain Kenneth Kobetitsch
NYPD Auxiliary Police Lieutenant Eric Mazzella
NYPD Sergeant Michael Rosenbluth
NYPD Sergeant/Dr. James Sullivan
NYPD Sergeant Daniel Farrell
NYPD Auxiliary Police Sergeant Brooke Webster
NYPD Detective Sam Difiglia
NYPD Detective Ben Pistilli

Dr. Harold Becker (RIP)
Dr. Joseph Ryan
Dr. Maria "Maki" Haberfeld
Dr. Ken Peak
Dr. Dilip Das
Dr. Morris Rossabi
Dr. David Lambert
Dr. Hasan Arslan
Dr. William Norton
Ms. Iraida Garcia
Ms. Ev Fedotova

NYPD Detective Joseph Fodera
NYPD Police Officer Michael Sanchez
Orange County (Florida) Sheriff's Office Reserve Chief/Dr. Ross Wolf
Delta (British Columbia, Canada) Police Sergeant/Dr. Rick Parent
German Police Chief Marcus Puerschel
German Police Commander Horst Bichl
Turkish Police Commander Cihan Akyildiz
Hungarian Police Chief Imre Pallagi
Hungarian Border Patrol Supervisor Miklos Pek
French Police Chief Daniel Condaminas
Montreal Transit Police Officer Jean-Guy Sabourin
Kosovo Police Chief Rrahman Sylejmani

I want to express my gratitude to them and others for guiding me when bumps were on the road and when questions arose as to which path to take, especially when the "weather" was not cooperating.

Editor

James F. Albrecht, PhD, is presently an assistant professor in the Department of Criminal Justice and Homeland Security at Pace University in New York. Dr. Albrecht received a prestigious Fulbright Fellowship in 1998 and worked as a professor at the National Police College of Finland, and is considered an authority in police use of force, community/zero tolerance policing initiatives, police response to terrorism, emergency incident planning and management, democratic policing, law enforcement leadership practices, corruption control, and international criminal justice and law enforcement issues. Dr. Albrecht has lectured at police facilities and universities in China, Taiwan, Russia, Germany, Austria, Sweden, Norway, Estonia, Finland, Italy, Turkey, Canada, Dubai, Kosovo, Macedonia, Malta, the Ukraine, Trinidad & Tobago, the United Kingdom, and throughout the United States, and has served as a consultant to the United Nations, the U.S. Department of Homeland Security, the International Association of Chiefs of Police, and the National Institute of Justice on terrorism and policing matters.

Dr. Albrecht earned bachelor's degrees in biology and German language and separate master's degrees in criminal justice, human physiology, and history. He earned a PhD in criminal justice from the University of New Haven in 2016. Dr. Albrecht is the recipient of a 2013 Embassy Policy Specialist Fellowship (USDOS/IREX) and was tasked with conducting research and making recommendations to improve law enforcement effectiveness and legitimacy in the Ukraine.

Dr. Albrecht served in the European Union Rule of Law Mission (EULEX) in Kosovo (former Yugoslavia) as the police chief of the EULEX Police Executive Department in charge of criminal investigations and tasked with coordinating international law enforcement cooperation and intelligence analysis from 2008 through 2010. He is also a 20-year veteran of the NYPD, and retired as the commanding officer of NYPD Transit Bureau District 20, responsible for the supervision and deployment of more than 300 police officers tasked with the prevention of crime and terrorism in the subway and Rapid Transit System in the borough of Queens, New York City. Dr. Albrecht was a first responder and incident command staff member at the September 11, 2001 terrorist attack on the World Trade Center and the incident commander at the November 12, 2001 commercial airliner accident in Queens, NYC. Dr. Albrecht has extensive law enforcement experience in the

NYPD, having served as an auxiliary police officer, patrol officer, community policing beat officer, police academy criminal law instructor, firearms investigator, sergeant patrol supervisor, press information officer, community policing unit commander, supervisory research analyst for the police commissioner, lieutenant platoon commander, special operations lieutenant, lieutenant detective commander of internal civil rights violation investigations, executive officer (deputy precinct commander), and duty captain (designated critical and emergency incident commander).

Dr. Albrecht is the editor and coauthor of two other books: *Effective Crime Reduction Strategies: International Perspectives* (CRC Press, 2011) and *Policing Major Events: Perspective from Across the World* (CRC Press, 2014), and has many published works dealing with law enforcement, community policing, legal history, corruption control, crime reduction strategies, justice-related gender issues, criminology, and international terrorism/counterterrorism.

Contributors

Christiaan Bezuidenhout, PhD, is a professor in the Department of Social Work and Criminology at the University of Pretoria in South Africa. He teaches psycho-criminology, criminal justice, and contemporary criminology on the undergraduate and postgraduate levels. Research methodology and ethics, psycho-criminology, and policing issues, as well as youth misbehavior are some of his research foci. During his academic career, Dr. Bezuidenhout has published numerous scientific articles in peer-reviewed journals and many chapters in books. He has also acted as editor-in-chief for various scholarly books. He is the program coordinator of the Criminology Honors Degree Program at the University of Pretoria. He has participated in national and international conferences and has been actively involved in various community projects focusing on crime prevention and has assisted the South African government in the development of different crime prevention initiatives. Dr. Bezuidenhout also does court work as an expert witness. He is currently the president of the Criminological and Victimological Society of South Africa (CRIMSA). He earned the following degrees: BA (criminology), BA Honors (criminology), MA (criminology), PhD (criminology), and also earned an MSc degree in criminology and criminal justice from the University of Oxford.

Mkay Bonner, PhD, is a licensed industrial organizational psychologist with expertise in police and public safety psychology, including preemployment, fitness-for-duty, and officer-involved shooting evaluations. Dr. Bonner is a police academy instructor and crisis intervention team (CIT) coordinator. Dr. Bonner is an associate professor in criminal justice at the University of Louisiana at Monroe, covering many psychology courses.

April Christman, MSW, earned her bachelor's of social work from Virginia Wesleyan College and her master's of social work from Smith College. She is currently employed in the mental health field.

George W. Cook, MBE, joined the Southend-on-Sea Borough Constabulary as a volunteer special constable in December 1963. He has been promoted through the ranks of the Volunteer Police Service, serving in many operational and management roles, achieving the rank of chief officer in 2004.

He remained in that post until retirement in 2010 after 47 years of service. His main achievement was founding and becoming the first chair of the Association of Special Constabulary Chief Officers (ASCCO). He was awarded an MBE (Member of the Most Excellent Order of the British Empire) by Queen Elizabeth for services in volunteer policing and fundraising for numerous charities.

Gary Cordner, PhD, is chief research advisor with the National Institute of Justice, the research arm of the U.S. Department of Justice, working on agency-based police research, and is also a senior police advisor for the International Criminal Investigative Training Assistance Program (ICITAP) (U.S. Department of Justice [USDOJ]) working on police reform in the Ukraine. Additionally, he is Professor Emeritus at Kutztown University and Foundation Professor Emeritus at Eastern Kentucky University, where he served as dean of the College of Justice and Safety. Dr. Cordner recently completed nine years as a commissioner with the Commission on Accreditation for Law Enforcement Agencies (CALEA) and served as co-primary investigator on the National Police Research Platform. He worked as a police officer and police chief in Maryland and earned a PhD from Michigan State University.

Annette Crisp, PhD, having originally come from a policing background, developed the first academic police training and Police Community Service Officer (PCSO) programs in Leicestershire, England, after having worked on the quality assurance audit of the British government's Initial Police Learning and Development Program (IPLDP) for police officers. She has recently earned a PhD, which examined the role of the PCSO as an exemplar of complex systems within community policing processes. Dr. Crisp is currently the program leader for academic programs in criminology and criminal justice at De Montfort University in Leicester, England.

Adam Dobrin, PhD, earned a bachelor's degree from the College of William and Mary in Virginia and both his master's and doctorate in criminology from the University of Maryland. He is an associate professor in the School of Criminology and Criminal Justice at Florida Atlantic University and volunteers as a reserve deputy in his local county sheriff's office.

Benjamin Dobrin, MSW, PhD, earned a bachelor's degree from the College of William and Mary in Virginia, his master's of social work from the University of Pennsylvania, and a PhD from the University of South Florida, College of Public Health. He is chair and Batten Professor of social work at Virginia Wesleyan College. He volunteers as an auxiliary police officer in his city's police department and has appointments to the marine patrol unit as well as the dive team.

Robert D. Hanser is the coordinator for the Criminal Justice Program at the University of Louisiana at Monroe. He is also the director of the Institute of Law Enforcement, established in 1991, which offers in-service training to police and related agencies throughout Louisiana, Arkansas, and Mississippi. Hanser was also a five-year administrator at the North Delta Regional Training Academy, a regional academy responsible for providing cadet-level training to police and correctional officers throughout northeastern Louisiana.

Desmond Tan Kay Heng has been a member of the Volunteer Special Constabulary (VSC) in the Singapore Police Force (SPF) for more than 10 years. Heng currently holds the rank of inspector of police and is the head of the volunteer unit in the Bukit Timah Neighborhood Police Center in the Tanglin Division. He has plenty of practical experience and has been performing police duties, including uniformed patrol duties as well as plainclothes operations. He has been part of the deployments in Singapore for major events, including the Singapore Youth Olympic Games, SEA Games, Singapore F1 night race, and the Singapore National Day Parade celebration. In his regular career, Heng is the regional head of Services Alliances for the Asian-Pacific region for a large IT multinational corporation.

Ron Hyman began his volunteer law enforcement career in 1975, retiring from the Portsmouth Police Department (Virginia) as auxiliary division commander in August 2016, and is currently an auxiliary captain with the Portsmouth Sheriff's Office. Captain Hyman is a retired U.S. Navy commander and a retired manager with Verizon. He serves on the board of directors with an international organization, the Volunteer Law Enforcement Officer Alliance (VLEOA).

Charles R. Jennings, PhD, is associate professor of Security, Fire, and Emergency Management and the director of the Christian Regenhard Center for Emergency Response Studies (RaCERS) at John Jay College of Criminal Justice of the City University of New York. He has worked in various capacities in fire and emergency services, including serving as deputy commissioner of public safety for the City of White Plains, New York. He is a chief fire officer designee from the Center for Public Safety Excellence and a Fellow of the Institution of Fire Engineers.

Mark S. Johnson is a 28-year veteran law enforcement officer. He has experience in patrol, narcotics enforcement, SWAT training, criminal investigations, patrol supervision, emergency operations and special event supervision, and crisis intervention team (CIT) training. Johnson retired in 2016 from a municipal police agency to accept an assistant director of police position at the University of Louisiana at Monroe. He earned an MA in criminal justice and is an adjunct professor at the University of Louisiana at Monroe.

Carol Borland Jones, PhD, has a background in tourism, and her husband's role as a former UK reserve police officer (special constable) for many years provided the foundation for her PhD and her interest in volunteer policing. She is a former consultant to Victim Support Mauritius and has presented in South Africa and Florida as well as at a number of conferences in the United Kingdom. She has undertaken research throughout her career for the Home Office and the Office of the Police and Crime Commissioner for the Gloucestershire Constabulary. She was, until July 2016, a senior lecturer (associate professor) of criminology in England before becoming an associate of the Institute of Public Safety, Crime and Justice researching special constables and police support volunteers.

Pal Kardos is president of the Budapest Auxiliary Police Federation. He graduated from the National University of Public Service, Budapest, Hungary. Kardos is very active in the international auxiliary police arena.

Wayne Koo has been with the Singapore Police Force Volunteer Special Constabulary (VSC) for over 18 years. He is currently commanding the volunteer unit in the Traffic Police Department and holds the rank of superintendent of police. Koo has also held various appointments ranging from head of the VSC of the Criminal Investigation Department and head of the VSC of the Tanglin Division. He has wide experience in patrol assignments, holding senior officer appointments in the Bedok Police Division and Airport Police Department, as well as the VSC headquarters. Koo is a Chartered Accountant of Singapore and a Certified Public Accountant.

Charles A. Lieberman, PhD, has more than 25 years of experience in the field of criminal justice, both as a practitioner and an academic. He spent nearly two decades with the NYPD, conducting investigations on almost every criminal offense and conducted research, designed training programs, and provided training of law enforcement personnel of various ranks and assignments. Dr. Lieberman earned a PhD in criminal justice, conducting research on policing and terrorism. He has coauthored numerous books, book chapters, and journal articles and has presented his research at both national and international conferences.

Melissa M. Miele, MA, earned her degree in forensic mental health counseling at John Jay College of Criminal Justice in New York. She is currently working as a correctional counselor in a women's correctional center in

Massachusetts providing counseling services to inmates struggling with addiction and mental illness. Miele has also worked as a therapist in a domestic violence clinic in New York City, providing treatment to court-ordered male domestic violence and stalking offenders.

Nathan R. Moran, PhD, is Senior Distinguished Professor of criminal justice and chairman of the Criminal Justice Department at Midwestern State University in Wichita Falls, Texas. Dr. Moran's research interests and areas of expertise are in comparative and international criminal justice, international crime, terrorism, organized crime, and research design.

Colleen Morin, JD, earned a juris doctorate from Gonzaga University and is an instructor in the Department of Criminal Justice at the University of Nevada, Reno.

Robert Morin, JD, PhD, earned a juris doctorate from Gonzaga University and a PhD in political science from the University of Nevada, Reno, and is a professor of political science at Western Nevada College.

Francis G. Olive III, PhD, is an assistant professor at Worcester State University in Massachusetts. He has a bachelor's degree in social work from Elms College, a master's degree in social work from Fordham University, and a PhD in criminal justice with a specialization in corrections from the University of New Haven. Dr. Olive previously worked as a correctional officer and then correctional counselor/correctional officer for the Hampden County Sheriff's Department in Massachusetts from 2007 through 2011.

Rick Parent, PhD, is an associate professor in the School of Criminology at Simon Fraser University. He completed 30 years of service as a police officer in the Vancouver area. His research and expertise focuses on the police use of lethal force, including the phenomena of suicide by cop. He was also a reserve constable with the Delta Police Department.

Steven Sheffer has been a volunteer in law enforcement since December 1982, when he joined the Florida Highway Patrol Auxiliary. Sheffer was promoted as the organization's director in April 2000. He is actively involved in recruitment, legislative, and technology issues in volunteer law enforcement programs and is credited with developing effective systems and processes to streamline administrative operations. Sheffer has worked in health care for more than 30 years, starting his career as a paramedic. He is a graduate of Jacksonville University (Florida), holding a master's degree in business administration with a concentration in management.

Marc Spigel began his interest in law enforcement as a Newton Police Explorer in 1972. He first volunteered as an auxiliary officer for the Newton (Massachusetts) Police in 1979 and later became a Framingham Police Auxiliary officer in 1985. With the Framingham Auxiliary Police, he was promoted to sergeant in 1989, lieutenant in 1993 and took command of the unit as captain in 1998. Spigel joined the Wellfleet Police Department in 2015 as a seasonal officer. He was a cofounder of the Volunteer Law Enforcement Officer Alliance in 2009 and the Massachusetts Volunteer Law Enforcement Officer Association in 2011, and is a member of the Massachusetts Citizen Corps Council. Spigel was selected in 2011 by the International Association of Chiefs of Police to be the state advocate for Massachusetts police volunteers. He earned a bachelor's degree in business administration from the University of Massachusetts Amherst in 1979. He earned a Certified Public Accountant designation in 1982 and works as a financial consultant for a large regional public accounting firm.

Beata Szoke earned an MA degree in psychology, specializing in the field of health and clinical psychology. She has worked as a criminal psychologist intern at the Public Prosecutor's Office in the 2nd and 3rd Districts of Budapest. Szoke is currently a member of the Organizational and Work Psychology Division of the Psychology Department of the Hungarian Defense Forces Defense Health Institute.

Theresa C. Tobin, PhD, is a 33-year veteran of the NYPD and currently holds the position of deputy chief. She earned a PhD and MA in criminal justice from the State University of New York at Albany, an MSW from Fordham University, and is a graduate of the FBI National Academy, the Police Management Institute at Columbia University's Graduate School of Business, and Harvard University's John F. Kennedy School of Government's Senior Executives in State and Local Government Program. She is an adjunct professor at Molloy College in Rockville Center, New York.

Paula Torn, PhD, has conducted extensive research on volunteer police personnel in Haaglanden in Belgium. She earned her doctoral degree from Rasmussen University in Rotterdam, Belgium.

Ronald Verbiest, PhD, recently retired from the Haaglanden Police in Belgium. His last position was as coordinator of international relations for the police in The Hague region. He earned a doctoral degree in administration from the University of Leiden and a bachelor's degree in public administration from Hague University.

Ross Wolf, EdD, is associate dean in the College of Health and Public Affairs and associate professor of Criminal Justice at the University of Central Florida. He also serves as division chief with the Orange County (Florida) Sheriff's Office Reserve Unit and has provided volunteer policing training for or worked with police agencies around the world, including agencies throughout the United States, in the Caribbean, the United Kingdom, Russia, Hong Kong, and Singapore. He was awarded the National Sheriffs' Association Medal of Merit and the Presidential Lifetime Call to Service Award for his work with volunteer and reserve policing. His research interests focus on volunteer/reserve policing, international policing, tourism-oriented policing, and police use of force.

John S. Young, PhD, a toxicologist and risk assessor by profession, has held positions in the private sector, in government, and in academia. His volunteer experience includes service with the Mishmar Ezrachi–Civil Guard in Jerusalem, Israel, as a commissioned officer in the Virginia Defense Force (State Guard of Virginia), and with the Marine Rescue Team of the Virginia Beach Department of Emergency Medical Services.

Introduction I

Introduction
The Obvious Need for Volunteers in Policing

1

JAMES F. ALBRECHT

Contents

1.1 Introduction

It is difficult to fathom what would entice an individual to volunteer without compensation for a position in which their lives would be placed at serious risk at any moment. And yet volunteer firefighters and police auxiliary and reserve officers as well as many other volunteers continue to enthusiastically accept and undertake this challenge. An effective police executive should take heed to harness this positive energy and enthusiasm and the opportunity to further strengthen collaboration between law enforcement and the community being served.

1.2 Textbook Overview

This book will endeavor to provide a comprehensive overview of the benefits, rewards, and challenges of developing, maintaining, and participating in a police volunteer program. At a time when most police executives and government leaders have been faced with the reality that they must "do more with less," there are numerous apparent benefits for incorporating a well-vetted, trained, and maintained complement of police volunteers into organizational operations.

In Chapter 2, Robert Hanser, Mkay Bonner, and Mark Johnson provide the basic outline of the Volunteers in Police Service (VIPS) program and the variety of volunteer programs that are commonly implemented within police departments across the United States. Chapter 3, by Ben Dobrin, Adam Dobrin, and April Christman, identifies many of the obvious and subtle benefits and challenges inherent in using volunteers to accomplish and to enhance police agency tasks and responsibilities.

Section II of the book examines the variety of police volunteer programs in place across the United States and includes options employed in state police and sheriff offices and county and municipal police departments. Chapter 4, by Marc Spigel, provides an insider's perspective into the police auxiliary program in Framingham, Massachusetts, and Jimmy Albrecht, in Chapter 5, provides a comparison with a similar long-standing institution within the New York City Police Department. Steven Sheffer, in Chapter 6, presents another experiential discussion about the highly regarded Florida Highway Patrol Auxiliary. In Chapter 7, Ron Hyman supplies an empirical overview of the Portsmouth Police Department Auxiliary Unit in Virginia, and in Chapter 8, Ross Wolf examines the deployment of police reserve officers within the Orange County Sheriff's Department surrounding Orlando, Florida. In Chapter 9, Jimmy Albrecht provides an outline of the diverse use of volunteers within the Aurora Police Department in Colorado and presents sensational insight into the effective response of those resources at the tragic movie theater massacre in 2012. In Chapter 10, Mkay Bonner, Mark Johnson, and Robert Hanser comprehensively outline the professional utilization of police reserves over a three-tier system within the Los Angeles Police Department. And finally, Colleen Morin and Robert Morin, in Chapter 11, convey the history and traditions of the use of volunteers in the Carson City (Nevada) Sheriff's Office.

Section III of the text provides a glance into the use of police volunteers internationally. Starting with Canada, Rick Parent, in Chapter 12, provides a detailed overview of the reserve police programs in place on the Canadian west coast in British Columbia. Pal Kardos and Bea Szoke examine the highly successful and touted auxiliary police program in Hungary in Chapter 13. Christiaan Bezuidenhout, in Chapter 14, outlines the long-standing use of police reserve officers within the South African Police Service. In Chapter 15, Paula Torn and Ron Verbiest provide insight into the use of volunteer police in the Netherlands and The Hague. Wayne Koo and Desmond Tan contribute an inside view into the deployment of police reserves in Singapore in Chapter 16, and the section continues in Chapter 17 with Charles Lieberman's outline of effective use of the Civil Guard in Israel as community cooperation and action is critical in any nation plagued by the threat of terrorism. Finally, Carol Borland Jones and Ross Wolf, in Chapter 18, provide a detailed overview of the long history and accomplishments of the Special Constabulary in the United Kingdom.

Section IV continues with a thorough analysis of other potential options for using police volunteers and other intermediary deployment alternatives to enhance organizational efficacy. Many police departments across the United Kingdom have improved community relations, not only through the Special

Constable (i.e., volunteer police) initiative, but also through the employment of community service officers. In Chapter 19, Annette Crisp delineates the program and its benefits in comprehensive detail. In contrast, Nate Moran and Rob Hanser, in Chapter 20, convey how many police agencies in Texas have developed a system wherein reserve police officers are routinely hired as part-time officers in times of need. Theresa Tobin, in Chapter 21, concludes with an overview of the New York City Police Department's initiative, following the September 11, 2001 terrorist attack, of maintaining a reserve corps of retired police officers for mobilization during large-scale incidents, disasters, and terrorist attacks.

Section V includes only one piece, Chapter 22, which describes the captivating experiences of a veteran member of the Special Constabulary of Essex Police Department in the United Kingdom, which is sure to be the highlight of this book.

Section VI examines the utilization of volunteers in other public service agencies. Chapter 23 by Francis Olive and Melissa Miele peers into the benefits and consequences of incorporating volunteers into the operations of correctional institutions. Theresa Tobin, in Chapter 24, thoroughly outlines the volunteer arm of the United States Coast Guard, the USCG Auxiliary. And Chapter 25, by Charles Jennings, analyzes the effective (and heroic) use of volunteers in firefighting across the United States; and John Young, in Chapter 26, conducts a similar evaluation of volunteer emergency medical personnel.

1.3 Conclusion

The book concludes with Chapter 27 in Section VII, which provides a summary of the most critical points highlighted within the chapters and provides recommendations for ensuring success, effectiveness, longevity, and efficiency in police volunteer programs. Government officials and police executives can take heed of one of the most trusted proverbs: "There is no need to reinvent the wheel." This book should pose potential prototypes for any leader seeking to develop or reorganize a police volunteer program.

Volunteers in Policing in the United States

Support from the Community Serving within the Agency

2

ROBERT D. HANSER
MKAY BONNER
MARK S. JOHNSON

Contents

2.1 Introduction

The use of volunteers in police agencies is not a new idea, but it has increasing appeal to agencies that are strapped for revenue in tough economic times. Although there may be some substantial public knowledge regarding the role of auxiliary or reserve police officers, their role being a bit more visible and recognizable, there is often little public awareness of the activities that numerous day-to-day citizens may perform for their local or regional police agencies. These activities are usually not immediately apparent to the public eye but, for administrators who are often overwhelmed with myriad details and duties, the work of volunteers who can attend to duties and functions that take time from front-line personnel to engage in direct services can be invaluable.

With this in mind, it is important to note that the value of volunteers in police agencies has not just been recognized on a local level; they have also been recognized throughout the entire United States as part of a nationalized initiative. Indeed, the term *Volunteers in Police Service* (VIPS) refers to a federal agenda that has its origins with the Citizen Corps, a nationalized effort started by then-President George Bush after the September 11, 2001 tragedy to help coordinate volunteer contributions throughout the nation. The Citizen Corps program was divided into five categories of volunteers, which include the Community Emergency Response Team (CERT), USA on Watch, the Fire Corps, the Medical Reserve Corps, and VIPS.

Thus, it can be seen that VIPS is, in actuality, a part of a much larger program designed to organize volunteer resources so as to utilize them in the most effective manner possible. Undoubtedly, this coordination of volunteers implies that their contributions are substantial enough to warrant national coordination. Specifically, the role of VIPS is as follows: *To enhance the capacity of state and local law enforcement to utilize volunteers.* Thus, the mandate of VIPS is both simple and very broad. Adding to the legitimacy of this coordinating effort is the fact that the VIPS program is managed by the International Association of Chiefs of Police (IACP) with financial support from the Bureau of Justice Assistance. This national system, to date, has registered more than 2,260 law enforcement volunteer programs that represent more than 256,000 volunteers (VIPS, 2012a). This is obviously not a small program.

Further, VIPS helps to recognize and showcase the contributions of police volunteer programs throughout the nation. On the VIPS website and in the organization's newsletters, individual volunteers as well as local programs are recognized for their efforts. Awards are given, and training opportunities are offered to volunteers in various areas of the nation and at different times throughout the year. Further, the VIPS program provides a variety of sample documents and forms, potential policies and procedures, training materials, screening forms, and other services for volunteer programs throughout the nation.

The VIPS program provides support and resources for agencies interested in developing or enhancing a volunteer program and for citizens who wish to volunteer their time and skills with a community law enforcement agency. The program's ultimate goal is to enhance the capacity of state and local law enforcement to utilize volunteers (VIPS, 2012a). Correspondingly, VIPS staff seek to do the following:

1. Learn about promising practices being used in existing VIPS programs and share this information with law enforcement agencies that want to expand their programs
2. Increase the use of volunteers in existing programs
3. Help citizens learn about and become involved in VIPS programs in their communities
4. Help agencies without volunteer programs get them started

It is clear from the above points that VIPS staff have an agenda that is broad and seeks to further facilitate the use of volunteers in police agencies. Aside from financial savings and similar tangible advantages, agencies also benefit from enhanced police–community relations when they have an active volunteer program in their jurisdiction. Thus, VIPS provides numerous benefits for agencies, both in direct and indirect terms.

This chapter provides a discussion of how volunteers in policing are utilized throughout the nation and will continue to do so with the VIPS framework in mind. The discussion that follows entails five separate and distinct sections, which are (1) guidance and program development offered through VIPS, (2) examples of various agencies recognized for excellence in integrating volunteers into their operations, (3) disaster response, (4) specialized programs, and (5) multicultural volunteer programming. Readers can refer to Table 2.1 (Some Common and Some Specialized Uses of Volunteers in Policing) for an overview of some of the means by which volunteers have been utilized in agencies. This is, by no means, an exhaustive list but is meant to simply demonstrate the multiple types of contributions that volunteers can provide to an agency. Last, this chapter provides a section on the use of volunteers with police agencies in other nations throughout the word, demonstrating how this idea has spread throughout the global community and is not restricted to the United States alone.

Table 2.1   Some Common and Some Specialized Uses of Volunteers in Policing

Volunteer Assignment	Duties and Responsibilities of Assignment
Administrative Duties	Assist with data entry of routine and confidential information; scan, copy, and file documents; conduct inventories; organize and maintain property room
Neighborhood Watch	Conduct watches of various locations, coordinate citizen watches in neighborhoods, coordinate neighborhood block parties and other similar activities
Traffic Assistance	Aid with auto accidents, help process reports, issue parking citations
Missing Persons Assistance	Assist parents in completing child identification kits; develop, post, and distribute posters and fliers; operate phone and command stations; stay in contact with families; and update case files
Crime Prevention	Conduct watches of various locations, help with target-hardening activities in the community, encourage community awareness, train community about common means by which crimes occur
Animal Control	Collect animals for potential adoption, clean cages, exercise animals, wash and groom animals
Disaster Response	Disaster preparation and response, first aid and triage, recovery from crises and disasters, crime prevention during times of disaster
Victim Assistance	Provide emotional support to victims, link victims to various community support programs, guide victims through crime victim compensation process
Bilingual and Cultural Response	Provide language translation assistance, engage in community relation building, provide officer training on various cultural norms, provide community training on police roles and services
Religious Chaplaincy	Provide spiritual counseling to officers and victims, educate cultural and/or religious membership on role of police, participate in ride-a-longs
Sex Offender Management	Assist with registration, community notification, address verification, and other monitoring and tracking efforts
Crime Scene Investigation	Investigate car thefts and other property crimes that sworn officers have not had time to address, collect fingerprints, take photos, gather forensic evidence
Cold Case Review and Processing	Administrative volunteers assist with copying statements and documents for review, discuss various cold cases and offer suggestions for solving and closing them
Education and Training	Volunteers assist with hosting Citizen Police Academies, provide community information brochures on police services, act as cultural liaisons in ethnic minority communities, assist in specialized training (for volunteers with special or technical skill sets)

Source: Volunteers in Police Service (2012b). *Volunteers in police service add value while budgets decrease.* Alexandria, VA: International Chiefs of Police (IACP).

2.2 Guidance and Program Development

Agencies that have a VIPS program and/or agencies who are interested in starting such a program will, upon visiting the VIPS website, quickly determine that they have numerous resources at their disposal. Programming for volunteer programs has become so extensive that the federal site for VIPS has publications that include model policies for starting and maintaining a volunteer program and example drafts and brochures from hundreds of agencies around the nation as well as specific publications that outline the use of volunteers in specific circumstances, such as with patrol operations or disaster response.

Typically, most agencies will have an administrator who is tasked to be the volunteer coordinator. This person has a significant responsibility in developing the program and its corresponding components. The volunteer coordinator will, in most cases, be responsible for the recruiting, selection, and training of volunteers. According to the model policy developed by the IACP, the volunteer coordinator will usually be responsible for the following:

1. Maintenance of employment records for each volunteer
2. Establishing and maintaining a volunteer handbook that clearly describes the expectations, policies, procedures, and responsibilities of volunteers for each post or duty to which they may be assigned
3. Maintenance of a record of the work schedules and assigned duties of volunteers
4. The continual completion of paperwork and reports necessary throughout the operation of the program
5. Coordinating special events, awards ceremonies, and recognition programs for the contributions that volunteers provide to the agency and the community
6. Dispensing administrative discipline when necessary
7. Providing performance evaluations on a schedule that is similar to those given to regular full-time employees

It is important to note that, when recruiting volunteers, agencies must adhere to equal opportunity and nondiscriminatory employment standards. From this point, the volunteer coordinator or other assigned agency staff must provide suitable screening of applicants that should include the following three key points of selection criteria: (1) an official application; (2) at least one face-to-face interview; and (3) a suitable background investigation that includes information on traffic violations and criminal activity, employment history and performance, and outside references. From this point, the selection and placement of volunteers into needed functions of performance is completed, followed by the appropriate training that is necessary for whatever position(s) to which they will likely be assigned.

Agencies should ensure that positions for volunteers are given a clear and detailed position description, just as would be provided for any paid position in the department. Although it may seem to be intuitively obvious, it should be mentioned that volunteers should only be used within the bounds of the job description that is given to them. Naturally, in the world of policing and agency day-to-day activities, some duties will vary and not always fall within a specifically identified guide, but the agency should make a good faith effort to ensure that activities of volunteers are at least reasonably related to a given job description. This is important from the standpoint of volunteer effectiveness as well as agency liability to the public (the consumer of the services provided by the agency and its volunteers) and to the volunteer (having a reasonable expectation to make contributions that are similar in scope to that which they have agreed to, in writing). The importance of this stipulation is clear when one considers that the model policy notes, "Volunteers shall not work without a written job description or outside the limits of job responsibilities specified in the job description" (IACP, 2004, p. 2). Last, it is important that all position descriptions are reviewed from time to time so as to ensure that listed responsibilities are still applicable to a given job assignment and to ensure that they correctly reflect the utilization of a given volunteer's time and work in the agency.

Once these basic aspects are in place, agencies and their volunteer coordinators must keep in mind that the initial fitness for duty of the volunteer is, of course, important and that fitness (physical, mental, legal, and so forth) considerations are not stagnant. In other words, periodic review of a volunteer's fitness for duty should be maintained through records checks and requirements that volunteers report any changes in their medical conditions and changes in residence or other life-course considerations, and they should report any traffic violations, arrests, or potential criminal charges that might develop.

In regard to training, agencies must provide an orientation program for volunteers that appropriately acquaints them with the agency and its personnel, policies, and procedures that have an impact on their work duties. Naturally, they should also receive position-specific training to ensure that they are competent in completing tasks that are required by an assigned duty position. Last, it is very important to note that volunteers are just that: They are *volunteers*. Thus, it must be made clear (in writing and through community awareness mechanisms) that volunteers are not sworn officers; they shall not represent themselves as such either by the commission or the omission of any given act or statement. To be more clear, volunteers have a responsibility to ensure that the public is not mislead, and they have a duty to inform persons with whom they interact that they are, in fact, volunteers with the agency and not sworn police personnel. This type of ethical bearing is very important, and if agencies discover volunteers within the ranks who are not conscientious of this, it is important to correct this misbehavior and, if it does not desist quickly, to remove the volunteer. In such cases, it is likely that the underlying motive for volunteering is not to aid the public welfare as much as it is to meet individual ego needs for recognition and prestige. Obviously, this is to be discouraged in the agency.

One other important area of focus when using volunteers is the dissemination of agency information (IACP, 2004). In some cases, volunteers may have various levels of security clearance and/or may have access to confidential information, including criminal histories or files with sensitive information from both previously closed and ongoing investigations. It is, of course, important that volunteers understand that access to such information is a privilege that entails a high degree of trust from the agency and the public. To make this clear, agencies should have all volunteers sign a nondisclosure agreement, and they should be made aware that unauthorized disclosures can be grounds for dismissal and even criminal prosecution, depending on the information that is leaked outside the agency.

Last, most departments will have policies related to dress codes and the use of agency property and equipment as well as other mundane aspects of running an agency. It is important that volunteers are made aware of these expectations so that they will be informed and able to provide the best contribution that is possible. Certainly, most volunteers wish to enjoy their experience and in all likelihood are motivated by intrinsic incentives. Ensuring that they are informed in regard to expectations allows them to operate with confidence and to have an experience in which the value of the work itself provides incentive for continued interest, uncontaminated by bad experiences that result from a lack of training or information from the agency.

2.3 Examples of Impressive Police Volunteer Programs in the United States

It is easy to identify volunteer programs of excellence in the United States due to the IACP's tradition of recognizing police agencies that have developed and implemented creative and/or effective volunteer programs. Specifically, the IACP and Wilmington University sponsors an annual award that is given to three recipient agencies each year as a means of showcasing the successful use of volunteers in policing. This annual award is known as the Outstanding Achievement in Law Enforcement Volunteer Programs Award, and it recognizes excellence in leadership through the implementation of an effective, high-quality volunteer program. This award helps to perpetuate and make permanent the theories and practices of the VIPS program, and at the same time, it recognizes agencies that successfully integrate and utilize volunteers into agency operations in a tangible manner that exemplifies the goals, concepts, and spirit of volunteerism.

During 2012, there were three agencies that were given this award with several others being given honorable mention. Because the Outstanding Achievement in Law Enforcement Volunteer Programs Award specifically showcases agencies that successfully use volunteers and because these recipient agencies have been recognized, it seems that these agencies (or others from recent past years) might be good examples to draw from. With this said, it is noteworthy that agencies chosen for this award tend to be diverse in location, size, and classification (i.e., rural, urban, or suburban). Thus, it is likely that this is representative of the full spectrum of police agencies.

2.3.1 Charlotte-Mecklenburg Police Department (North Carolina)

In 2012, the Charlotte-Mecklenburg Police Department (CMPD) in North Carolina was a winner of the Outstanding Achievement in Law Enforcement Volunteer Programs Award (VIPS Newsletter, 2013b). This department serves a population of 785,000 with a staff of 1,752 sworn and 464 non-sworn employees. The department's policing strategy places an emphasis on engaging citizens as active partners in problem identification and crime reduction, raising the perception of safety and utilizing enforcement actions and partnerships that target priority chronic offenders. In 1994, the CMPD Volunteer Partnership Program was created to make use of citizens' talents to support departmental initiatives. Due to growth and increased public interest in this program, a more formalized system of volunteering was established.

The CMPD Volunteer Unit was formally established in 2000, and a volunteer liaison officer position was created to oversee the unit. Today, the CMPD Volunteer Unit has more than 600 volunteers. Volunteers are trained to enforce accessible parking and fire lane ordinances, complete data entry and administrative assignments, and provide retail support in the CMPD gift shop. Citizens on Patrol volunteers are assigned to a patrol district and work with a partner to perform such duties as traffic direction at crash scenes, assisting disabled motorists, checking abandoned vehicles, and citizen welfare checks.

The CMPD also utilizes a specialized group, the Bilingual Volunteer Unit (BVU), that has volunteers who fluently speak a foreign language as assistants for patrol officers and detectives whenever there is a need for interpretation or translation that the department cannot typically fulfill (VIPS Newsletter, 2013b). The BVU translates requested information on the scene and at the agency when investigations are being conducted. These volunteers also aid the department with community meetings, conduct case follow-ups, provide crime prevention education with non-English-speaking communities, and conduct license checks within immigrant communities. This last function, as a product of enforcement, is conducted by persons known to the community and done as a means of encouraging immigrants to obtain valid identification. This is, of course, a sensitive function from a community relations perspective, and the BVU plays a mitigating role between the need to conduct license checks and maintain effective relationships in the community, including the immigrant community, who may even consist of persons who do not legally reside within the nation's borders.

Another program that gains substantial support from agency volunteers is the Animal Care and Control Division (VIPS Newsletter, 2013b). Volunteers within this division assist staff with the intake of more than 18,000 homeless animals annually. These volunteers collect animals for potential adoption, clean cages, exercise animals, wash and groom these animals, and even provide basic training to these animals in the hope that they will have future homes. On occasion, volunteers for this unit will support veterinarian staff at more than 250 clinics to spay or neuter and vaccinate found animals. In order to find animals homes with loving owners, volunteers assisted at two offsite adoption events each month. This service is one that provides a benefit to the welfare and humane conditions of the community. This service also saves the agency time and resources for a function that, although necessary, often goes beyond the capabilities of agency staffing.

One last program in which volunteers make contributions is the Homicide Cold Case Unit, which joins volunteers with a variety of backgrounds and experiences in local, state, and federal levels of law enforcement (VIPS Newsletter, 2013b). These volunteers are brought together in teams that review and discuss various cold cases and offer suggestions for solving and closing them. These volunteers work with Cold Case Unit detectives and even summarize the facts and circumstances for these cases as a means of providing focus, additional review, and consideration of possible explanations for each case. From this point, administrative volunteers assist with copying statements and documents for review. In the past, it often took detectives up to two months to review cases, but now, with the work of volunteers, these cases are often reviewed and presented to detectives in two or three weeks. Going further, a long-term goal of the Cold Case Unit is to complete a team review for all open homicide cases. Since 2003, this unit has reviewed 127 cases, and of these, 34 have been cleared, two are pending trial, and another 22 resulted in arrests leading to a 100% rate of conviction. Last, this volunteer unit has been instrumental in resolving cold cases in a variety of other states, including Louisiana, Maryland, and Texas.

Last, the 600 or so volunteers of the CMPD have contributed nearly 54,000 hours of service in 2011, a value of more than $1.1 million when calculated at the national hourly value of volunteer time (VIPS Newsletter, 2013b). Many units within the agency have recognized the benefits of volunteer service, including increased visibility and higher efficiency with volunteers performing tasks that do not require an officer's attention. With the support of the Volunteer Unit as one important component of the agency's crime prevention strategy, the City of Charlotte as well as the County of Mecklenburg reported a drop of nearly 20% in crime statistics during the past three years. This is obviously an indicator that these programs are beneficial to the agency and to area taxpayers in terms of an improvement to public safety.

2.3.2 Fresno Police Department (California)

Within the Fresno Police Department, there are more than 700 sworn and nearly 200 non-sworn staff. These numbers, in actuality, reflect a reduction of 100 officers and 275 civilian staff due to the current economic climate. Due to this reduction in paid personnel, volunteers have become a vital resource in helping the department continue to provide professional, timely, and effective service while also maintaining trusting relationships with residents (VIPS Newsletter, 2013b).

This police department has historically included volunteer partnerships to the point that this feature is a part of the organizational culture of the agency. This agency began the use of volunteers in 1947 during the later part of World War II for its Reserve Officer Program. This program was established to fill in the patrol ranks that had been depleted due to military drafting of many full-time officers to fight in the war overseas. From this point, the number of active volunteers has grown considerably. For instance, the neighborhood watch program in Fresno currently has more than 18,000 members and maintains leadership and commitment levels similar to the program's earlier years of development; interest in volunteering has not waned.

One specific program, the Citizens on Patrol program, was started in 1997 and still continues to be a very important tool for the agency. This program aids officers in activities such as crime scene preservation, helping at DUI checkpoints, conducting missing person searches, and a variety of functions related to traffic accident response. Another unique program entails volunteers who are given the task of checking community gas pumps for credit card skimming devices and another in which citizens observe and enforce compliance with disabled parking requirements. These volunteers are trained and respond to nonemergency reports so that full-time sworn officers are able to focus on emergency calls for service. In 2012, volunteers with Citizens on Patrol assisted with more than 3,000 calls for service and the towing away of more than 900 vehicles, including abandoned vehicles (VIPS Newsletter, 2013b).

Other areas in which volunteers have proven to be extremely helpful to the agency are in the realm of administrative assistance. Indeed, the number of administrative projects that utilize volunteers has doubled in size and mission scope during the past few years. These programs include 71 regular volunteers whose duties are to develop and maintain databases, complete filing and reception services, develop outreach materials, and photograph special events. To demonstrate how these volunteers provide a variety of benefits, consider one volunteer who worked on the manual entry of pawn slips and identified suspicious patterns in these ticketing slips, a pattern that uncovered and traced more than $200,000 worth of stolen property.

Last, one unique feature of this agency's volunteer program is the degree to which volunteers cross-train between public safety and disaster response programs. To further refine this aspect of volunteer contribution and inclusion, one of the agency's Police Officer Standards and Training (POST)-certified instructors developed a 24-hour course that helped to coordinate agency volunteers with volunteers in the Citizen Corps in a variety of security roles related to crime prevention during times of disaster, disaster preparation and response, and recovery from crises and disasters. Further, the classroom training is combined with ride-a-longs with patrol officers and sit-a-longs with agency emergency dispatchers. This further bridges this dual role of volunteers and provides them with knowledge of the inner workings and routine decision making associated with the full-time personnel of the department.

2.3.3 Grapevine Police Department (Texas)

The Grapevine Police Department (GPD) employs 93 sworn officers and 40 civilians. This department began the use of volunteers in 2006 when it was determined that their use in selected activities could expand and bolster the agency's service to the public. With the GPD, volunteers are organized into two distinct categories called "VIPS 1" and "VIPS 2," and each category is based on the type of work that they are assigned (VIPS Newsletter, 2013b, p. 8). The VIPS 1 volunteers are assigned to external programs that include activities that augment car and foot patrols. This program utilizes reconditioned police cars, and volunteers in this program perform vacation, security, and neighborhood checks. They often assist motorists in need and conduct a number of other activities that range from the collection of pawn tickets to the delivery of needed supplies and commodities to the local jail. In many cases, they may deliver supplies to officers who are on scene and in need of specialized equipment or other tools that are not immediately available to the officer.

VIPS 1 volunteers also support the department with traffic speed surveys and even assist in candidate testing processes. They also help to organize a program called Project Lifesaver, which locates missing persons (VIPS Newsletter, 2013b). In many cases, these missing individuals will have some debilitating state of declined functioning, such as Alzheimer's disease or some type of other mental health problem. Because of this, the volunteers may also be trained in appropriate means of response to these populations.

The second category of volunteers, VIPS 2, utilizes volunteers for internal operations and administrative functions. In reality, this category is the entry point from which all volunteers start with the agency. These volunteers are required to complete FEMA's IS-100 Introduction to the Incident Command System course and a four-hour course on handling sensitive or confidential information. After they complete this initial training and a period of observation, these volunteers can staff the main desk or other similar functions on their own, and they are able to work in other areas throughout the agency that are part of the VIPS 2 program. Their duties can include anything from staffing the information and animal control desks to providing dispatch assistance, scanning classified documents, and fingerprinting of personnel or suspects. Once an individual has completed the VIPS 2 training and has worked in any VIPS 2 position for at least two months, he or she can apply for the VIPS 1 program if desired. Thus, all VIPS 1 personnel have been, at one time or another, in the VIPS 2 program of training with the GPD. Although many do go on to VIPS 1 training and assignments, it is important to note that some volunteers do not, and they, instead, choose to stay within the VIPS 2 category of service. These services are certainly needed and aid the agency greatly, and over time, these individuals develop a great degree of competence related to internal administrative processes within the agency. Even though they may choose to stay within the VIPS 2 category, after two months, they are also eligible to take an optional two-hour foot patrol training course as well as the Sky Watch mobile watchtower training program. They are then qualified to work in these activities as well, should they desire.

Since this program began in 2006, volunteers with the GPD have contributed 59,000 hours of service. They have also filled in for more than 650 crossing guard shift assignments, thereby freeing up sworn officers for other emergency or investigation-related duties. In addition, they have conducted more than 7,000 security checks, 1,700 neighborhood checks, and responded to more than 3,000 citizen requests for assistance (500 being motorist-related), and they have also assisted in more than 150 crash incidents (VIPS Newsletter, 2013b, p. 9). These numbers make it clear that volunteers in this agency have made a huge impact on the quality of service delivery performed by the agency in only a few short years.

2.4 Disaster Response

Volunteers who assist with emergency response may also frequently be involved with the regional CERT program, which is discussed earlier in this chapter as one of the five categories of the Citizen Corps program established after the 9/11 World Trade Center tragedy. Disaster response teams may also include volunteers who are also members of the area Red Cross and may, therefore, have a great deal of training (and cross-training) due to these other similarly aligned volunteer organizations.

In general, these volunteers will aid in providing food and water, clothing, and other donated items of relief to persons who have been impacted by a disaster (VIPS, 2012b). They may also provide various forms of victim triage and first aid until adequate medical attention can be obtained. These volunteers may conduct damage assessments and provide persons who have been impacted with additional services (such as temporary housing or transportation) and will often work at distribution centers where persons can come to receive basic supplies during an emergency or where supplies can be transported to persons who are in need.

During emergencies, volunteers may work at makeshift staging areas where supplies are provided but also where electric generators function. Unique features may include mobile traffic signals that operate off generators so that traffic will continue to move safely during times of power loss. They may also provide support assistance to first responders, relaying information to and/or from families, fetching tools or equipment not at the scene, or any other sundry array of tasks and activities that may be needed (VIPS, 2012b). Naturally, these types of coordinated efforts require extensive training on the part of the volunteers, and as with paid staff, different volunteers will have different qualifications and skill levels that will likely dictate the particular role that they play during disaster response efforts.

2.5 Specialized Programs

Undoubtedly, there are a number of means by which volunteers may be utilized. In this section, we provide some very specialized programs that integrate unique skill sets of volunteers, address specific types of threats to public safety, or address aspects of the criminal justice system that often do not get adequate attention. Three examples are provided, each demonstrating unique types of programming for which volunteers are utilized.

2.5.1 Volunteer Chaplaincy

The Vineland Police Department in New Jersey has a specialized program known as the Chaplain Program, which began in 2007 under the coordination of the chief of police and the now senior chaplain (VIPS Newsletter, 2010a). Ordained chaplains who are interested must submit a letter of intent to the Chief of Police and must submit a full application that includes a membership application to the International Conference of Police Chaplains (ICPC). If approved, their applications are then sent to the senior chaplain.

Accepted chaplains are provided an orientation from the chief and the senior chaplain, who cover a range of policies and procedures and also introduce the new volunteers to the referral assistance program for employees of the department. The agency provides volunteer chaplains with a membership to ICPC, a uniform that is distinct from the colors worn by officers of the agency, funding to attend regional training events, and access to any in-service training that is hosted by the agency. Volunteer chaplains participate in ride-a-longs when attending daily roll call. These volunteers must complete a curriculum provided by the ICPC before going on ride-a-longs, and the City of Vineland is able to provide insurance for these volunteers while they are in transit to and from their assignment as well as when they are on duty.

Further, volunteer police chaplains are active in interventions addressing minor juvenile offenders. This program is known as the Station House Adjustment Program and is designed to redirect first-time juvenile offenders who have committed minor offenses away from formal court proceedings. Generally, when a young person is arrested for a minor crime, such as a city code violation or petty disorderly conduct offenses, he or she is given the option of participating in this program. This program involves the offender, the parent or guardian, and the arresting department's juvenile officer. Upon arrest of the juvenile, a chaplain is called to meet the juvenile at the station along with the parent or guardian. Chaplains, with their training, have the ability to counsel juveniles and their parents. Chaplains explain their role in the process and outline the rules and options for the adjustment program. The chaplain meets the minor at his or her community service assignment (if recommended) and is present when the service is completed. It is very important to note that, as of 2007, none of the youth who have successfully completed this program have been known to recidivate.

2.5.2 Sex Offender Monitoring

Another specialized type of volunteer programming is designed to address the challenges posed by the ever-growing numbers of registered sex offenders who must be tracked. Some agencies have enlisted the assistance of volunteers to support and enhance agency efforts to manage the sex offender population. These volunteers play a key role in maintaining public safety and ensuring compliance with sex offender mandates. In such cases, they will usually provide assistance with registration, community notification, address verification, and other activities designed to reinforce the monitoring and tracking of these offenders.

One example of such a program can be found with the Itasca (Illinois) Police Department, which has implemented the Enhanced Surveillance of Registered Sex Offenders program to monitor registered sex offenders. These volunteers routinely monitor registered sex offenders' residences, document vehicle information, and/or note any suspicious activity. In addition, they patrol schools, day care facilities, parks, and other locations where children congregate and where sex offenders on supervision might look for victims. Any information gathered is organized into binders that are kept in program vehicles and at the police department. These volunteers maintain this binder of information, "which includes procedures, suspect bulletin form with photo; vehicle photos with tags clearly visible; and locations of schools, day care facilities, parks, apartment playgrounds, baseball and soccer fields" (VIPS Newsletter, 2010a, p. 3). Further, "if a registered sex offender or their vehicle is observed in a prohibited location, volunteers immediately contact dispatch so that an officer can investigate the matter" (VIPS Newsletter, 2010a, p. 3). Last, these volunteers provide a valuable community service by improving public safety through this monitoring process. In addition to helping the police and the public, they also help to fill in gaps that community supervision agencies (i.e., probation and parole) might experience, providing an additional layer of observation and monitoring to further limit the offenders' ability to reoffend.

2.5.3 Domestic Violence Victim Assistance

Criminal investigations are often time-consuming and detailed, often making it difficult for police to meet the physical and emotional needs of victims who have been impacted by crime. This is true with victims of domestic violence as well as with other crimes. However, domestic violence calls happen to be the largest category of calls received by police agencies, and given that these crimes are violent and potentially lethal, safety concerns for the victim necessitate appropriate follow-up with the victim's case (VIPS Newsletter, 2011).

The Chicago Police Department has initiated the use of domestic violence subcommittees, which are tasked with providing support for victims. Each district of the city has its own domestic violence subcommittee. These subcommittees bring community volunteers to educate the public and raise awareness about domestic violence issues. The domestic violence program manager oversees the administration of the program, but each individual subcommittee functions independently with the support of an assigned domestic violence liaison officer (DVLO). The DVLO receives monthly training on domestic violence issues, including legal cases and developments. The DVLO for each district then, in turn, trains volunteers, other officers, and community members to ensure that the information is circulated throughout the district.

Subcommittees plan their own events and promote awareness of the rights and resources available to domestic violence victims. Many events are held in April in recognition of Sexual Assault Awareness Month and in October in recognition of Domestic Violence Awareness Month. In addition, many volunteers also bring a multicultural perspective to these events, being that many are persons with disabilities; are members of the lesbian, gay, bisexual, and transgender community; or are members of various ethnic minority groups throughout the city. In some cases, these subcommittees will make concerted efforts to reach these specific groups of citizens.

While engaged in outreach, volunteers provide education resources and referrals, but they are not expected to provide actual victim counseling. However, many of these volunteers work for local domestic violence agencies and are professionally trained in domestic violence counseling. Nevertheless, many of the volunteers who are active in this initiative also happen to work in agencies or nonprofit organizations that address domestic violence. As such, they are often professionally trained and are qualified to conduct domestic violence counseling. Thus, even though volunteers are not expected to provide victim counseling, these subcommittees do try to staff events so that there is a professional available to talk, should this be desired by a victim.

It is in this manner that community awareness is developed in Chicago and by which citizens are encouraged to report acts of abuse. These subcommittees bring together volunteers, law enforcement, and the community to develop this sense of awareness. "With officers, community organizations, subcommittee volunteers, and residents working together…" the Chicago Police Department "…maintains a broad network to help victims access services and to spread that message that domestic violence will not be tolerated in Chicago" (VIPS Newsletter, 2011, p. 6).

2.6 Multiculturalism and Volunteerism in Policing

According to the 2008 U.S. Census American Community Survey, of the 304 million persons in the United States, 12.5% were foreign born. This rapid growth in immigrant populations is expected to continue to increase. With this changing cultural landscape, many law enforcement agencies are building trust and preventing crime by reaching out to immigrant communities. In connecting with the minority population, the agency must place a priority on having culturally competent means of public response. Volunteers can be a key resource for law enforcement in building relationships with diverse communities and helping to empower immigrant groups to overcome their apprehension and possible distrust of law enforcement. Volunteers are also a resource that can help provide culturally competent service responses, when appropriate. We provide three specific programs as examples of how volunteers can aid law enforcement agencies in providing culturally competent responses in the communities they serve.

2.6.1 Bilingual Volunteer Assistance

As an example, consider the Spanish-Speaking Ride Along Program, which was developed by the Tulsa (Oklahoma) Police Department (VIPS Newsletter, 2010b). This program was developed amid budget cuts and departmental reorganization, which left one Tulsa police sergeant in charge of both the VIPS program and the Hispanic outreach program. Recognizing the potential for crossover, the Spanish-Speaking Ride Along and Interpreter Program was developed to both build trust in the Spanish-speaking community and to bring new volunteers with valued language skills into the VIPS program. This program provides Spanish-speaking citizens with an opportunity to assist Tulsa police officers in better communicating with the Hispanic community. Bilingual citizens or legal residents who volunteer for this program ride with on-duty officers and utilize their language skills as needed.

Importantly, volunteers who work with the Spanish-Speaking Ride Along Program quite often live right in the communities where they assist law enforcement. Thus, they are recognized by others in the community, which helps to diffuse tension and prevent misunderstandings. In addition, these volunteers, in tandem with patrol officers, provide presentations to Spanish-speaking groups in the city as a means of cultivating positive police–community relations while also providing the Spanish-speaking community education on basic crime prevention. These presentations also serve as very effective tools for recruiting other volunteers for the Spanish-Speaking Ride Along Program.

2.6.2 Cultural Liaisons and Cultural Committees

In Westbrook, Maine, a growing African American and Middle Eastern refugee population has led to the development of volunteer programs designed to be culturally specific to these diverse citizen groups (VIPS Newsletter, 2010b). Rapid demographic changes in many neighborhoods led to increased misunderstandings and challenges. With the goal of preventing and avoiding conflict, this agency began to recruit volunteers to act as cultural liaisons. These volunteers are on call to support officers with language and cultural interpretation. Volunteers go through a selection process during which they must provide an application and driver's license and undergo a criminal background check. Likewise, the police department makes a point to check with members of cultural organizations to ensure the volunteers are well-respected members of their communities. In the past, cultural liaison volunteers have effectively translated police department brochures into a variety of languages. These brochures outline the services available to residents to foster knowledge and understanding of police services. Full-time officers carry these brochures and interpreter lists while on patrol so that the services can be accessed during a traffic stop or at the scene of a call. These volunteers have provided help in a variety of capacities related to public safety and human service issues.

2.6.3 Immigrant Communities and Ethnic-Specific Responses

During the early 1990s, the City of Delray Beach, Florida, experienced a large influx of immigrants from Haiti. This immigration trend continued through the 2000s, and today, approximately 13% of the city's population are of Haitian ethnicity. Many of these immigrants arrived with little understanding of law enforcement in the United States and, due to experiences in their home country, distrusted the police of Delray Beach. Likewise, during these years of transition, the area saw a rise in the rates of crime victimization experienced throughout the Haitian community, much of this being due to intra-ethnic feuding and conflict. As a result, the Delray Beach Police Department sought out leaders in the Haitian community and also visited Haitian churches to build partnerships and enhance communication between the police and this community.

Over time, the Delray Beach Police Department developed a volunteer program known as the Haitian Roving Patrol, which is used to supplement patrol efforts of the police and to also enhance the relationship between the Delray Beach Haitian population and the local police. All volunteers are carefully screened, and each must meet requirements established by the agency, which are identical to those of fully sworn officers on patrol. Volunteers patrol in pairs every evening. Those vehicles used by volunteers are clearly distinguished from typical departmental patrol vehicles by an amber light bar and large-face decals identifying these personnel as volunteers.

In Sacramento, California, one particularly unique program exists that addresses diversity in the community and the need for culturally competent police response. It is important to note that Sacramento is one of the most diverse cities in the United States. Indeed, this city is home to persons from approximately 48 different cultures, including Hmong, Vietnamese, Slavic, and Mien. Because of the diversity of the city, the Sacramento Police Department, as a means of showing understanding and responsiveness to the city's demographic features, transformed its standard police academy into one that is well suited for a variety of different cultures. This academy, named the Cultural Academy, has hosted a number of ethnic groups, including the Mien and the Hmong as well as Slavic communities. These cultural academies are held one evening a week over a six-week period. The academy includes a field trip to the communications center and the training academy. The inclusion of these types of observational field trips allows citizens to see their police department at work and also demystifies the agency and its role in the community. Rather than standing apart from the surrounding community, the agency is transformed into one that is actually part of the community, including the diverse minority and/or immigrant population.

The process for application is made deliberately simple to encourage and welcome interested individuals to the cultural academies that are offered. In addition, it is important to note that these academies do not include a background check. Food is provided at each academy session to help bring individuals together, build trust, and facilitate a relaxed atmosphere of open communication. The Sacramento Police Department has up to 50 participants per each academy session, and they are held in a very large community room at the agency's headquarters that is fully equipped with audiovisual equipment. This equipment is important because, with the use of headsets, participants can hear simultaneous interpretations of the English version of the presentation in their own primary language.

2.7 Global Examples of Successful Police Volunteer Programs

Although it should be clear, at this point, that the use of volunteers in police agencies is a concept that has been fully embraced in the United States, it is important to also note that this practice has been implemented in a number of other countries around the world. For instance, Gravelle and Rogers (2009) conducted peer-reviewed research on the use of volunteers who are utilized by police in the nations of England and Wales. Economic challenges throughout the global economy have been cited as the primary impetus to these agencies adopting this practice. These researchers conducted an economic costing analysis using a specialized statistical model to piece out the variety of economic advantages using volunteers. Further, Gravelle and Rogers (2009) provide support for an increase in public confidence and better-developed police–community relationships. Naturally, these findings are very similar to what has been discussed in prior parts of our discussion showing that, in the United States, improvements in police–citizen relationships have been touted as a reason to encourage the use of volunteers in police agencies.

Likewise, in the territory of New South Wales, Australia, volunteers in policing are described as being extremely important to police, serving in more than 120 locations throughout New South Wales (New South Wales Police Force, 2013). In this area of Australia, the Volunteers in Policing (VIP) program began in 1995 as a means of empowering community members to assist police by performing tasks and functions that are important but are not the core duties of the police alone. Since 1995, VIP has become an integral part of the New South Wales police operation, and through their contributions, full-time salaried police are able to better concentrate on their core duties of crime reduction throughout the region. In this region, these volunteers commonly assist and support victims of crime, provide security and assistance to drug court programs throughout the region, aid in times of disaster, and provide mentoring and assistance to youth programs in the region. All volunteers are given specialized training at their regional police command agency to be fully prepared and competent in the duties that they perform.

Last, in Vancouver, Canada, VIP has been in existence since 1986 with one program in particular, the Citizen's Crime Watch (CCW) Program, proving to be quite successful in aiding Vancouver police (VIPS Newsletter, 2013a). This program has grown to more than 100 volunteers who provide police with "extra eyes and ears on city streets on Friday and Saturday nights" (VIPS Newsletter, 2013a, p. 5). These volunteers patrol in pairs within their own personal vehicles. Their geographical assignments are logically placed based on crime analysis data with which the agency predicts the likelihood of future crime in a given area. These individuals work under the guidance of a CCW coordinator who is a full-time police officer on duty while volunteers go on patrol in various areas of the jurisdiction. The CCW program has been touted as being quite successful in a number of efforts to reduce crime and/or resolve criminal cases in the Vancouver area.

2.8 Conclusion

It is clear from the examples that have been provided that volunteers make significant contributions to police agencies across the nation. In fact, the use of VIP is a practice that is quite common, not just in the United States, but in other areas of the world as well. This should not be surprising given the current economic climate, police agencies now face times of limited resources, and at the same time, criminal activity is an ever-looming threat to the public welfare. These same economic and criminogenic phenomena are experienced around the globe, and just as agencies in multiple countries have partnered to fight crime, it only stands to reason that agencies in various countries might also tap into their own communities and citizenry who are willing and able to provide assistance.

Further, the use of VIP is an official and endorsed practice by the IACP. This is important for at least two (if not more) reasons. First, this demonstrates that this practice has official sanction and should actually not just be considered a variant of policing but should probably be considered an indicator of a highly successful agency. In other words, it is perhaps one of the best practices in police agency administration and should be touted as such. Second, the fact that the IACP, an international organization, has adopted these practices speaks even further to the likely global trend that will emerge in using community members as volunteers in differing capacities to help fight crime and operate day-to-day aspects of the police agency.

In addition, this chapter demonstrates that the use of volunteers can be integrated through a large variety of methods. The types of programming and the level to which an agency integrates volunteers is, perhaps, limitless. All areas of agency operation can benefit from volunteers, and as we have seen, everything from administrative work to on-scene assistance can be provided by volunteers. In fact, many agencies also have auxiliary or reserve police officers who are sworn into service but are volunteers as well. However, it was the point of this chapter to focus exclusively on the contributions of volunteers who are not the typical officer on patrol. This is important because the contributions of these individuals are often not known by the public. If they are not known so well, then this also means many citizens may not realize their contributions are welcomed if they desire to assist their local agency.

In closing, volunteers provide numerous hours of service that, when factored at a standard rate of pay for similar services, would tally up into millions of dollars across the nation. Further, their services impact on and assist in a wide array of agency operations, including crime fighting, public safety, and victim service functions. Further, the efforts of volunteers also help to bridge relations between the police agency and the outlying community. Specific examples have been provided in which agencies have successfully utilized volunteers as a means of improving cultural competence and service delivery to ethnic minority and other community niche populations with which effective partnerships have been otherwise difficult to develop. This, combined with the community education feature associated with volunteers, provides yet another benefit for the police agency and the general public welfare. Thus, it would seem that the benefits to the continued use of volunteers far outweighs any potential concerns, and it would also seem that this is a trend that will likely remain within the realm of agency operations for years, if not generations, to come.

References

Gravelle, R. & Rogers, C. (2009). The economy of policing: The impact of the volunteer. *Policing: A Journal of Policy and Practice, 4*(1), 55–63.

International Association of Chiefs of Police. (2004). *Model Policy*. Alexandria, VA: International Chiefs of Police (IACP).

New South Wales Police Force. (2013). Volunteers in Policing. Parramatta,
    Australia. Retrieved from http://www.police.nsw.gov.au/can_you_help_us
    /volunteers_in_policing

Volunteers in Police Service (VIPS). (2012a). *About VIPS*. Alexandria, VA: Inter-
    national Chiefs of Police (IACP). Retrieved from http://www.policevolunteers
    .org/about/

VIPS. (2012b). Volunteers in Police Service Add Value While Budgets Decrease.
    Alexandria, VA: International Chiefs of Police (IACP).

VIPS Newsletter. (2010a). Innovative Ideas: Engaging Volunteers in Unique Positions.
    Alexandria, VA: International Chiefs of Police (IACP).

VIPS Newsletter. (2010b). Bridging the Gap: Engaging Volunteers in Multicultural
    Outreach. Alexandria, VA: International Chiefs of Police (IACP).

VIPS Newsletter. (2011). Volunteers Expand Law Enforcement Response to Victims.
    Alexandria, VA: International Chiefs of Police (IACP).

VIPS Newsletter. (2013a). International Volunteers Share a Universal Commitment
    to Public Safety. Alexandria, VA: International Chiefs of Police (IACP).

VIPS Newsletter. (2013b). Outstanding Achievement in Law Enforcement Volunteer
    Programs Award 2012. Alexandria, VA: International Chiefs of Police (IACP).

Rewards and Challenges of Using Volunteers in Policing

3

BENJAMIN DOBRIN
ADAM DOBRIN
APRIL CHRISTMAN

Contents

3.1 Introduction

Being a police officer presents different meaning to different people, but shared cultural meanings exist that are mentioned here. First and foremost, however, the job of police officer often connotes the concept of "authority." Policing is one of the few jobs that convey state-sanctioned authority: the authority to enforce the rule of law, the authority to arrest, and the authority to use force—up to and including deadly force. This can bring with it associated attention, respect, fear, derision, and even attraction from community members. Volunteer police* officers reflect the same societal meanings as full-time paid police officers, but differences exist between volunteer police officers and full-time paid police officers given the voluntary and part-time nature of their policing participation. Some differences voluntary police encounter are discussed here.

As mentioned previously, policing is a considerably unique job. In an oft-quoted list that can be traced back to Dan Goldfarb, PhD (1987), 10 major differences between police and other jobs are noted:

1. Law enforcement officers are seen as authority figures. People deal with them differently and treat them differently even when they are not working.
2. They are isolated. The wearing of a badge, uniform, and gun makes a law officer separate from society.
3. Law enforcement officers work in a quasi-military, structured institution.
4. Shift work is not normal, and the "rotating shift" schedule is very taxing on an officer's life.
5. Camaraderie can be a double-edged sword. The law enforcement job nurtures a sense of teamwork, but it also stimulates a sense of belonging that can create an "us and them" view of the world.
6. Officers have a different kind of stress in their jobs, called "burst stress." There is not always a steady stressor, but at times, there is an immediate "burst" from low stress to a high-stress state.
7. Officers need to be in constant emotional control. Police officers have a job that requires extreme restraint under highly emotional circumstances.
8. There are no gray areas. The law enforcement officer works in a fact-based world with everything compared to written law. Right and wrong is determined by a standard.
9. The "at-work" world of the officer is very negative and often includes interacting with the bad part of society. This may skew the officer's opinions on the character of the average human being, creating cynicism and a critical view of the world.

---

* For purposes of this chapter, the phrase "volunteer police" means only those volunteers who are sworn police officers who generally wear identical or very similar uniforms as regular paid officers, are armed, and have either full or reduced arrest authority. It does not include other volunteer police positions, such as neighborhood watch liaisons, community service aides, explorers, citizens on patrol, search and rescue teams, chaplains, senior volunteers, and so on. "Reserve" and "auxiliary" police are often used synonymously with "volunteer police" but this sometimes may include part-time paid officers—hence the use of "volunteer police" for this chapter. "Volunteer police" may also include sheriff's deputies when performing the roles associated with policing (which may exclude courtroom or jail responsibilities).

10. Even their children are affected. To a young child, the police officer parent is seen as holding a prestigious, desirable position as a
minor celebrity, a person of great respect. To a teenager, the parent is
part of the authority of society, potentially causing double rebellion
against the parent both in their role as caretaker and as a symbol of
the authority of society.

3.2 Issues Unique to Volunteer Police

Although all of the aforementioned issues might not affect volunteer police
to the same degree as full-time officers, they all do have some impact on
volunteer officers. However, additional issues impact volunteer officers that
full-time officers do not face.

3.2.1 No National Standard of Volunteer Law Enforcement

The lack of national standards for training or expectations of volunteer police
officers presents one of the most striking characteristics of volunteer policing at a national level. Although differences in standards of volunteer law
enforcement exist between states (including what sort of academy training is required before one can become a volunteer officer), differences even
exist within states, such as differences in regulations and policies in different
departments. Some departments may train and equip volunteers no differently than their paid counterparts; other departments have minimal training requirements and often different equipment standards. When discussing
volunteer police with researchers and practitioners from across the country,
it becomes exceptionally confusing rather quickly on what each person and
each organization does. Volunteer policing is a patchwork of policies and
expectations.

3.2.2 Treated Differently by State Codes

Along those lines, different states abide by different laws and regulations
concerning volunteer police. Without commonality between states, we cannot achieve a comprehensive understanding of volunteer policing. Recent
court rulings in Michigan (Hall, 2015) posit that volunteer police are not
afforded the same protections while on duty as paid officers. On the other
hand, other state (such as Virginia) codes outline that volunteer police, by
code, are afforded the same rights and protections as their paid counterparts
(Virginia Code §15.2-1731). Volunteer police are specifically mentioned, for
example, as an included class in the capital murder law in Virginia (Virginia
Code §18.2-31).

3.2.3 Roles Are Different within Departments for Volunteers

Among volunteers, vast differences exist regarding the experience of the officers as well as time committed to the department. Some officers volunteer
30–40 hours a week, and some donate minimal to no time. Some volunteer
officers are retired or former full-time officers, and others present with a
strictly volunteer-based experience with possibly limited training and experience. All of these factors lead to different roles for the volunteer officers
even within the same department. Some volunteer officers might be happy
working special security details, such as parades or football games, and others might work more specialized assignments (such as dive team, boat team,
investigations, tactical teams, helicopter, or mounted units). Some volunteer
officers in some departments work in a solo capacity on the street while, even
in the same department, other volunteer officers might work with the direct
supervision of a paid officer. The role of the volunteer officer can be confusing as there are many different roles they can take on even within the same
department.

3.2.4 Different Levels of Volunteers

Some states have variations of training, certification, and authority for volunteer police officers. In Florida, for example, there are three types of police
officers: full-time, part-time, and auxiliary. Florida statute refers to these as
"law enforcement officer," "part-time law enforcement officer," and "auxiliary law enforcement officer" (Florida §943.085-943.255). Full-time and part-
time officers share the exact same training and requirements, and there is
no mechanism to count how many of the part-time officers are volunteers.
Auxiliary officers are most likely to be almost exclusively volunteers. They
require only entry-level training and take a 319-hour training academy with
identical high-liability requirements as the full academy, and they do not
have to take the state officer certification exam. They also have to be under
the direct supervision of a full-time or part-time law enforcement officer to
have the authority to arrest and perform law enforcement functions (Florida
§943.10 [8]). As such, in different states and agencies, there are varied levels of
training, certification standards, and authority for police volunteers. In other
states, there may be no training requirements for volunteer officers, and with
the approval of the police chief or sheriff, they can be sworn in and given
policing authorities simply based on the authority of the chief or sheriff.

3.2.5 Two Chains of Command

The notion of two chains of command is one of the more confusing aspects
of volunteer policing. Police departments are paramilitary in nature with a

strictly structured and organized chain of command. Commonly, volunteer units possess their own unique place in the departmental organizational hierarchy with their own internal chain of command. Ideally, the two chains of command (one for the entire agency, one within the volunteer unit) work together in a parallel manner to ensure a smooth and uninterrupted command structure. Different agencies abide by different administrative mechanisms in order to ensure the parallel structure works, which sometimes can lead to confusion or conflict. For example, a volunteer police officer might pursue a task as assigned from the volunteer command. While doing this task, the officer may be tasked with another duty from a full-time officer. In many volunteer units, orders from a full-time officer (regardless of rank) outweigh the orders from the volunteer command, even those with high rank. Thus, the volunteer officer is retasked, leaving the original task unaddressed and disobeying the original orders from the volunteer command. Due to service of two, sometimes conflicting, chains of command, the volunteer office may experience confusion and internal conflict.

3.2.6 Us versus Them, Part One: At Work

Volunteer police experience a dualism in their lives with which full-time paid officers do not contend. Although social friction between police and nonpolice during the officers' off-duty lives exists (see Us versus Them, Part Two), volunteer police receive greater amounts of time "off duty" and less "at work" social support. When at work, full-time officers find themselves surrounded by other like-minded people. Full-time officers' workmates are fellow police officers and police support staff: generally, a very pro-police group of people with empathetic experiences of the realities of police work. Volunteer police officers experience the benefit of empathic comrades when doing their police duties; however, when in their nonpolice (i.e., their full-time) jobs, the reality of such peer support presents as unlikely. In the current climate within the United States, there are likely many workplaces that have neutral to strong antipolice sentiments. For the volunteer officer, this could prove to be exceptionally stress-inducing and might potentially lead to hiding the fact that he or she volunteers as a police officer. Paid officers do not need to hide this aspect of their lives in order to avoid being denigrated at work from their colleagues for their policing roles. Volunteer officers volunteer their time to a uniquely difficult job and, as a result, may face negative repercussions at their workplace (and other social environments) for their altruistic commitment.

3.2.7 Us versus Them, Part Two: General, Off Duty

Due to the aforementioned issues, some volunteer police officers may keep their status as a volunteer officer compartmentalized (or even secret) in other aspects of their lives besides their day-to-day jobs. Those volunteer officers who share their volunteer status with coworkers, neighbors, and other associates inevitably encounter confusion or outright hostility about working as a police officer for free. Volunteer police officers truly lead a double life.

3.2.8 Us versus Them, Part Three: On Duty

Tensions may exist between full-time paid police officers and volunteer officers—perhaps the least talked-about aspect of volunteer policing. Officially, everyone within the police department loves volunteer police officers. Volunteers offer great work for a great price and satisfy the evolving needs of the department. Unofficially, there is often discord among the paid officers about volunteers. This conflict may be based on financial concerns— the perception that the volunteers are taking away paid overtime or part-time opportunities from the paid officers. Most volunteer departments go out of their way to ensure that they have no negative financial impact on individual officers, that the volunteers do not take money from their paychecks. On the contrary, volunteer officers, by doing certain work for free, free up more monies for salaries of the paid cadre.

Another criticism made from paid officers regarding their volunteering counterparts is that volunteer officers lack enough street experience to know how to handle themselves. Different departments enforce different requirements for the amount of time the volunteers spend on their duties during the month or year. If volunteers lack the competency to do police work because they do not work the street enough, they should be required to work more to maintain proficiency. However, this brush is often very broad, and volunteers who volunteer many hours are included in this generalization. The reality is that many volunteer police officers have worked the streets more recently and do it more frequently than command staff, training staff, or many other office jobs at the department. Paid officers do not question the command staffs' abilities even though many of them have not been on the street for years. Departments must realize, from the command staff to the newest recruit, that volunteer police officers often have the same training as the paid full-time officers, and many have more recent experiences than other officers on the paid staff. If the training for volunteers is not held to the same standard as for the full-time officers, then this needs to be addressed at the command or state policy level and not used as a mechanism to denigrate the efforts of the volunteer officers.

3.2.9 Normal Stressors

Life is stressful. People have the normal stressors of work, family, financial and medical issues, household responsibilities and costs, and so on. Volunteer police officers have all of those normal stresses, plus they have the additional stress of being a police officer and leading their double life. They work a second "job"—a potentially extremely risky, emotionally taxing, physically demanding, fraught with potential liabilities, and sometimes unpopular job. The support systems for this volunteer job lack ever-presence as for a paid officer, and the nondisclosure of this second life may certainly increase their day-to-day stress.

3.2.10 Primary Job Does Not Offer Support Inherent in Police Departments

When there is any sort of traumatic event for police, the department will become a strong support structure for its members. The law enforcement "family" is considerably protective of its members and will come to the aid of officers in times of need. Although part of this family while doing police work, volunteer police officers do not receive this valuable social support while at their full-time jobs. As mentioned previously, some volunteers do not share their involvement with the police at their paid jobs. Even if they do, non-law enforcement present with limited connection or understanding of what happens to police. The inherent support in police departments does not exist outside of the department. When at their paid jobs, volunteer police officers can feel isolated, alone, and unsupported, which can drastically increase their stress in times of need.*

3.2.11 Volunteer Police Programs Are Often Unknown to Many

There are fewer more recognizable workers in the modern world than the police officer. Police officers are such a ubiquitous image that, regardless of variations in uniforms, car paint schemes, and equipment, they are immediately recognizable to all. The concept of a community without police escapes imagination. The same does not hold true for volunteer police. Although they, of course, are recognized as police given the same (or very similar) appearance, anecdotal inquiries reveal that almost no community members are aware that there is such a person as a volunteer police officer. Even more surprising, many full-time police officers themselves are unaware that there are people doing the same job, for free—even in their same department!

---

* For example, as a member of his agency's dive team, Ben Dobrin retrieved the bodies of several deceased people. The two different retrievals of boys, similar in age to his own son, proved emotionally taxing. Despite the occurrence of emotional trauma, as soon as the retrieval process ended, he immediately went to his full-time job, where the other employees were unaware of the emotionally traumatic events he just endured.

3.2.12 Volunteer Police Are Volunteers

The most obvious unique characteristic of volunteer police officers that separates them from full-time officers is that they volunteer. The time they put into training, education, patrol, and other policing responsibilities is done without remuneration. They work for free. Volunteering is a popular activity for Americans with more than a quarter (26.5%) of adults in 2012 volunteering through a formal organization, totaling almost 8 billion hours (Corporation for National and Community Service [CNCS], 2014). This was worth $175 billion with national estimates of value being $22.55 per hour (Independent Sector, 2014). The rate of volunteering for those born between 1965 and 1981 displays a steady increase, going up almost 6% in the past 11 years. Parents with children under 18 volunteer more than people without children (33.5% compared to 23.8%) (CNCS, 2014), perhaps highlighting that those with a vested stake in the future are more willing to donate their time and labor. Additionally, volunteers are twice as likely to donate financially to charities than those who don't volunteer (CNCS, 2014), indicating that the desire to help is probably a stable personality trait revealed in multiple outlets. Volunteers are more likely to "exhibit positive emotions and social skills including openness, agreeableness, and extraversion" than nonvolunteers (Matsuba, Hart, & Atkins 2007, p. 903). Sullivan and Transue (1999) recognize that the key to optimal governance and oversight is the participation of those governed in the process of oversight. Democracies depend on an ethic of civic participation. Volunteerism is this belief in action, and volunteer police are a perfect manifestation of these ideals.

3.3 Conclusion

Volunteer police officers not only share some of the strenuous characteristics of working in law enforcement as do full-time paid officers, but volunteer officers experience additional factors that collectively compound the difficulties police officers experience on the job. The life-saving public service of volunteer police officers often goes unrecognized by the very recipients of said service, and yet volunteer officers continue to demonstrate dedication to public service.

References

Corporation for National and Community Service. (2014). *Volunteering and civic life in America 2013, national, regional, state, and city information.* Retrieved from http://www.volunteeringinamerica.gov/

Florida State Statute §943.085-943.255 Chapter 943 Department of Law Enforcement. Retrieved from http://www.leg.state.fl.us/Statutes/index.cfm?App_mode =Display_Statute&URL=0900-0999/0943/0943.html

Goldfarb, D. (1987). Ten reasons why police work is different. Presented at the Suffolk Country Police Conference, NY.

Hall, C. (2015). Court: Resisting reserve police officer not a crime. *Detroit Free Press* (9/21/2015). Retrieved from http://www.freep.com/story/news/local/michigan/2015/09/21/reserve-police-officer-michigan-resisting-statute/72586134/

Independent Sector. (2014). Retrieved from http://www.independentsector.org

Matsuba, K., Hart, D., & Atkins, R. (2007). Psychological and social-structural influences on commitment to volunteering. *Journal of Research in Personality,* *41*(4): 889–907.

Sullivan, J. L., & Transue, J. E. (1999). The psychological underpinnings of democracy: A selective review of research on political tolerance, interpersonal trust, and social capital. *Annual Review of Psychology, 50*: 625–650.

Virginia Code §15.2-1731. Establishment, etc., authorized; powers, authority and immunities generally. Retrieved from https://vacode.org/15.2-1731/

Virginia Code §18.2-31. Capital murder defined; punishment. Retrieved from https://vacode.org/18.2-31/

Police Volunteer Programs in the United States

II

Police Auxiliaries in Framingham, Massachusetts

4

MARC SPIGEL

Contents

4.1 Introduction

The Framingham Auxiliary Police was established in 1942 in order to assist the Framingham Police Department and Civil Defense Agency during World War II. The Framingham Auxiliary Police is comprised of trained volunteers who give of themselves to make Framingham a better place to live and work. It is the policy of the Framingham Police Department to provide guidance to members of the Framingham Auxiliary Police through various policies, procedures, and regulations, which have been established to direct members in the performance of their duties and responsibilities. The mission of the Framingham Auxiliary Police is to be prepared to assist the Framingham Police Department in the event of a civil or natural disaster or in the event that additional personnel are needed by the Framingham Police Department to carry out its assigned duties. The Framingham Auxiliary Police is a part of the Framingham Emergency Management Agency and is organized under the Massachusetts Civil Defense Act of 1950. As last measured in 2011, Massachusetts has 77 law enforcement agencies with volunteer police programs with approximately 1,200 auxiliary, reserve, and special officers. Of these programs, 56 agencies participated in a survey that showed 1,029 auxiliary, reserve, and special officers volunteered 124,338 hours in 2010, equating to $3.3M of services at the established volunteer rate of $26.18 per hour.*

4.2 History of the Agency

The Town of Framingham is a diverse community located 20 miles west of Boston. Framingham has 67,000 residents with a daytime population estimated at 100,000. Framingham is the largest municipality in Massachusetts that has a town meeting form of government.

At the first town meeting in 1700, three individuals were elected town constables. At that time, constables and volunteers from the community had the responsibility to keep peace and order in the town. The advent of trains brought crime into the community from the outside, and the existing part-time constables were no longer able to cope with the "vagabonds and vagrants." One hundred seventy-one years later, in 1871, the Framingham Police Department was established. Officers during this time had no formal training and had to provide their own equipment and uniforms except for their badge. Many officers would travel to Boston and buy used police uniforms from the then well-established Boston Police Department, the first professional police department in the country. Officers in this era worked alone. There was no concept of roll call or backup. You were on your own to effect law and order. The department slowly grew in size over the course of many years; a sergeant was added in 1909, and pension benefits were afforded in 1925. A review of the history of the department shows that police officers often faced many of the same issues and dangers that the officers face today. For example, in 1923, while on routine patrol, Officer William H. Welch stopped a suspicious person for questioning. He took the suspect to a boarding house and called the station for assistance. The suspect fled, and Officer Welch pursued the suspect, who drew a concealed revolver and shot Officer Welch at point-blank range, killing him.[†]

Today, the Framingham Police Department is recognized as a leading and innovative law enforcement agency in Massachusetts. The Framingham Police Department is charged with protecting and serving those who live, work, and travel in Framingham. The department accomplishes its mission by establishing partnerships with the community, using innovative

---

[*] Survey conducted in the fall of 2011 by the Massachusetts Chiefs of Police Association, www.masschiefs.org, in conjunction with the Massachusetts Volunteer Law Enforcement Officer Association www.mavleoa.org.
[†] Framingham Police Department 1871–1994 Commemorative History Book by Orlo H. Coots, Jr.

problem-solving approaches, and recognizing the value of strong leadership and organizational accountability.* Led by Chief Steven B. Carl, the men and women who are the Framingham Police Department are consummate professionals who work tirelessly to serve and protect the citizens of Framingham. The Framingham Police Department has been accredited by the Massachusetts Police Accreditation Commission since 2005.

4.3 Overview of the Framingham Police Auxiliary Program

The Framingham Police originally established an auxiliary police program in 1942, during World War II, as part of the nation's Civil Defense program. The first duty of the auxiliary officers was to enforce the blackout, serving as Civil Defense air raid wardens. Following the war, auxiliary officers continued to serve the town but with a different focus. Instead of being on the watch for blackout violators, the auxiliary officers began patrolling town-owned properties, watching for vandalism and checking for improperly secured buildings. Auxiliary officers continued to help the Framingham Police Department in whatever capacity was necessary and remained prepared to assist in times of disaster. In 1953, natural disaster struck the town in the form of a tornado, and Chief McCarthy praised the auxiliary police for their efforts: "On this occasion the emergency auxiliary groups responded over and above the call of duty. The auxiliary police have been a great source of help as a uniformed outfit. They are second to none."† These deep traditions continue as the Framingham Auxiliary Police continued to evolve with the times and is currently recognized as a leading auxiliary police unit in Massachusetts. Although our selection process has become more rigorous and our standards of training have increased significantly, auxiliary officers today have the same values and desires as our predecessors: to make Framingham a better and safer place to live and work while being prepared to assist the Framingham Police Department as needed.

4.4 Present State of Affairs

By the end of 2012, we had 20 auxiliary officers in Framingham. During 2012, we contributed more than 4,000 hours of service to our community. Our strength fluctuates between 20 and 25 officers. Framingham has 115

---

* Framingham Police website: www.framinghampd.org.
† Framingham Police Department 1871–1994 Commemorative History Book by Orlo H. Coots, Jr.

full-time sworn officers, so our auxiliary force brings approximately a 20% increase of manpower reserve to the department in times of emergency.

Becoming an auxiliary officer in Framingham is not an easy task. In order to achieve excellence, we start with a selection process that helps choose only the finest recruit officers. We administer three separate tests to all candidates: the Laser Associates entry-level law enforcement examination, the Inwald Personality Index (IPI), and the Johnson and Roberts Personal History Questionnaire (PHQ). Our goal is that any officer that we accept as a volunteer should be of the same caliber that would be hired for a full-time position by the Framingham Police. Candidates who successfully pass these tests are then subject to a background investigation and are interviewed by a board of auxiliary officers and the Framingham police liaison officer. Our recruit selection process helps us to select quality volunteers for our organization to continue achieving its goal of excellence and professionalism. Of those candidates who express an interest and sit for the tests, we only select about a third of the candidates. An average of 50% do not pass the entry-level law enforcement examination, and of those who do, not all make it through the remainder of our review.

After selection and prior to being issued a uniform, our auxiliary officers all attend the Massachusetts Municipal Training Committee Reserve Intermittent Academy. This is currently a 242-hour academy. After completion of the academy, our officers attend a 24-hour orientation program conducted by auxiliary officers and, last, are issued a uniform. At this time, these officers can start participating in field training. Every Friday and Saturday night from approximately 7 pm to midnight, a senior auxiliary officer is paired with a junior officer for a training patrol. During the evening, the auxiliary officers will check on critical infrastructure in town and assist the police department as requested.

The Framingham Auxiliary Police is committed to a community policing philosophy. In fact, our very existence demonstrates community policing in action. We express our commitment by contributing actively to the quality of life in Framingham through our role as auxiliary police officers by providing our volunteer services for many community activities and events. There are several ongoing activities that we provide services for regularly. During the summer, we are proud to provide traffic assistance at the town's Concerts on the Green. As requested, we distribute winter parking notifications before the annual winter parking restrictions take effect and carry out door-to-door community notifications. In addition to these ongoing activities, in 2012 we provided assistance with 29 separate community, charitable, and safety events in Framingham. Without our assistance, some of these events would have been difficult to conduct safely, or Framingham Police resources would have needed to be reassigned from patrol to provide the needed services.

4.5 Accomplishments and Success

The overriding success of our auxiliary police program can be attributed to the enhancement of our training and recruit selection processes that professionalize our organization and which started in the early 1990s. The enhancements were made in advance of the Framingham Police Department's decision to become accredited and were instrumental in our accreditation success.

4.6 Training

Prior to 1992, required training for our auxiliary officers was only a few hours in length, which was just long enough to cover an introduction to the role of an auxiliary police officer. At that point, you were issued a uniform and were scheduled to assignments. Hands-on training continued during these assignments and were supervised by a superior officer. To this day, there is no training requirement for auxiliary police officers in Massachusetts. Around 1990, the ranking officers of the Framingham Auxiliary Police determined that the limited training that our officers received was inadequate in relation to our responsibilities and that one day we could find the unit disbanded as a result.

The best available training was offered through the Massachusetts Criminal Justice Training Council (now known as the Municipal Police Training Committee). The Training Council offered a state-sponsored Reserve Intermittent Academy. This training academy is designed for part-time officers in Massachusetts and is delivered during "reserve-friendly" times (nights and weekends). In addition to the academy training, additional training in CPR and use of force was determined to be a necessity before an officer could be considered to have had sufficient training. Our policy was changed in 1991 to give all current auxiliary officers a two-year period of time to complete the training program. All new officers had the same time deadline. At the end of the two-year period, we instituted a new policy under which all the preliminary training was required prior to issuing a uniform to a new officer.

Since 1993, all of our auxiliary officers have completed the Reserve Intermittent Academy along with CPR, which now includes AED as well as training and certification in all use-of-force options that they carry. During the transition period, we sponsored a Reserve Intermittent Academy in Framingham. The full-time officers observed firsthand the commitment our auxiliary officers were making as well as seeing that we were being trained by the same instructors that they had in their academy. This observation made a lasting positive impact on the relationship between auxiliary and full-time officers of the department. Annually, we conduct an in-service training program that complies with Municipal Police Training Committee guidelines as well as

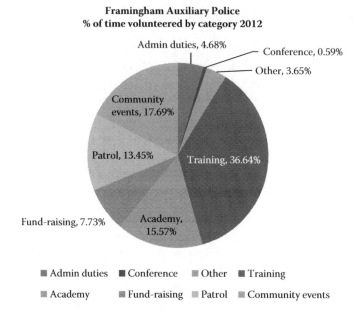

Figure 4.1 Total 2012 hours (4,050) presented as a percentage by category of service.

recertification programs as required. By examining Figure 4.1, it is obvious that the Framingham Police Department has recognized the relevance of professional instruction and development through the extensive academy and in-service training hours it continues to provide to the Framingham Auxiliary Police.

4.7 Selection Process

Prior to 1998, our selection process consisted of a review of the applicant's criminal history and an informal interview. We determined that we needed to create a selection process that mirrored the Framingham Police recruit selection process. However, the Framingham Police is a civil service department, so the same tests were not available for use. In 1998, we enhanced our selection process by adding an entry-level police officer exam, a formal oral board interview, and a thorough background investigation. The goal we set is that anybody who we accept as an auxiliary officer would be of the same caliber that the Framingham Police Department would hire for a full-time position.

4.8 Accreditation

There is a myth that needs to be busted. The myth is that a department with an auxiliary police unit cannot be accredited. The myth is not true. The auxiliary unit must meet or exceed accreditation standards, which should be the goal even if your department is not seeking accreditation.

In 1999, the Framingham Police Department established a goal of becoming an accredited agency. The accreditation was to be conducted by the Massachusetts Police Accreditation Commission (MPAC), which follows national Commission for Accreditation of Law Enforcement Agencies (CALEA) standards as modified by the MPAC. It was the news that all auxiliary and reserve police units generally fear as it has been the demise of many volunteer units, which is a practice that unfortunately continues to occur in 2013.* Our challenge was not to be an obstacle in the Framingham Police Department's accreditation as we fully understood what our fate would be if we were in the way.

Our first step was to contact the now-defunct Massachusetts Auxiliary Police Association to determine what other auxiliary units and the association were doing in regards to preparing for accreditation. I was advised by the association president that accreditation was the way that auxiliary police units would be eliminated in the state, and the association would offer no help. Finding no help locally, our next step was to identify armed auxiliary or reserve units that were part of accredited departments. Our information source was the book *Reserve Law Enforcement in the United States* by Dr. Richard Weinblatt.† Through the book, we identified that the Florida Highway Patrol Auxiliary was very similar to the Framingham Auxiliary Police in both training requirements and scope of duty. We contacted the Florida Highway Patrol Accreditation manager and the auxiliary coordinator. They were very helpful and sent me both the Florida Highway Patrol policies and the Florida Highway Patrol Auxiliary policy manual. Much later in the process (in 2005), the Florida Highway Patrol helped again and explained their program, policies, and procedures to the MPAC during our accreditation. We also contacted CALEA, which was very helpful in explaining the accreditation standards.

We then conducted a self-assessment and found that the Framingham Auxiliary Police measured up well to the accreditation standards. There were small gaps that would be easy to fill. The self-assessment was submitted to our accreditation manager, where it sat from 1999 to 2002 as the department worked on policy and physical changes to the police station that would be needed to fulfill accreditation standards.

In the fall of 2002, the Framingham Police Department had its first in-house meeting with MPAC. The focus of discussion quickly turned to the

---

* Glen Rock New Jersey Disbands Auxiliary Police Unit 2-3-13 http://www.northjersey .com/news/189549041_Glen_Rock_disbands_auxiliary__police_unit.html.
† Reserve Law Enforcement in the United States: A National Study of State, County and City Police & Sheriff's Reserves—ISBN-10: 0982869738.

Framingham Auxiliary Police program. The commission had yet to find an armed auxiliary program operating under the Civil Defense Statutes. The very next day, the MPAC commissioners had a scheduled meeting, and the deputy chief, who was also the accreditation manager, was asked to meet with the commission to discuss the auxiliary police program. For two hours, the deputy chief defended our professional auxiliary program before the commissioners, who had many questions. By the end of the meeting, the commissioners still did not understand the concept of unpaid volunteer officers, and it became clear that having the auxiliary police unit be part of the accreditation was not going to be easy.

In January 2003, the department was asked to attend a commission meeting to further explain our program. The liaison to the auxiliary police program, police department attorney, and auxiliary police commanding officer attended the meeting, and they made a presentation about the Framingham Auxiliary Police to the commissioners. There was much debate among the commissioners, none of which was terribly positive toward auxiliary police programs. At the end of the meeting, it was determined that we would be assessed against the Auxiliary Police Standards, which are less of a hurdle than the Reserve Police Standards.

It was clear that we were going to be the test case for the state, and we had to develop a strong policy for the department, backed up by statutes and case law. Throughout 2003, extensive legal research was conducted by the department's attorney, and support for this effort was given by the police chief, both of whom were former auxiliary officers. From this research, a Framingham Police policy on auxiliary police was written and adopted by the time the assessors arrived in September 2004.

The assessors conducted their review, including the auxiliary police. They found no flaws in the auxiliary policy and records as compared to the accreditation standards. We thought we were all set, but the commissioners needed to review the assessment and make their final determination.

In October 2004, the commissioners met and did not approve the Framingham Police accreditation. They noted a few small items and one big one. The big item in their view continued to be the Auxiliary Police Program. At the October 2004 meeting, the commissioners determined that the bar would be raised on the auxiliary program, and we would need to meet the reserve standard.

The next few months were very active, and the Framingham Police policy was revised to reflect the reserve standards. These changes were positive changes compared to some of the requirements of the auxiliary standards. As we were really at the accreditation reserve level, this was a great outcome. The commissioners requested that we use the same application as the Framingham Police and add two additional entrance exams to our selection process.

On March 10, 2005, the MPAC voted to award state accreditation to the Framingham Police Department.

The success of the Framingham Auxiliary Police being included in the accreditation process is the clear result of the professionalism of the men and women who volunteer their time to make our community a better and safer place to live and work.

4.9 Summary, Conclusion, and Recommendations

A successful volunteer police program begins with support of the command staff of the agency and the respect of the officers. This can be obtained by developing a program that has standards that are in compliance with accreditation standards whether your agency is seeking such status or not. This starts by selecting volunteers that the agency would hire for a full-time sworn position if they were to apply for that position. Hold your volunteers to the same high standard. The next step is to provide training that meets or exceeds the training needed to complete the volunteer assignments that the officers will be given. The training should be provided in a professional environment with high standards, preferably by the same authority that is responsible for training full-time officers. Once the initial training is completed, ongoing continuing education should be in place to maintain certification. The other element to include is a way to thank your volunteers for their efforts.

Abundance of Auxiliary Police and Volunteer Personnel in the NYPD

5

JAMES F. ALBRECHT

Contents

5.1 Introduction

The New York City Police Department, with the largest police complement in the United States, also boasts the largest cadre of active police volunteers. The NYPD oversees a number of volunteer initiatives, the two most notable involving the more than 4,000 auxiliary police officers (APOs) who patrol in uniform in all communities across New York City, and more than 10,000 retired NYPD officers who remain trained and ready for active service under the Retiree Mobilization Plan. In addition, the NYPD continues to operate successful volunteer programs that involve local religious clerics and adolescent explorers, among others, in community events.

5.2 NYPD Auxiliary Police Program

The NYPD Auxiliary Police Program traces its roots back to the last century and the need for a competent team of community volunteers to assist in public safety during the challenging wartime and cold war periods. Although many volunteers assisted in routine public safety functions during World War I and World War II, the practice was formalized in 1941 by the federal statute that developed the United States Citizen Service Corps and later, in more detail, by the Federal Civil Defense Act of 1950, developed in response to the perceived nuclear threat during the early years of the Cold War (Executive Order 8757, 1941). The NYPD has maintained its Auxiliary Police Program since 1951, after the enactment of the New York State Defense Emergency Act. The program was initially created to assist in the response to civil defense emergencies or natural disasters; however, those responsibilities were expanded in a New York City Mayoral Executive Order to specifically include uniformed patrol and crime prevention under the supervision of the NYPD (Kelly et al., 2008).

As a result, the NYPD Auxiliary Police Program flourished due to matching federal grants, and the number of auxiliary police personnel continued to increase until the late 1970s, when they were stifled by the budgetary crisis. Rising serious crime and violence rates and a call for stronger community–police partnerships throughout the 1980s* and 1990s, later coupled with the tragedies of September 11, 2001, continued to highlight the enhanced need for the incorporation of volunteers into public service agencies, and the NYPD was not unresponsive to this need. The number of APOs within the NYPD has ranged from a high of more than 8,000 at the turn of the century to the present level exceeding 4,000.

5.3 Auxiliary Police Program Guidelines and Training

NYPD APOs must be between the ages of 17 and 60, live or work within New York City, and pass a background investigation. In 50 hours of training over a 16-week period, the candidate receives instruction on the New York State Penal and Criminal Procedure Laws, baton and self-defense tactics, first aid, police procedures, traffic control, and other related topics. The APO can then be assigned to a patrol precinct, transit (subway) district, or socialized housing police service area, usually at their request and likely in their own residential neighborhoods (Kelly et al., 2008).

---

* The author served as an NYPD APO for three years during the early 1980s in the 112th Precinct before moving on to become a career NYPD officer.

5.4 Mission of an NYPD APO

New York City Police Department policy delineates the specific mission of these highly committed volunteers:

1. To assist the NYPD in deterring crime by having auxiliary police perform uniform patrol
2. To help bridge the gap between the NYPD and the community and improve community relations
3. To maintain a large team of trained APOs that would assist the NYPD in the event of an emergency or natural disaster

5.5 Responsibilities and Restrictions

NYPD APOs routinely patrol within all NYPD precincts and jurisdictions in uniform and generally on foot patrol. Some perform highway, mounted, harbor, or bicycle patrol. However, of paramount importance is that NYPD APOs do not possess arrest or law enforcement authorities, are not armed with firearms, and can merely "observe and report" criminal acts and illegal behavior to the NYPD radio dispatcher. They have been instructed to act solely as additional "eyes and ears" for the NYPD. In addition, court decisions have delineated that APOs within the state of New York cannot be used as substitutes for police officers nor be assigned to hazardous and dangerous duties. Agency procedure mandates that NYPD APOs cannot be assigned to solo patrol assignments and emphasizes that they cannot act as primary response personnel to radio calls or assignments (Kelly et al., 2008). By legislation, NYPD APOs can be granted "peace officer" status by the NY State Criminal Procedure Code during declared states of emergency.

Even given these restrictions, the NYPD Auxiliary Police Program cadre contributes more than a million hours of volunteer service each year and has been a key component to enhancing community safety and providing a visible police presence at parades, street festivals, schools, and neighborhood activities throughout communities across New York City (Kelly et al., 2008).

5.6 NYPD's Retiree Mobilization Plan

In addition to the auxiliary police program, the NYPD, in 2006, initiated the Retiree Mobilization Plan (RMP) in order to maximize organizational efforts to respond to critical incidents and large-scale emergencies with experienced and trained first responders. The RMP volunteers, comprised of retired NYPD officers, receive routine training but are activated only under exigent circumstances. The Personnel Bureau of the NYPD maintains a database outlining the expertise and specialization of each RMP member, and if mobilized, the NYPD incident commander at the scene of an incident would determine which assignment would best benefit the effectiveness of that particular mission. The NYPD RMP program presently consists of more than 10,000 retired NYPD officers who do not have arrest or law enforcement authority, are not financially compensated, and likely participate to maintain the esprit de corps experienced across the law enforcement profession (NYPD Operations Order 16, 2006).*

5.7 When Tragedy Strikes

On March 14, 2007, a major tragedy struck New York City as two auxiliary police heroes, APO Nicholas Todd Pekearo and APO Yevgeniy Marshalik, were savagely killed while attempting to engage a suspect involved in a disturbance in midtown Manhattan. The suspect had just committed a robbery at a Greenwich Village pizzeria, where he murdered the employee by shooting him 15 times.

After hearing the suspect's description over their police radios, foot patrol partners APO Pekearo and APO Marshalik approached the suspect a few blocks from the scene of the crime. Both officers ordered the suspect to drop a bag he had been holding. The killer initially complied but then punched APO Marshalik in the face, knocking him to the ground. The killer fled on foot with both APOs in close pursuit. Seeing that capture was likely, the suspect drew a firearm and opened fire on the officers. APO Pekearo took cover behind a parked vehicle, but the suspect approached from behind, shooting him six times and killing him almost instantly. The suspect then attempted to again flee the scene, but noting that APO Marshalik had just taken cover, he approached him and assassinated him with one shot to the head. Responding officers from the local NYPD precinct opened fire on the suspect, who repeatedly opened fire on NYPD personnel. The suspect was quickly shot and killed in the ensuing gun battle. After searching the suspect's bag, it was revealed that the suspect had one secreted handgun in addition to the second one that he used in the gunfight. Both of the heroic APOs have been recognized, not only by the City of New York and the NYPD, but also by the federal government for their sacrifices.

---

* A separate chapter will thoroughly outline the more specific aspects of the NYPD Retiree Mobilization Plan.

5.8 Terrorism and Natural Disaster Are Met with Heroism and Commitment

5.8.1 September 11, 2001

Although New York City fortunately possesses the largest police agency in the United States, the NYPD has been notably supported by their highly respected volunteers during critical incidents.

On September 11, 2001, the first responders of New York City responded to the dramatic and challenging circumstances that quickly unfolded as the result of the terrorist attacks in Manhattan. Even with more than 40,000 active police officers and 10,000 career firefighters, the City of New York was strained to the limit. Not only were the rescue operations at the collapsed World Trade Center pressing, the NYPD was tasked with securing the entire municipality from further attack and for carrying on routine police responsibilities. As a result, the New York City Police Department called upon the thousands of available APOs to respond and assist in completing these strenuous tasks.* Although many held full-time positions and had family obligations, APOs in the thousands regularly worked hundreds of volunteer hours after the tragedy to maintain a safe and secure environment across the city.

5.8.2 Hurricane Sandy

On October 29, 2012, Hurricane Sandy struck America's northeastern coastline, wreaking havoc and causing mass destruction and casualties. New York City was directly in the path of this tropical storm, which destroyed thousands of homes and flooded coastal areas and most of the island of Manhattan.

Fortunately, as in the case of many natural disasters, there is advanced warning, and jurisdictions can properly prepare for many of the anticipated exigencies. This was the case with Hurricane Sandy. The New York City Police Department activated all police resources, including auxiliary police and RMP personnel. This option provided the City of New York and the NYPD with a large reserve, numbering thousands, who were properly trained and capable of addressing the many challenges facing this large metropolis before, during, and after this tragic event. As a result, and in line with the successful transitions observed after the September 11, 2001 tragedy, the City of New York returned to a general sense of normalcy within two weeks of this disaster. This is an astounding accomplishment given that the population of

---

* At the time of the September 11, 2001 attacks in New York City, the author was an NYPD precinct commanding officer, who utilized the transit district's auxiliary police team to conduct routine patrols and to provide relief breaks to police officers on patrol. These APOs proved to be force multipliers and enhanced command capabilities at a time when the need was most evident.

New York City approaches 10 million with approximately 3 million more visiting on a daily basis. And this is clearly indicative of the levels of sacrifice and commitment that NYPD auxiliary police and RMP personnel regularly dedicate to the public safety and well being of the Big Apple.

5.9 Conclusion

There is no doubt that maintaining a properly vetted, trained, and recognized cadre of volunteers can positively impact police organizational performance and reputation. In line with Sir Robert Peel's principles of law enforcement (Lee, 1901, p. 7) outlined in 1829, all police agencies are obligated "(t)o maintain at all times a relationship with the public that gives reality to the historic tradition that the police are the public and that the public are the police…"

References

Executive Order No. 8757, 6 Fed. Reg. 2517 (May 20, 1941).

Kelly, R. et al. (2008). *NYPD Auxiliary Police Program Overview 2008*. New York Police Department, New York. http://www.nyc.gov/html/nypd/downloads /pdf/careers/nypd_auxiliary_police_overview_2008.pdf (accessed January 16, 2016).

Lee, W. L. M. (1901). *A History of Police in England*. Methuan and Company: London.

NYPD Operations Order 16, March 14, 2006.

Florida Highway Patrol Auxiliary

6

STEVEN SHEFFER

Contents

6.1   Introduction: The Use of Volunteers in State Law Enforcement

Since the tragedy of September 11, 2001, an emphasis has been placed on homeland security, law enforcement, and public safety volunteerism. In conjunction with the International Association of Chiefs of Police and the Bureau of Justice, the Volunteers in Police Service (VIPS) has been working to promote and enhance the local, county, and state law enforcement to utilize volunteers. The concept of volunteers in policing is not new, but the role and scope of these programs is evolving.

An informal survey by the Council of Law Enforcement Reserves attempted to quantify the actual number of reserve police serving in the United States. As there is no formal tracking of reserve law enforcement officers, the council collected data from state-level standards and training organizations. The 2011 estimate is more than 86,000 volunteer officers although the vast majority of programs are at the municipal and county level, and the concept of using volunteers at a state level is somewhat limited.

Across the nation, state-level programs once flourished; however, today, only a handful of these programs survive. Programs were established by states in Alabama, Arizona, Connecticut, Florida, New Hampshire, Ohio, South Carolina, and Vermont. The Alabama, Ohio, and Florida programs are very active.

This chapter presents information on one of the largest state-based volunteer programs in operation: the Florida Highway Patrol Auxiliary (FHPA).

6.2 Overview and Early History

The FHPA is a professionally trained, all-volunteer, statewide law enforcement organization dedicated to providing direct assistance and operational support to the Florida Highway Patrol (FHP). Formed by an act of the Florida legislature, the FHPA is patterned after the Ohio State Highway Patrol Auxiliary, which was formed in 1942.

The State of Ohio had great success utilizing members from local VFW posts to support its troopers. A member of the Ohio program, Ronald Johnson, played a key role in moving the Florida program forward. Johnson served as chairman of the Florida Law and Order Committee and past commander of VFW Post 14 in St. Petersburg, Florida. At its 1954 Florida convention, the VFW supported the FHPA concept. Subsequent meetings were also held in St. Petersburg between Colonel N. H. Kirkman, the first director of the Highway Patrol and the American Legion (Flying Wheel, OSHP, May 1955). An act authorizing the creation of the FHPA was passed by the Florida legislature and signed into law by Governor Leroy Collins on May 14, 1957. Today, the Ohio and Florida auxiliary programs share many similarities and maintain strong relationships.

The director of the FHP appoints FHPA members. As volunteers, auxiliary members serve without compensation although statute allows a member to serve with or without compensation. As a result of the success of the FHPA program, the Florida Department of Environmental Protection, Florida Fish and Wildlife Commission, and Florida Department of Law Enforcement Capitol Police have functioning reserve programs although they are smaller in scale.

Since 1994, the Florida legislature has provided more than $3,000,000 in direct funding. State funds are earmarked for training and equipment. All uniforms and weapons are provided. In recent years, this amount has been reduced in response to state budget pressure.

The FHPA has a similar organizational structure to that of the FHP. The director of the FHP appoints an auxiliary director who, up until 2011, held the rank of colonel. The position of auxiliary director was rebadged at the rank of lieutenant colonel. The FHPA's director has an executive staff that assists in overseeing the 10 troops that, in turn, support 28 districts.

The command staff oversees field operations, recruitment, training, the auxiliary's budget, and a volunteer auxiliary surgeon program. Bureau chiefs oversee supply, logistics, and their assigned budgets along with the technology infrastructure that links the entire organization statewide. Auxiliary troops are commanded by majors and districts by captains. The local FHP staff officers at the district level directly supervise FHPA members.

6.3 FHPA Mission

The primary duties of the auxiliary are to assist the FHP in the performance of their regularly constituted duties. These include the following:

- Safety augmentation and operational enhancement by riding with FHP troopers on patrol
- Communication center operations
- Operation of chemical test equipment to assist troopers in the detection of impaired drivers
- Traffic details and special enforcement/safety campaigns
- Aircraft operations

FHPA members respond to emergency situations or statewide response situations when such action is appropriate or requested. This includes such emergencies as hurricanes and wildfires, which occur in Florida.

Auxiliary troopers are responsible for various specialized details and assignments across the state. Troopers assist with a wide variety of public safety campaigns and educational events such as child-seat education, seat belt/vehicle rollover simulation, and DUI awareness programs. With the high volume of large-scale public sporting events in Florida, the FHPA supports local jurisdictions with traffic control and enhanced patrol presence. Combined with full-time troopers, the FHPA is often utilized as a force extender, thus allowing the state to provide mutual aid assistance by quickly deploying hundreds of troopers. This manpower surge is especially critical for ensuring a sustained presence at major special events, critical incidents, or for regional scale emergencies.

6.4 Duties and Statutory Authority

Florida statute defines an auxiliary officer as any person employed or appointed who serves with or without compensation and who aids or assists a full-time or part-time law enforcement officer. Florida statute does not specifically create a reserve officer category. Individual department policy establishes the scope and duties of its reserve or auxiliary officers. Some agencies have adopted the term "reserve officer;" however, the FHP's volunteer program retains its original 1957 designation as "auxiliary." Florida statute only defines sworn peace officers as full-time, part-time, or auxiliary officers. Auxiliary officers have the authority to arrest and perform law enforcement functions while under the supervision and direction of an FHP trooper, which was defined by a 1993 advisory opinion by Florida's attorney general (AGO 93-64).

Members of an auxiliary also have the same protection and immunities afforded full-time troopers.

6.5 Relevant Florida Statutes

321.24   Members of an Auxiliary to Florida Highway Patrol

(1) The director of the Florida Highway Patrol is hereby authorized to establish an auxiliary to the Florida Highway Patrol to be composed of such persons who may volunteer to serve as members of an auxiliary to the Florida Highway Patrol as defined in s. 943.10(8).

(2) Members of an auxiliary serving with the Florida Highway Patrol shall at all times serve under the direction and supervision of the director and members of the Florida Highway Patrol. After approval by the director on an individual basis and after completion of a firearms course approved by the director, members of an auxiliary, while serving under the supervision and direction of the director, or a member of the Florida Highway Patrol, shall have the power to bear arms and make arrests. Members of an auxiliary shall have the same protection and immunities afforded regularly employed highway patrol officers, which shall be recognized by all courts having jurisdiction over offenses against the laws of this state.

(3) The director of the Florida Highway Patrol shall determine the fitness of persons to serve as members of an auxiliary, shall require their completion of a regularly prescribed course of study for members of an auxiliary as established and conducted by the Florida Highway Patrol. The total number of members of the auxiliary to the Florida Highway Patrol shall be limited to 5 times the total number of regularly employed highway patrol officers authorized by law.

(4) No member of the auxiliary shall be required to serve on any duty of and for said auxiliary without his or her consent thereto. The duties of the auxiliary shall be limited to assisting the Florida Highway Patrol in the performance of its regularly constituted duties.

(5) Notwithstanding any other law to the contrary, any volunteer highway patrol troop surgeon appointed by the director of the Florida Highway Patrol and any volunteer licensed health professional appointed by the director of the Florida Highway Patrol to

work under the medical direction of a highway patrol troop surgeon is considered an employee for purposes of s. 768.28(9).

(6) The director of the Florida Highway Patrol may present to an officer who retires from the Florida Highway Patrol Auxiliary after a minimum of 20 years of service one complete uniform, including the badge worn by that officer; the officer's service handgun, if one was issued as part of the officer's equipment; and an identification card clearly marked "RETIRED."

943.10   Law Enforcement Definitions

(1) "Law enforcement officer" means any person who is elected, appointed, or employed full time by any municipality or the state or any political subdivision thereof; who is vested with authority to bear arms and make arrests; and whose primary responsibility is the prevention and detection of crime or the enforcement of the penal, criminal, traffic, or highway laws of the state. This definition includes all certified supervisory and command personnel whose duties include, in whole or in part, the supervision, training, guidance, and management responsibilities of full-time law enforcement officers, part-time law enforcement officers, or auxiliary law enforcement officers but does not include support personnel employed by the employing agency.

(8) "Auxiliary law enforcement officer" means any person employed or appointed, with or without compensation, who aids or assists a full-time or part-time law enforcement officer and who, while under the direct supervision of a full-time or part-time law enforcement officer, has the authority to arrest and perform law enforcement functions.

The FHPA designates four tiers of qualification for its members:

Level I–Non-sworn (or civilian volunteer): Assists with non-law enforcement duties (administrative/clerical)*

Level II–Auxiliary trooper: Patrol with zone troopers and assist FHP as directed at checkpoints and with other enforcement duties

Level III–Limited scope patrol (LSP) auxiliary trooper: High-visibility patrol, assist disabled motorists, assist/back up zone troopers

Level IV–Senior LSP auxiliary trooper: Selective enforcement, noncriminal traffic crash investigations, citations

---

* Level I is reserved for civilian volunteers who wish to contribute their time and talent to the FHP.

All serve a valuable role in non-law enforcement and administrative capacities and provide a wide range of support services. Additionally, sworn members may revert to Level I status and continue to contribute their experience with a non-sworn status. This has been particularly helpful with retaining older members who wish to remain active within the FHPA but wish to no longer perform in a law enforcement role.

FHPA recruits who complete the basic auxiliary recruit training course or who already have current full or auxiliary police standards certification in Florida enter at Level II status. Most auxiliary troopers ride with other FHP troopers, forming two-officer patrol units. After a year's probation and an additional two years of service as a Level II trooper, members may take advanced in-service and field training and move to Level III, performing LSP. More than 150 auxiliary troopers are today designated to patrol independently, covering assigned zones. This program was implemented on New Year's Eve 1996 and resulted in the apprehension of four impaired drivers in its first eight hours of existence. The LSP program is designed to create a high-visibility patrol presence and especially to assist in zone coverage on long stretches of rural Florida interstate.

6.6 Training

Once an applicant has successfully passed the background investigation and all physical and mental testing, they are permitted to enter the recruit academy program. This basic training academy consists of a minimum of 319 hours of law enforcement training, which is conducted regionally at districts across the state. Topics include the following:

- Civil and criminal law
- NCIC/FCIC operations
- Intoxilyzer operations
- Defensive tactics
- Domestic violence/human diversity
- Laser/radar ops
- Crash investigation/report writing
- Human diversity
- First responder
- Professional traffic stops
- Juvenile sexual offender
- PR24 baton and TASER
- Emergency vehicle operations
- HAZMAT
- Aerosol subject restraint

Applicants must meet the same eligibility requirements as an applicant for full-time positions with the FHP. Only after successfully navigating the rigorous background investigation, physical and mental testing, and academy training as well as passing the state's certification exam will the applicant be appointed.

Recurrent or annual training is conducted by FHP troopers assigned to support each FHPA district as instructors. Instructors volunteer for this additional duty, and the agency provides shift-schedule flexibility that allows these FHP troopers to deliver training. Instructors are state-certified by the Florida Criminal Justice Training Commission and additionally are supported by FHP's training academy. FHPA members may also obtain state certification as an instructor and assist with delivery of training.

6.7 Recruiting

As with all law enforcement agencies, the recruiting and appointment of qualified candidates is a major challenge. The FHPA is fortunate to have members who take on the additional responsibility of managing the recruitment and background process for prospective members. Ongoing, there are approximately 50 individuals who are in the process to become an auxiliary trooper statewide. Auxiliary applicants come from many different backgrounds, including businessmen, attorneys, pilots, teachers, physicians, students, hospital administrators, firefighters, paramedics, master tradesmen, former law enforcement, and military personnel.

The FHPA utilizes a variety of platforms to search for volunteers, and these include recruitment literature and posters, public safety displays, and the media. One of the more powerful recruitment tools is the organization's dedicated recruiting website at www.FloridaStateTrooper.org. Here, interested applicants review preliminary information about the FHPA. They then may request information and make contact with their local auxiliary unit. Once they have been successfully screened, candidates then complete a secure, online application. All of this is done on the Internet. On average, the FHPA website has more than 100,000 new visitors each month.

Once an applicant has expressed interest in joining the FHPA, basic screening is done to identify any obvious disqualifications (e.g., being underage, being a convicted felon, domestic violence, etc.). To be considered, an applicant must also be a U.S. citizen and at least 19 years old with a valid Florida driver's license. An individual must also possess a high school diploma or GED and needs to have accumulated qualifying experience: This can be one year of ongoing public contact, 30 college semester hours, or two years of military experience with honorable discharge status.

In the final screening phase, a full background investigation takes place involving the candidate's credit, criminal history, polygraph, psychological exam, physical abilities test, and physical and eye examinations as well as a drug screening. Finally, an applicant is expected to successfully complete a basic aptitude exam.

6.8 Volunteer Service Requirements

Auxiliary troopers are required to volunteer a minimum of 24 hours per calendar quarter and attend monthly district meetings and all required training events. However, members typically volunteer more than 40 hours each month. In 2012, auxiliary troopers volunteered more than 132,732 hours of public service. These hours were accumulated through community details, support services, training, limited scope and law enforcement patrol, and other assigned activities. Law enforcement hours totaled nearly 64,123 hours. Another 16,808 hours were devoted to recurrent or annual training. Those officers qualified for LSP activities patrolled more than 565,000 miles of Florida highways and responded to more than 14,680 motorist assistance contacts.

6.9 Noteworthy Events

FHPA Sergeant Apprehends Robbery Suspect

On Saturday, June 26, 2010, FHPA Sgt. Wayne Hunter was assisting on an FHP detail at the Tack Shop off SE 60th Ave. in Ocala. While on the detail, some IHOP restaurant employees ran up to him and shouted "stop that man, he just robbed us." The alleged suspect was walking across the parking lot, and Sgt. Hunter shouted, "Stop, Florida Highway Patrol." The suspect began to walk faster, and a pursuit was underway. Sgt. Hunter chased the man approximately three blocks and was assisted by a citizen in apprehending the suspect. Sgt. Hunter placed the man in handcuffs and told the man he was being detained until other officers arrived. In short order, officers from the Ocala Police Department and FHP Sgt. Rick Norris arrived on scene. After receiving information from witnesses and questioning the suspect, he was placed under arrest by the Ocala Police Department and charged with strong armed robbery. After searching the suspect, drugs were also found in his possession. Congratulations to FHPA Sgt. Wayne Hunter on being alert and apprehending an armed robbery suspect! (FHPA, www.floridastatetrooper.org)

Two Suspects Arrested in Boat Theft

On Monday, October 12, 2009, FHP Auxiliary Sergeant Mark Malvin was patrolling busy Interstate 95 through Broward County when he noticed a Chevy Suburban that had entered the apex at the exit to State Road 736. The vehicle was pulling a trailer and boat with no visible license tag. It was approximately 11:40 PM, and Auxiliary Sergeant Malvin pulled behind the trailer and immediately noticed that the boat was significantly oversized for the towing vehicle, to the extent that the rear of the Suburban was within inches of the pavement. He approached the vehicle and reported the tag to the FHP Regional Communications Center and advised that the vehicle was occupied by two Hispanic males who were attempting to remove the trailer from the tow vehicle. When asked what they were doing, one male indicated they were picking up this boat for his boss and that the boss was en-route to their location with a bigger truck. When asked where he picked up the boat, one male replied, "He didn't know the address." The communications center reported that the tow vehicle tag was reported lost or stolen out of Miami earlier. Backup troopers were requested and dispatched. FHP Auxiliary Trooper Wayne Melzer was first on scene followed by FHP Corporal G. Slayten. An officer from Davie Police Department was also dispatched and assisted. Both subjects were placed under arrest by FHP Cpl. Slayten and transported to jail by Auxiliary Sergeant Malvin. The boat was valued at $385,000.

In 2008, significant state budget cuts impacted each agency, and the use of highly trained law enforcement volunteers has become increasingly advantageous. In the FHP, the auxiliary trooper concept has been successfully time-tested for more than 50 years. Today, every year, more than 45 million out-of-state motorists travel on Florida's state roadways and interstate highways, underscoring the need for a visible presence by state law enforcement on these heavily traveled corridors.

Most importantly, it is the role of the auxiliary trooper patrolling in-car and alongside FHP troopers that contributes directly to officer safety and to the FHP's mission. There is no question that the added presence of a second trooper in a vehicle or the close proximity of a zone backup provided by LSP auxiliary troopers has had a significant positive impact on our officers' safety. Each year, members of the FHPA quietly and consistently donate time and personal resources to the benefit of Florida and its citizens. For these and so many other reasons, the auxiliary program in Florida serves its mission well and will continue to earn the support of the FHP's troopers as well as the admiration and respect of Florida's citizens.

6.10 Current Status

At one point in the organization's 50-year history, there were more than 1,000 members in the 1970s to an average of low to mid-400s through most of the 10-year period between 2000 and 2010. Over the past decade, membership had drastically declined. With current membership strength dropping well below 300, many factors are driving this downward trend. Aging membership, diminished department resources, declining recruitment support, increased training requirements, and lack of expanding roles all are affecting both the recruitment and retention of membership.

However, the overall picture in Florida is promising as more local and county jurisdictions are expanding their volunteer programs. According to the Florida Department of Law Enforcement, there are more than 345 agencies in the state with 305 utilizing volunteers in either law enforcement or support capacities. With proper leadership and focus, the agency can continue to thrive and meet its mission.

Despite the current program challenges, each member of the FHPA continues to serve the citizens of the state of Florida. Each has a different story as to how they came to the auxiliary, but all have a common story about why they give their time: They want to help the people who live in their community and state. These members, along with all the others who serve to support law enforcement, are true patriots; they deserve our respect and admiration.

Reference

Ohio State Highway Patrol. (1955). *Flying Wheel.* Vol. 5 Columbus, OH: Ohio State Highway Patrol.

Portsmouth (Virginia) Police Department Auxiliary Unit

7

RON HYMAN

Contents

7.1 City of Portsmouth (Virginia) and Police Department History

The City of Portsmouth is a small, independent, deepwater port city in the southeastern part of Virginia. It is located in the geographic center of a metropolitan area known as Tidewater or Hampton Roads, which also consists of the much larger cities of Norfolk, Virginia Beach, Chesapeake, Suffolk, Hampton, and Newport News. The city is 33.2 square miles and has a population of 96,000. The Portsmouth Police Department (PPD) is authorized to have 263 paid officers and is currently at 238. Additionally, there are 108 civilian employees employed by the PPD (http://www.ports mouthva.gov/history).

Since 1871, the PPD has lost nine sworn officers killed in the line of duty. The first Portsmouth police officer killed in the city was Patrolman John Wilson, who was shot and killed during a political rally in downtown Portsmouth on November 11, 1871. Officer Wilson is believed to be one of the first African American police officers to serve in the United States and one of the first believed to be killed in the line of duty (http://www .odmp.org/officer/14345-patrolman-john-wilson). On November 23, 2005,

Patrolman Richard Spaulding suffered a fatal heart attack shortly after being involved in a vehicle and foot pursuit. Patrolman Spaulding had served with the PPD for nine years; six years as a full-time officer and three years as one of the auxiliary police officers (http://www.odmp.org/officer /18030-patrolman-richard-lee-rick-spaulding).

According to city code, the department is authorized to have as many as 100 auxiliary police officers and currently has 19 sworn auxiliary police officers. The City of Portsmouth has a city manager form of government, which includes a city manager, mayor, and city council. The mayor serves with six other elected citizens to form the city council. The chief of police reports directly to the city manager.

The history of Portsmouth is significant to the development of the United States in terms of the early shipping industry. According to the City of Portsmouth website,

> Portsmouth was founded as a town in 1752, on 65 acres of land on the shores of the Elizabeth River. The town was founded by William Crawford, a wealthy merchant and ship owner who at various times had held office as the Norfolk County presiding court judge, high sheriff, militia lieutenant colonel and representative to the House of Burgesses. Because of his militia service, he is frequently referred to as "Colonel Crawford." The 65 acres were part of Colonel Crawford's extensive plantation and were constituted as a town by an enabling act of the General Assembly of Virginia. The town was named after the English naval port of that name, and many of the streets of the new town reflected the English heritage. The town already had a rich history by the time it was separated from the county government and given status as an independent city in 1858. Its location as an East Coast deepwater port has been the common denominator of the City's development throughout its centuries of growth.

7.2 PPD Auxiliary Unit

The PPD's auxiliary unit was formed during World War II and was originally a part of the Civil Defense Organization. Later, in the early 1960s, the auxiliary unit was placed under the division of police by an act of the city council. Training and outfitting of the personnel in the unit has mirrored that of the full-time paid police officers. Auxiliary officers are authorized to work in all areas of the PPD except for the K-9 and strategic traffic unit's motorcycle squad. Auxiliary officers are selected for assignments based on their desire and department need. Currently, auxiliary officers are serving as school resource officers, bike patrol officers, background investigators, cold case homicide squad investigators, narcotics investigators, property crimes investigators, strategic traffic unit investigators, pawn enforcement investigators, fugitive apprehension unit investigators, and training coordinators. All auxiliary officers serving as investigators still have the primary responsibility to support the uniform patrol division, working special events, parades, festivals, and special details requiring a uniformed officer presence. The unit supports an average of 30 of these special events each year, occurring year-round. These events require police resources for crowd control, traffic control, and security for visiting dignitaries.

The auxiliary unit has a rank structure that provides a chain of command within the unit. Currently, there are two sergeants, one lieutenant, and a captain who functions as auxiliary bureau commander and who reports to a full-time paid captain. Auxiliary officers wear the same uniform as full-time paid officers and are issued the same police badge and identification cards. This has helped to eliminate the "us and them" problem that happens in many police agencies in which the volunteer officers often feel "separate and unequal."

Auxiliary police officers are recruited through advertisements on the PPD's web page, general recruitment at job fairs, law enforcement seminars, and word of mouth. The PPD's web page provides the capability for interested auxiliary applicants to send an e-mail to the auxiliary bureau commander (captain). The auxiliary captain monitors this city e-mail account daily and immediately responds to all requests from citizens asking how to become a volunteer police officer. Each person inquiring about the program is called by the captain, and the program is discussed in detail with him or her. If it appears that the person can meet the rigid entrance requirements, the application packet is then e-mailed to the prospective applicant.

The selection process for becoming an auxiliary officer is the same as it is for full-time paid officers with the exception of the written civil service exam, which is waived. As auxiliary officers receive no pay, the Civil Service Commission does not require volunteers to take the civil service exam. The selection process begins with each applicant completing the four-page "application for position of auxiliary police officer" form. Each applicant must also submit signed and notarized copies of two release forms for appropriate record checks, such as credit checks, driving record, criminal history, and so on. Each applicant also completes a 17-page background investigation package, which is used for the interview and pre-employment polygraph exam. This package is reviewed for accuracy by the auxiliary captain and then submitted to the lieutenant in charge of police recruitment and backgrounds. The applicant then begins the background investigation process. His or her driving record, credit report, and criminal history information is screened, followed by a pre-employment interview and polygraph exam. Each applicant is then scheduled for a full "fit for duty" medical exam followed by a physical agility test. Once all of the background and entrance components are successfully completed, the applicant is accepted and scheduled for the Auxiliary Police Academy and is officially an auxiliary recruit.

Entrance and training requirements have dramatically changed and improved since the auxiliary unit was placed under the control of the PPD in the 1960s. From the 1960s through the mid-1970s, applicants were given a routine background examination and were then placed into an auxiliary academy that ran for approximately 180 hours. The class covered routine police duties, firearms, report writing, and basic self-defense. Once completed, the officers were given their uniforms and hit the street, riding with full-time paid officers who completed their field training.

Today, auxiliary police applicants face extensive background investigations and polygraph exams. Each applicant must also pass a structured physical agility test that must be completed within a specified time limit. If he or she fails to complete an individual event or fails to complete the agility course prior to reaching the maximum time limit allowed, he or she will receive a "did not finish," and this will disqualify them from any further processing as an auxiliary police applicant.

The physical agility test consists of the following events, which are part of a total quarter-mile course that must be completed within five minutes. The stations in sequence are the following:

1. 80-yard run/walk
2. Stair climb (6 steps up, 6 steps down)
3. 40-yard run/walk
4. 50-foot dummy drag (100–150 lbs)
5. 25-yard run/walk
6. 35-yard sprint
7. 6-foot metal chain link fence climb (must get over)
8. 70-yard run/walk
9. 35-yard run walk
10. 60-yard run/walk
11. Stair climb (6 steps up, 6 steps down)
12. 15-yard run/walk
13. 4-foot horizontal jump over sand pit
14. 15-yard run/walk
15. 45-yard sprint
16. Dry fire a provided Glock 9 mm pistol (5 trigger pulls with the right hand, 5 trigger pulls with the left hand)

7.3 Auxiliary Police Unit Training/Police Academy

Auxiliary officers must pass the same entrance and background requirements as full-time paid officers. As previously mentioned, they must pass a thorough physical exam, physical agility test, background investigation, and a pre-employment polygraph exam. Now as auxiliary recruits, they must also attend and pass the Virginia State Certified Department of Criminal Justice Services (DCJS) Police Academy that is held at least annually on three week-nights, four hours each night, and on most Saturdays for eight hours. The auxiliary academy, which has the same DCJS syllabus as that of the full-time career officers' academy, is approximately 680 hours in length. Prior to the start of their academy, auxiliary recruits are issued a recruit uniform and basic gun belt with handcuffs, baton, pepper spray, and a Glock handgun. In order to successfully graduate, recruits must pass a comprehensive final written exam, consisting of 200 questions, administered by the Commonwealth of Virginia's DCJS. Once the certification exam is passed, they are appointed as auxiliary police officers by the city manager, given their oath, and sworn in by the chief of police. They are presented with their badge at a formal graduation and pinning ceremony. After graduation from the auxiliary police academy, auxiliary officers must then ride with a field training officer (FTO), and they will receive their field training. Field training usually consists of another 390+ hours of street patrol in uniform. Field training and all related checklists must be satisfactorily completed and signed off on by the auxiliary officer's assigned FTO within 12 months of graduation from the academy. Once the FTO training is completed and signed off, the full-time paid lieutenant or sergeant in charge of training conducts a final check ride. If passed, the auxiliary officer is DCJS certified as a law enforcement officer (LEO), released from field training, and interviewed by the chief of police, who signs his or her final release paperwork. Only then is the officer allowed to ride alone, commonly referred to as riding solo. Annual training and recertification of the auxiliary officers follows the same mandates as that for full-time paid officers. Auxiliary officers are also eligible for any training that interests them or meets their career path goals or desires within the PPD.

The police department's training unit tracks training hours for auxiliary officers along with their mandatory DCJS in-service training requirements. Each auxiliary officer must complete 40 hours of DCJS in-service training within a two-year period. This training includes mandatory training required by the PPD chief of police, which is often held during the weekdays. This requires auxiliary police officers to take time off from work, often unpaid, to maintain their training and certifications. Training includes recertification with firearms, including the 9 mm Glock pistol, 12-gauge shotgun, and if carried, the .223 carbine. Each must recertify with the ASP baton, TASER, OC (pepper spray), ground fighting, defensive tactics, less-lethal weapons, legal training, and diversity courses. Auxiliary police officers must be first aid, CPR, and AED certified. Although the auxiliary police captain supervises the overall work of its members, full-time paid supervisors of the units to which the auxiliary officers are assigned are responsible for the daily supervision of each officer's activities, just as they are with their paid officers.

Each auxiliary police officer is required to work a minimum of 24 hours per month or 72 hours per quarter. This is required to maintain proficiency in police reports, procedures, services, and department practices. The number of hours each auxiliary officer works is reviewed monthly by the auxiliary captain to ensure that each officer is maintaining accountability. Most auxiliary officers routinely work double or triple the required number of hours needed per month. A few auxiliary officers work as much as 35–40 hours per week.

7.4 PPD Auxiliary Unit Organization, Assignments, and Work Hours

The PPD auxiliary unit falls under the guidance of the special operations division (SOD) commander, who is a career PPD captain. The auxiliary captain supervises the auxiliary unit and reports to the SOD commander. The auxiliary police program is tracked and monitored in many ways. All auxiliary officers must post their work hours in a logbook in the operations support center (OSC) at police headquarters. The auxiliary captain tracks these logged hours monthly and submits a monthly time and status report to the chief of police, assistant chief of police, SOD commander, and the city's volunteer coordinator. At the end of each calendar year, the auxiliary captain completes an end-of-year report for the auxiliary unit that lists the hours worked, special events supported, and significant accomplishments of the unit. This report lists the members assigned, the headcount losses and gains, and includes an assignment organization chart as well as charts on hours worked. This information is included in the overall end-of-year departmental report, which is assessed by the city.

Auxiliary police officers are assigned to work in uniform patrol for their first year of solo police work. After one year in uniform patrol, they may request transfer to any specialized unit where a need exists, and a unit "fit" is observed. Auxiliary officers are ultimately qualified to ride alone and have the same powers of arrest as any certified law enforcement officer in Virginia. Unlike most other police agency assignments of auxiliary police officers, Portsmouth auxiliary police officers are completely integrated into the police department.

Auxiliary officers reporting to work in uniform first report to the OSC, where they check out a radio, laptop computer, TASER, and a police vehicle. They then contact a beat sergeant or lieutenant who assigns them a beat and a beat number. Once on the street, they call dispatch to go in-service and start receiving calls. Auxiliary officers who are designated as detectives report in plainclothes to their respective squad or unit and work as assigned by their supervisor.

The PPD patrol officers previously worked an 8.5-hour shift for day and evening shifts. The midnight shift worked as long as 10.5 hours. However, this recently changed in January 2011 when the department switched to 12-hour shifts. This placed more patrol officers on the street 24 hours a day, seven days a week. These overlapping 12-hour shifts allowed the officers in those squads to handle normal calls for service. A third squad of officers was utilized for special assignments in high crime areas of the city, using more of a "strike force" approach to crime hot spots in the city.

Auxiliary officers usually have full-time paid jobs and cannot work an entire 12-hour shift in uniform or an eight-hour shift in plainclothes. Minimum work hours for each auxiliary officer are 24 hours per month or 72 hours per quarter. They are allowed to work as their personal schedule permits. Auxiliary officers can work two 12-hour shifts per month, three eight-hour shifts, four six-hour shifts, or a blend of hours. Their DCJS in-service training time counts as work hours, and court attendance counts as well.

7.5 Auxiliary Unit: General Information

Auxiliary officers are not paid to attend the police academy, refresher training, mandatory in-service training, or to attend court. Auxiliary officers are not allowed to work any job off duty, with or without pay, representing themselves as a police officer. After one year in uniformed patrol, auxiliary police officers may carry the city-issued Glock handgun off duty for self-protection along with their police identification card, which also serves as their concealed weapon permit in the Commonwealth of Virginia.

The PPD provides each member of the auxiliary police unit with new equipment at the time of issue rather than surplus or used equipment. The department has provided a private office for the auxiliary unit, equipped with an office telephone line and computer. The auxiliary police line officers are provided with assigned portable radios, and the auxiliary captain is issued a PPD official cell phone. The auxiliary captain attends the chief's general staff meetings and is provided full information on departmental operations appropriate to his grade of captain. Each member of the auxiliary unit is provided with access to the city e-mail system with remote access from home.

The auxiliary captain maintains contact with the auxiliary lieutenant and sergeants daily via e-mail, cell text messaging, and telephone, concerning details about upcoming work events and personnel issues. The auxiliary lieutenant is the acting unit commander during the absence of the auxiliary captain. The auxiliary lieutenant is assigned as the training coordinator for the FTO program and has recently been assigned to the cold case homicide unit. The auxiliary sergeants function as the unit special events coordinators, calling and e-mailing unit members to ask about their availability to work special events and special training evolutions. They also monitor performance of the officers during special events. One sergeant is assigned to the strategic traffic unit as an investigator, and the other sergeant is a detective assigned to the fugitive apprehension unit.

The auxiliary program also brings a highly trained influx of civilian skills into the police department, and this aids in the day-to-day operations of the PPD. Auxiliary officers, as volunteers, have been utilized as photographers, airplane and helicopter pilots, lawyers, engineers, medical personnel, and military experts in special weapons, tactics, and counter-terrorism. Many of these auxiliary officers have become DCJS instructors and have taught other officers in formal classroom settings.

A potential outcome of any volunteer program is the transformation of a volunteer to a paid position. This has occurred in the PPD many times since the inception of the program. Many auxiliary police officers find that they enjoy their law enforcement career to the extent that they become full-time paid officers. During the years, many of the former auxiliary police officers who became full-time paid officers have become ranking officers up to the level of chief of police. This is truly a remarkable positive outcome for this program.

7.6 PPD Auxiliary Unit Awards and Recognitions

From December 1991 to December 2011, Portsmouth auxiliary officers have worked in excess of 206,906 hours, saving the city more than $4,744,000 in equivalent wages. The auxiliary unit has been recognized by the city and was presented with the "outstanding job performance by a unit" award in 2003 for its service to law enforcement. The auxiliary unit is a certified organization under the Presidential Volunteer Service Award Program and is certified with Gold Status in the President's Volunteer Service Award.

The auxiliary police unit has been recognized by city council for outstanding service, and city council enacted a resolution in 2004 making auxiliary officers, for purposes of workman's compensation and health care, employees of the city. The chief of police has recognized and honored the auxiliary unit by his actions and deliverance of speeches throughout the city and the state of Virginia. The ultimate form of acceptance comes from the full-time paid officers, who work hand-in-hand as peers with the auxiliary officers, showing no resentment or animosity toward them. We often hear that this is a problem among other auxiliary officers across the nation, but it does not occur at PPD. The program is so well accepted by full-time paid officers in the department that many retire from full-time paid service, go on to other careers, and then become members of the auxiliary unit themselves.

Awards and recognition of auxiliary officers are presented during the police department's annual awards and retirements banquet. Each year at the department's annual awards ceremony, all auxiliary officers are awarded a certificate for their years of service to law enforcement. The dinner banquet meal is provided by the city at no cost as a "thank you" for their service. One auxiliary officer is awarded the Auxiliary Police Officer of the Year along with the related Medal of Merit. This award is received after a letter of nomination is written from a member of the police department recommending the officer for the award. Auxiliary officers are eligible for all awards that full-time paid officers can obtain, such as the Lifesaving, Medal of Valor, and so on. After 20 years of satisfactory auxiliary police service, auxiliary officers may retire. Upon retirement, they will receive a retired identification card identifying them as a retired police officer and receive a retired gold badge in their grade (i.e., police officer, sergeant, lieutenant, and captain). The Commonwealth of Virginia State Code §59.1-148.3 also allows the city police departments to sell a retired police officer or auxiliary police officer his or her service/duty weapon upon retirement. Four auxiliary officers have retired after 20 or more years of service and have purchased their service/duty weapon.

The auxiliary police program is registered with the Volunteers in Police Service (VIPS) program and has qualified for the Gold Level Award with the President's Volunteer Service Award program. Five members of the unit have been awarded the President's Call to Service Award, for volunteering more than 4,000 hours of service as an auxiliary police officer. The VIPS website states, "Recognizing and honoring volunteers sets a standard for service, encourages a sustained commitment to civic participation, and inspires others to make service a central part of their lives. The President's Volunteer Service Award recognizes individuals, families, and groups that have achieved a certain standard—measured by the number of hours of service over a 12-month period or cumulative hours earned over the course of a lifetime." Our auxiliary unit exemplifies this statement.

Each member of the auxiliary unit helps to promote volunteerism within the city and assists in bridging the gap often seen between civilians and sworn law enforcement officers. The auxiliary unit has been awarded the President's Volunteer Service Medal (Gold Level) for the sixth year in a row. The auxiliary unit has improved the working conditions and lives of their full-time paid counterparts and the citizens of Portsmouth by providing needed manpower during critical times and special events as well as during local disasters.

Members of the auxiliary unit are actively involved in educating the community. They frequently attend civic league meetings, school events, church meetings, and other public forums at which they are able to promote the program. Auxiliary officers teach at the citizen's police academy, where they encourage participants to be a part of the "thin blue line" by becoming a police volunteer officer. They set leadership standards in their neighborhoods and serve by example.

The auxiliary unit captain has appeared on local television stations and in the local newspaper in order to publicize the program. There are also two taped programs about the unit that run on the city access cable TV channel, which is used as a recruitment tool. In the recent past, auxiliary officers volunteered their time at Portsmouth's NEAT Summit, which is a crime prevention and community involvement seminar, where they worked a booth handing out PPD auxiliary unit recruitment information.

The citizens of Portsmouth show their acceptance of the auxiliary unit by their support and attendance at community service events where the auxiliary unit is participating. Citizens also comment directly to the members of the unit, the city manager, and members of the city council and the mayor about their positive experiences with the auxiliary unit and its officers. The PPD also offers a "citizen's police academy" several times each year, which brings citizens into the police department. The PPD's website states,

> This community-oriented program is designed to provide private citizens and members of the business community with an insider's perspective of police work and the legal system. During the ten-week academy, participants are exposed to all areas of the criminal justice system. Police Department instructors will cover a variety of topics, such as officer recruitment, Uniform Patrol duties, functions of investigative units, Crime Prevention, and drug use and abuse information. Several classes will involve actual demonstrations by special units, including SWAT, K-9 and Mounted Patrol. Hands-on classes also are provided in firearms training and traffic stop exercises. A ride-along experience with patrol is offered as well, to allow participants to observe first-hand officers' response to police calls for service. The citizens' Police Academy will assist ultimately in the reduction of crime, through the forging of a partnership between the community and the Police Department. This partnership is the most practical, efficient, and powerful tool in the fight against crime. (http://portsmouthpd.org/?page_id=440)

The Auxiliary Police Unit is provided the opportunity to showcase the auxiliary unit to the citizens of Portsmouth at the citizen's academy and has repeatedly received high praise from citizens attending the academy.

7.7 PPD Auxiliary Unit Success Stories

PPD Auxiliary police officers have responded to many emergency situations on the street. On May 3, 2010, at 1900 hours, while on a directed patrol, Auxiliary Officer Robert Griffin observed a minivan stop in traffic in the northern part of the city. He noticed the driver's side rear door slide open and saw a woman who was holding a small infant out of the door by its legs shaking it up and down. Auxiliary Officer Griffin pulled up behind the van, activated his emergency lights, exited his police car, and ran to the side of the vehicle where he saw an infant that was not breathing and turning blue in color. The woman, who was the infant's mother, was hysterical at this time. Auxiliary Officer Griffin took the infant from the mother and gave the infant three to four light blows to his back, performing an infant version of the Heimlich maneuver. Suddenly, the infant coughed up a thick mucus plug that had obstructed his airway and began breathing on his own. His color quickly returned to normal and the mother took the baby and Auxiliary Officer Griffin placed them in his patrol car and stayed with them until the medics arrived. The child survived due to the fast action by Auxiliary Officer Griffin. He was subsequently awarded the Police Department's Lifesaving Award at the annual awards ceremony.

While on routine patrol on Sunday, March 10, 2002, Auxiliary Officer Tim Schaffer heard a call on the radio in reference to a shooting/homicide at a major intersection in the city of Portsmouth. Rather than rush to the crime scene, the well-trained veteran auxiliary officer used his years of experience and made the decision to stay on patrol on the perimeter of the crime scene thinking that the two suspects would be fleeing the area. They did indeed, and they headed directly to where he was traveling. While he was traveling westbound, he observed a group of young males chasing the two suspects through a shopping center parking lot. The pursuing group caught the two running suspects, holding one down while the other suspect attempted to free his partner in crime. Auxiliary Officer Schaffer entered the parking lot at this time, and the suspect being held broke free and ran. Auxiliary Officer Schaffer observed the fleeing suspect trying to stuff something down his pants while running, and he subsequently commenced a foot pursuit. He chased the suspect across a major four-lane highway, where other officers stopped him at a nearby intersection. While the first suspect was being detained by the officers, the second suspect approached Auxiliary Officer Schaffer and stated, "That ain't the dude with the gun, he didn't shoot the kid." This statement proved to be very incriminating as no police officer on the scene had made any statements or asked any questions about the shooting. Both suspects were taken to police headquarters, and after investigation, they positively identified the shooter and an arrest was made. Thanks to Auxiliary Officer Schaffer's training and initial involvement, he was critical in providing the witnesses who identified the suspect and aided in solving the tragic slaying of a young high school student. The shooter was identified, arrested, and convicted.

One auxiliary officer, Richard Huneycutt, is a retired Portsmouth school teacher with 30 years of service. He works as an auxiliary police officer in the assignment of school resource officer. From 2001 through 2011, this volunteer officer worked 11,975 hours or more than 8,807 hours in excess of his required minimum hours. His expertise in handling juvenile issues in the school system is unsurpassed! In 1976, Auxiliary Officer Huneycutt was also the very first mounted patrol police officer in Portsmouth. Police work runs in his family. His grandfather, Charles Henry Krouse, was a mounted patrol police officer in Richmond, Virginia, in the early 1900s. He was shot from his horse in 1906 and died a few years later from the bullet that had remained in his body. Auxiliary Officer Richard Huneycutt has been an auxiliary police officer for more than 37 years. His love of the auxiliary unit and the police department is extraordinary. Each year for 37 years, Auxiliary Officer Huneycutt has worked Christmas Day on street patrol, allowing a full-time paid officer to have the day off with his family. Christmas Day in 2010 was special for him and to a family of a missing elderly Alzheimer's patient.

While working uniform patrol on Christmas Day, Auxiliary Officer Huneycutt was notified by the sergeant at police headquarters that an elderly lady from Rocky Mount, North Carolina, was missing and was last seen in the Cradock area of Portsmouth three days before Christmas. She suffered from symptoms of Alzheimer's disease. The Rocky Mount Police Department had called the PPD to ask that we please look for her in our city as it was suspected that she had remained in the area. Auxiliary Officer Huneycutt was given her name and a description of the car she was last seen driving. He went to the house in the Cradock section of the city where she was last seen and started his search. No one was home at the house, so Auxiliary Officer Huneycutt talked with several neighbors, none of whom had seen her. He drove through Cradock but could not locate her. He then decided to drive into the adjoining city of Chesapeake and check the local motels, which were not far from Cradock. The first motel that Auxiliary Officer Huneycutt checked had a car that fit the description of the lady's car. He contacted Chesapeake Police Department, and they arrived and went to the room where she had registered and located her. Auxiliary Officer Huneycutt contacted her family; they went to the hotel, and they were all reunited. She had been alone in the hotel for several days, lost and confused.

The above are just a few examples of the many ways Portsmouth's auxiliary officers serve the city and the public each day.

7.8 PPD Auxiliary Unit Challenges

As with any volunteer organization, recruitment of volunteers and managing headcount loss is a major concern. The auxiliary police academy can only be held once per year due to the length of the school, which is 10 months. Entry requirements are very stringent, and it takes a continuous pool of prospective auxiliary applicants to make sure growth in the unit continues.

Losses average six auxiliary officers per year. Figure 7.1 shows the resignations, retirements, terminations, and transfers from the auxiliary unit for the period of March 2000 to December 2011.

Resignations usually result from auxiliary officers who are in the military and receive orders permanently moving them out of state; civilian job transfers; auxiliary officers who are unable to meet the demands of attending court, training, and so on; and those who resign due to losing interest in the program.

Terminations from the auxiliary unit rarely result from any misconduct, but they usually occur because of the officers' failure to maintain their required minimum work hours or failure to be able to qualify on the firing range or maintain their DCJS certifications.

The last bar on the chart designated "full-time" are losses that occur when an auxiliary officer becomes a full-time paid officer. These are auxiliary officers who love police work so much that they quit their civilian jobs and transfer from the auxiliary unit to being a full-time paid police officer. Although this is a loss to the auxiliary unit, they are a tremendous gain to the police department.

Auxiliary officers do not need to attend the police academy again in order to transfer to the department as a full-time paid officer as many other police departments require. They must take the written civil service exam and compete with applicants for a full-time paid position. If they rank within the accepted score range on the exam, they will have an updated background investigation completed, a "fit for duty" medical exam, another agility test, and a follow-up polygraph exam. They will then transfer and become a full-time paid member of the police department. Many of the department's sergeants, lieutenants, captains, and even chiefs of police have been former members of the auxiliary police unit.

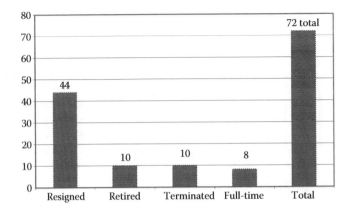

Figure 7.1 Auxiliary police losses March 2000 to December 2011.

7.9 PPD Auxiliary Unit Hours Served and Agency Cost Savings

Time records and hours worked have been obtained as far back as 1991. Figure 7.2 highlights the auxiliary unit's annual work hours from January 1991 until December 31, 2011. Work hours have exceeded 206,900 hours.

Figure 7.3 outlines the auxiliary police hours worked from January 1991 to December 31, 2011. These hours were converted to estimated equivalent wage savings, based on the loaded labor rate for a police officer. This rate is currently $40.50 per hour and was adjusted for the lower labor rate going back to 1991 on a graduated scale. As one can see, the cost savings to the city is tremendous! The cost to initially outfit an auxiliary officer with uniforms, weapon, training, and so on, averages around $5,000 per auxiliary officer. Each auxiliary officer must work a minimum of 24 hours per month or 288 hours per year. Based on a minimum of

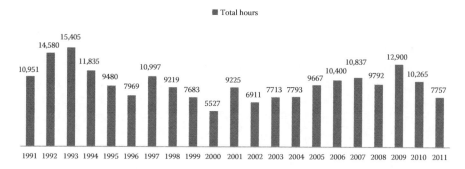

Figure 7.2 Total hours from 1991–2011: 206,906.

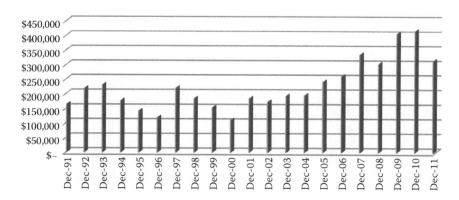

Figure 7.3 1991–2011 cost savings: $4.744 million.

288 hours × $40.50 per hour, current cost savings per officer is $11,664 per year. Based on this average rate, each auxiliary police officer returns the initial investment back to the city within six months of commencing volunteer police work.

7.10 Successful Integration of Auxiliary Police Officers

Based on information received during conferences over the last decade, many items have come to light that appear to be instrumental in making the successful integration of auxiliary police and reserve officers with career full-time paid officers a reality and quite successful. The PPD has incorporated each and every item on this list, making its unit extremely successful.

For the successful integration of auxiliary officers and reserve deputies, recommended strategies and policies include the following:

1. You must have 100% buy-in from the chief of police/sheriff, the executive command staff, city manager, mayor, and city council.
2. Entrance requirements and training must mirror that of full-time paid officers.
3. It is strongly recommended that the uniform, patch, badge, and ID card be the same as their full-time paid counterparts.
4. Recommended is a command structure within the auxiliary (captain–lieutenant–sergeant) for chain of command acting as the unit's line officers.
5. Recommended is that disciplinary actions be the same for auxiliary and reserve officers. This, however, can be a challenge. How do you discipline a nonpaid volunteer?
6. Incorporate your auxiliary officers into the police department's or city's awards ceremony and generate an "Auxiliary Police Officer of the Year" award. Give each auxiliary or reserve an annual certificate of service for their years of service as a volunteer officer.
7. If budget allows, hold an auxiliary police annual banquet or incorporate them into any annual city or police awards banquet as a way of saying "thank you."
8. If possible, try to provide a small office for your auxiliary unit line officers.
9. Make sure that your auxiliary officers and deputies are not issued old, used, secondhand equipment. Used equipment would suffice for attending the academy, but trade it in at the end of training once the academy has been successfully completed.

10. Your decision to allow your volunteer officers to ride solo should be based on departmental policy, training level, and the philosophy of your agency.

11. Allow your auxiliary officers, after a probationary period, to transfer to specialized units such as traffic, narcotics, SWAT/TRU, special investigations, and the detective bureau.

12. Establish minimum work hour requirements such as 24 hours per month or 72 hours per quarter. This should be tracked monthly by the auxiliary unit commander and reported monthly to the auxiliary coordinator.

13. Integrate the auxiliary line officers into any regular weekly or monthly line officer/staff meetings.

14. Provide auxiliary personnel, consistent with their position in the unit, with a city-issued cell phone, pager, and assigned portable radio.

15. Off-duty arrest power will be determined by state code, city code, and department policy. Some auxiliary police and sheriff's units have full arrest power 24/7.

16. Allow for a seamless transition from the paid force to the auxiliary unit for officers who wish to retire or resign and remain as auxiliary officers and vice versa.

17. Make sure your volunteers are properly covered by medical insurance, workman's compensation, city liability insurance, and so on.

18. Register your program with the VIPS program at the International Association of Chiefs of Police. This allows departmental recognition as well as rewards for each of your volunteer officers (e.g., President's Volunteer Service Award). Each will receive a certificate from the President and a pin for their uniform.

19. Establish a retirement program for your auxiliary officers. After a preset number of years of satisfactory service (10, 15, or 20 years), allow auxiliary officers to retire and get a retired badge and ID card. Also, if state and city codes permit, allow your retired auxiliary officers to purchase their duty weapon. Under H.R. 218, the Law Enforcement Officers' Safety Act, and S. 1132, the Law Enforcement Officers' Safety Improvements Act, retired auxiliary officers and deputies, as sworn LEOs, may now carry a concealed weapon anywhere in the United States.

Auxiliary police work today is indeed a career even though no money is earned by the volunteer officer. When we, as auxiliary police officers, are asked, "Why do you place your life on the line without pay for a total stranger?", our reply is usually, "If I have to try and explain it to you, you probably would never understand. Personal satisfaction for helping the community and doing what is needed and right is all the pay I need."

It is an honor to be able to wear the uniform of an auxiliary police officer and to be accepted and treated with dignity and respect by our brothers and sisters within the law enforcement community who perform their tasks day after day, keeping all of us safe.

Who and what are auxiliary police officers? We are people just like you. We are your friends, your neighbors and your co-workers, who have decided to take a stand against crime and volunteer our time to aid the citizens of Portsmouth and the Commonwealth of Virginia by working as Volunteer Law Enforcement Officers.

Auxiliary Captain Ron Hyman

References

http://portsmouthpd.org/?page_id=440 (p. 15) Citizens Academy

http://www.portsmouthva.gov/history (p. 1) City of Portsmouth and Police Department History

http://www.odmp.org/officer/14345-patrolman-john-wilson (p. 1) Police Department History

http://www.odmp.org/officer/18030-patrolman-richard-lee-rick-spaulding (p. 1) Police Department History

Civic Volunteerism in Orange County (Florida) Sworn Police Reserves in a Metropolitan Sheriff's Office

ROSS WOLF

Contents

8.1 Introduction

Florida statute has very specific definitions about certifications for law enforcement officers. Police academy training programs for full certification are approximately 800 hours and require a state exam. Florida statute defines "law enforcement officer" to include "full-time law enforcement officers, part-time enforcement officers, or auxiliary law enforcement officers" (F.S.S. §943.10(1)). A "part-time-law enforcement officer" is defined as "any person employed or appointed less than full time, as defined by an employing agency, with or without compensation, who is vested with the authority to bear arms and make arrests" (F.S.S. §943.10(6)). An "auxiliary law enforcement officer" is defined as "any person employed or appointed, with or without compensation, who aids or assists a full-time or part-time law enforcement officer and who, while under the direct supervision of a full-time or part-time law enforcement officer, has the authority to arrest and perform law enforcement functions" (F.S.S. §943.10(8)). Therefore, although auxiliary, part-time, and full-time officers in Florida all have the authority for arrest and all have the same responsibilities related to firearm carry, auxiliary officers can only take law enforcement action when under the direct supervision of a full-time or part-time officer. Florida auxiliary academies are about 400 hours in length and do not require a state exam. Agencies that utilize volunteer law enforcement officers in Florida have different policies and procedures concerning their utilization and post-academy training but all are governed by the state definitions and court interpretations of their authority.

In 1964, then-Sheriff Dave Starr first authorized 10 "reserve deputies" to supplement the 25 full-time deputies in Orange County. Legal requirements in Florida for acting as a reserve or auxiliary officer at that time were vague, and many reserve deputies began their law enforcement positions with little or no training. For the next 20 years, deputies who were classified by agency policy as "reserve" or "auxiliary" were required to purchase their own weapons, uniforms, and duty gear. During this time period, Orange County auxiliary deputies wore a six-pointed sheriff's star, and fully certified reserve officers and full-time agency personnel wore a traditional Florida five-pointed sheriff's star. Orange County reserve and auxiliary deputies also had slightly different uniforms than their full-time counterparts, identified during the terms of various elected sheriffs by different colored shirts, different uniform patches, or different uniform markings (such as pocket flaps and pants-leg striping). Until the early 1990s, reserves and auxiliaries were still required to purchase their own duty weapons and flashlights, but the agency provided uniforms and duty gear (Wolf & Beary, 2010).

Requirements, training, and agency support have changed a lot since the unit's early development. Today, the OCSO reserve unit has two classifications of volunteers based upon the state definitions of auxiliary and part-time officers; agency policy labels these as "Reserve 1" and "Reserve 2." Reserve 1 volunteers have completed a state auxiliary academy, and Reserve 2 volunteers have completed the full state basic law enforcement training academy and have successfully completed the state exam for law enforcement officers. In the early 1990s, the sheriff's office developed a training program that required exactly the same field training for Reserve 1 and Reserve 2 deputies as was required for full-time deputies within the agency. This training program has 320 hours of post-academy classroom instruction, followed by 560 hours with a field training officer on patrol. With such high training standards and vetting of personnel in the employment process, the uniforms of all members of the reserve unit are now virtually the same as the uniforms of full-time deputies. The only difference in uniform is that reserve deputies wear silver-colored badges (regardless of rank) and Reserve 1 deputies have "Reserve Deputy" under their name on their name plate. The agency also provides the same equipment to volunteer deputies that are provided to full-time deputies, including radios, handguns and shotguns, duty gear, ballistic vests, personal safety equipment, electronic control devices, and agency laptops. Reserve deputies may also be authorized to carry additional weapons (such as M-16s) or be issued additional equipment (such as radar units, ticket-writing hardware and software, etc.) if requested and if the reserve has received the necessary training. The unit also has 11 marked cars that are used solely for reserve unit functions, reserve special enforcement details, reserve working patrol, and other approved purposes.

8.2 Management and Organization

Although early volunteers with the OCSO were lumped into two different organizations based on their classification as part-time or auxiliary officers by state statute, today the agency merges the two classifications into one unified entity. Reserves with both full and auxiliary certifications are welcome to serve in leadership capacities. The reserve unit organizational structure closely mirrors the chain of command at the OCSO in both the amount of responsibility and authority for each rank. The reserve unit is led by a bureau chief (unit commander) and a division chief (assistant unit commander) and four captains (administration, training, special operations, and platoon). The unit also has two field training lieutenants, a special operations lieutenant, platoon and staff lieutenants, and squad sergeants and corporals with approximately six to eight deputies assigned to each squad. Corporals and sergeants are assigned duties related to the administration of the unit; this includes the dissemination of urgent information, the collection of volunteer time sheets, and conducting annual performance evaluations. However, squad supervisors are also often assigned to lead special details, vice or decoy operations, or road patrol details. Lieutenants are given responsibility related to the management of three squads and performance evaluations of squad supervisors. There is also a designated full-time agency lieutenant who acts as a liaison assigned to the specialized patrol division of the sheriff's office that coordinates promotion boards and unit requests for equipment or training.

Although every reserve is assigned to a squad and platoon within the unit's organizational chart, reserves are free to volunteer their time in a variety of capacities. Reserves who have less than 20 years of experience as a sworn deputy with the OCSO are required to volunteer at least 16 hours per month, of which at least 12 must be in road patrol. Reserves who have more than 20 years of experience as a sworn deputy with the agency must still volunteer 16 hours a month but are free to donate that time in an area in which they have the most experience or interest. This is when the individual specializations of reserve personnel are best put to use by the agency. Members of the reserve unit often come to their volunteer positions with an array of individual experience.

Individuals within the unit often put their expertise and/or full-time employment to the benefit of the agency. One member of the reserve unit owns several fast food restaurants. When the agency is called upon to deliver police services for extended periods of time (such as during natural disasters, hostage situations, or perimeters), the reserve coordinates with agency command staff to be sure that food is delivered to all personnel at no cost to the agency. This may be in the form of a centralized location, such as a mobile mess hall, or to individual officers who cannot leave their posts. Another example is a reserve who is a full-time pastor; this reserve serves in a dual role of chaplain for the agency and as a reserve police officer. A firefighter who serves as a reserve deputy has successfully completed the entire course of training to serve as a tactical medic on the OCSO SWAT team. A former full-time detective who now serves as a reserve volunteers his time to the OCSO human resources department as a background investigator for new hires and conducts polygraph examinations. A former marine and full-time agency supervisor who is now an OCSO reserve serves on the OCSO Homeland Security Task Force and coordinates large-scale details for the unit and the agency.

8.3 Becoming a Reserve with the OCSO

The OCSO has very high standards for full-time deputies, and this high standard is also applied to applicants for sworn volunteer positions. Applicants for the reserve unit are required to meet the same physical skills assessment, psychological testing, background investigation, medical screening, and interview panel requirements as full-time recruits for the agency. In addition, applicants for Reserve 2 status are required to meet the same educational/experience requirements as candidates for full-time positions. This can create problems for recruiting volunteers as applicants may be qualified to hold paid positions as well as volunteer positions, but it is an area that the agency is not willing to diminish. Many of the same screening problems seen with applicants for full-time positions are also seen in applicants for volunteer positions. Seemingly well-meaning volunteer candidates are rejected due to credit history problems, prior traffic citations or minor drug use, lack of employment history, or even for minor criminal histories.

As part of the application process, panel interviews are conducted by reserve unit supervisors who work in cooperation with the agency's human resources division. The panel interview is conducted in exactly the same format as the panel interview for full-time personnel. If the candidate passes all of the agency-required exams and screenings, all applications are reviewed by the sheriff for final approval. Once sworn in, the reserve unit conducts an orientation class for all newly sworn in reserve recruits, and each new reserve deputy is assigned to an experienced reserve who acts as a mentor to guide them through what can be a very long training phase. Although reserves are welcome to complete their orientation phase and field training phase at the same rate as full-time deputies, this is often impossible for volunteers who have paying jobs and careers. Therefore, most reserves complete the training on a part-time basis, and almost all take approximately two years to finish the training. All reserves who have not completed field training must work under the supervision of both the reserve chain of command and the OCSO full-time training coordinator and are not authorized to work any of the reserve unit special details or in any capacity in which they are not accompanied by an agency field training officer.

About half of the members of the reserve unit, however, are prior full-time deputies from the sheriff's office who have retired or resigned from the agency in good standing. In order to successfully transfer from full-time status to the reserve unit, the individual must submit a memorandum through their chain of command requesting to remain sworn with the agency as part of the reserve unit. Many of the current reserves who served as prior full-time deputies held high-ranking positions with the agency and continue to volunteer their time as reserves.

Some applicants for reserve positions within the sheriff's office hope to use the position as a step up to a paid position in a law enforcement agency. The OCSO understands this and supports reserves who apply for full-time positions for which they qualify. The human resources division sees this as an opportunity to evaluate the potential of a deputy without the expense of paying a salary. Reserves often move from volunteer positions to full-time positions in road patrol and in court services. Unless there is a dire immediate need for qualified applicants, however, the agency requires that all reserves complete field training before they are eligible to apply for full- or part-time paid positions within the agency.

8.4 Utilization of Reserves

The OCSO reserve unit is a respected part of the agency with a specific objective to support uniform patrol. However, members of the unit are also eligible to participate in other non-uniform or specialized assignments. This confidence in the abilities and commitment of the reserve unit has been earned by years of responsible service, including assistance in times of crisis. Starting in 1998, the reserve unit initiated "squad relief" operations in which reserve deputies and reserve supervisors take over for a patrol squad for an entire shift. This has allowed full-time squads to focus their energies on proactive patrol, high-incident areas, or squad-level training. However, it has also been an important function when the agency has been reeling from the death of an officer, a circumstance that has happened far too often. On several occasions, the reserve unit has taken over patrol duties within the jurisdiction of Orange County for sheriff's office patrol squads or for municipal or state agency police department patrol units after a line-of-duty death.

Additionally important to the sheriff's office in a major tourist destination such as Orange County, Florida, the reserve unit adds to the entire agency manpower for large-scale events that take place within the county. The unit has been called upon during U.S. presidential visits, athletic events, and major entertainment performances to add to the total number of uniformed agency personnel and police presence. Although rarely publicized, reserve deputies have been on the front line for several high-visibility events that have occurred. Reserve deputies in these instances, including homicides, have not been identified by the news as anything other than a well-trained part of the agency and are identified by the media as "deputies" and nothing more.

The unit has also provided supplemental road patrol during SWAT hostage negotiation callouts and coordinated and participated in multijurisdictional law enforcement operations, terrorism threats, and after natural disasters. OCSO reserves are continually recognized for their work with the March of Dimes, Bacchus, Boy Scouts of America, Children's Miracle Network, Hispanic Celebration, Walk America, Mothers Against Drunk Driving, Give Kids the World, Diabetes Walk, local parades and festivals, local Public Broadcasting System events, and local church and community festivals. The community relies on the OCSO reserve unit for these events, and requests for assistance are constantly under consideration. In its history, the OCSO reserve unit has coordinated hundreds of events such as these, by which millions and millions of dollars have been raised for charitable functions with the security and traffic handled entirely or largely by the reserve unit.

8.5 National and International Involvement

Involvement in the law enforcement community does not end at the county line for the members of the OCSO reserve unit. The reserve unit has participated in numerous law enforcement tasks through mutual aid requests; this includes involvement with relief efforts in southwest Florida after the devastation of Hurricane Andrew; Hurricanes Charlie, Francis, and Jeanne in central Florida; and other unusual events. When unable to respond to an emergency elsewhere in the state or country, the unit has offered assistance in different ways. In 2005, the unit pooled resources and raised money for OCSO's "adopted" Waveland (Mississippi) Police Department after the devastation of Hurricane Katrina. While the OCSO donated vehicles to replace the WPD vehicles lost, the reserve unit resources helped provide for the cost of new uniforms.

The reserve unit also proudly serves as host for national and international conferences for police reserves and welcomes police reserve units from around the world to learn firsthand about volunteer policing in Orange County. This international outreach has extended to the Caribbean, the United Kingdom, and to Singapore. The OCSO reserve unit command staff has helped the Virgin Islands Police Department overhaul the training required for its auxiliary police program, developed and administered training on the island of Saint Lucia for upcoming major sporting events, and hosted an international delegation from Singapore about volunteer policing. Reserve command staff members have presented about volunteer policing management throughout the United States and in the United Kingdom. Reserve command staff personnel serve as members of the National Sheriff's Office Committee on Reserve Law Enforcement Officers and as members of several national and international reserve policing organizations.

8.6 Ongoing Contributions

Approximately 100 members of the reserve unit are proud to serve the citizens of Orange County and the OCSO as "citizen police officers." Each year, these volunteers participate in enforcement-related details and community charitable event details. As a condition to maintain state certification and to adhere to agency requirements, reserves also participate in Florida Department of Law Enforcement or agency advanced or continuing education (such as Active Shooter, NCIC/FCIC, firearms, Law Enforcement Vehicle Operations, and Hazardous Materials training classes, scenario training, ethics courses, and more). This training is provided at no cost to the reserve unit membership. Reserves are also authorized to submit training requests for local or out-of-town specialized training through the agency training division.

Unit volunteers also participate in recruiting, mounted patrol, marine patrol, motors unit, criminal investigations, homeland security, and other divisions of the agency. These contributions total more than 30,000 hours of volunteer time annually. Although federal law allows that volunteers in the public sector are entitled to reimbursement from out-of-pocket expenses, such as mileage, the OCSO does not offer reimbursement to the reserve unit members.

Although each deputy in the reserve unit has a unique background and a distinctive reason for being a part of the team, all members of the unit give something back to the community due to their participation. OCSO reserves hold full-time careers as ministers, business owners, contractors, educators, realtors, pilots, lawyers, mechanics, and firefighters, among many others. Reserves are encouraged to utilize their outside work experience in the duties they provide as deputy sheriffs, and many take the initiative to seek advanced training or assignments related to these experiences or personal interests.

References

Florida Statutes, Title XLVII Criminal Procedure and Corrections. §943.10 (2011). Available at http://www.leg.state.fl.us/Statutes/

Wolf, R., & Beary, K. (2010). The Orange County Sheriff's Office Reserve Unit: A strong cohesive volunteer unit able to handle multiple functions. *Deputy and Court Officer,* 2: 26–30.

Police Volunteers Can Effectively Impact Mass Casualty Incidents
The Aurora (Colorado) Police Department Faced the Challenge

JAMES F. ALBRECHT

Contents

9.1 Properly Prepared for the Unforeseen

Although many will say that no one can be properly prepared for the overwhelming and the unforeseen, particularly when the scenario involves mass casualties, the Aurora Police Department (APD) in July 2012 proved that it was the ultimate exception to this belief. On July 20, 2012, members of the APD, including their many community volunteers, were called to service to deal with the mass shooting at a movie theater that left 12 dead and 58 wounded—one of the largest mass shootings in modern U.S. history. Handling a quickly developing and dangerous scenario of this extent, although trying, ultimately resulted in successful concerted effort to deal with numerous victims, concerned family, and a quick media onslaught while expeditiously apprehending a criminal that clearly threatened the lives of first responders and others in the area. And the volunteers of the APD played a considerable role in dealing with this tragedy.

9.2 APD in Colorado

9.2.1 Agency Characteristics and Description

Founded in 1891, the City of Aurora was originally named Fletcher by its founder, Mr. Donald Fletcher. In 1907, the town changed its name to Aurora. Known as the "Gateway to the Rockies," this all-American city lies on the eastern edge of the Denver–Aurora metropolitan area.

In 1907, the APD was established to provide law enforcement services for the City of Aurora, Colorado. Currently, more than 335,000 residents choose to live in Aurora, making it the third largest city in Colorado and the 58th largest in the United States. It's also the eighth safest city of its size in the nation. Aurora also has a broad diversity with more than 100+ languages spoken. In 2012, the APD handled nearly 427,458 incidents, including calls for service and self-initiated activity. The city covers 155 square miles and is located within three counties: Arapahoe, Adams, and Douglas. Aurora is a home-rule city, with a council/city manager form of government with a mayor, six ward members, and four at-large members.

The APD is quickly growing and now has more than 667 sworn members and 131 civilian employees. The APD has been nationally recognized for its innovative approaches to law enforcement and community policing, and it has continually met the high standards of the Commission on Accreditation for Law Enforcement Agencies (CALEA). Also, the department is a full-service police department with a full range of special units that include K-9, a full-time SWAT team, vice and narcotics units, a traffic unit, and so on. The city is divided into three different police districts, each providing full-time police services to its residents.

9.3 Consistent Use of Police Volunteers

9.3.1 History of the Volunteer Program Development

In keeping with its community policing philosophy, the APD is committed to strengthening its bonds with the citizens of Aurora. Effective policing relies on a mutual dependency between the police and the community. In support of this philosophy, many Aurora citizens with a variety of skill and abilities regularly give of themselves by serving as volunteers. The spirit of volunteerism in the APD began in 1972 when a group of volunteers was formed to assist victims of crimes of sexual assault. Over the years, the volunteers were trained in crisis intervention, and increased calls for service were made for numerous incidents involving trauma to victims. In 1990, the group was reorganized as the Victim Services Unit. Today, approximately 40 volunteers assist as victim advocates in 24-hour, on-call shifts, 365 days a year.

Since 1982, volunteers have been donating thousands of hours at the APD headquarters to assist officers and support staff in a variety of assignments. In 1988, research was done, and the information collected was utilized to plan and implement Aurora's current volunteer program, which includes five different units with a total of 331 volunteers (and which continues to grow on a weekly basis).

9.4 Types of APD Volunteers

The APD utilizes community volunteers, who are mainly recruited from the agency's Citizens Police Academy or Senior Citizens Police Academy to assist the agency with numerous responsibilities, including the following:

9.4.1 Volunteer Positions and Activities

- *Alert Team*: The Alert Team is a group of Aurora Citizens' Police Academy Alumni Association member volunteers who are organized and willing to serve the department in specialized, usually unplanned functions.
- *Citizens Missing/Abducted Response Team (CMART)*: Volunteers who work side by side with APD's Emergency Response Team (ERT) in search and evidence detection in missing children cases.
- *Computerized Composites*: Volunteers who meet with witnesses or victims, one on one, to develop a composite drawing of a suspect or person of interest from a crime.
- *District 1 Patrol Assistant*: Volunteers who are assigned to the District 1 Patrol Bureau to assist the patrol administrative assistant with a variety of clerical duties.
- *Fingerprint Specialist*: Volunteers who provide fingerprint services for civilian applicants and also for children and parents of children at various safety fairs.
- *Foot Patrol Assistant*: Volunteers who assist foot patrol officers with filing and clerical assistance.

- *Graffiti Off Neighborhoods*: Volunteers who assist a project coordinator in the removal of graffiti throughout the community in response to citizen requests.
- *Pawn Unit Assistant*: Volunteers are trained to provide filing, sorting, data entry, and tracking of hundreds of pawn slips received weekly.
- *Property Section Data Entry Clerk*: Volunteers assist with the data entry of property information, property storage, and documentation of evidence. They assist with in-processing of evidence, relocating evidence to new storage locations, pulling out evidence for destruction, assisting officers and detectives in preparing evidence for court, drug destructions, gun destructions, preparing evidence for donations and auctions, NIBINS testing, and the filing and scanning of paperwork.
- *Range Assistant*: Volunteers are assigned to the training academy firearms range to assist employees in a variety of qualification functions, such as sorting, filing, and clerical duties.
- *Records Assistants*: Volunteers who assist record's staff in a variety of clerical functions.
- *Traffic Assistants*: Conduct vehicle window tint re-inspections for the APD traffic unit.
- *Vehicle Impound Assistant*: Volunteers who scan reports, do quality checks of scanned reports, and enter data into Versadex. They may assist with checking vehicles into the impound lot by verifying input information as well as general office and clerical work.
- *Victim Advocate Volunteer*: Volunteers who are specially trained to provide support to victims and witnesses of crime.
- *The Neighborhood Watch Program* was established in 1984 and has an estimated 500–600 volunteers who are the "eyes and ears" for the APD as well as for the City of Aurora.

9.5 Accomplishments of the APD Volunteer Programs

9.5.1 Volunteer Program Achievements

Over the past 40 years, the Volunteers in Policing Program has grown into an active, effective, and professional program that expands and enhances police services provided to the community and its citizens as well as its visitors.

In 2012, five specific groups of volunteers (totaling 471 volunteers) donated 31,003.29 hours (331 volunteers in 2011 donated 29,600), saving the city $675,562 (over half a million dollars). The five volunteer groups consists of 105 headquarters volunteers who donated 14,436 hours, providing clerical and support services in a variety of assignments throughout the department;

35 victim services volunteers who provided 2,500 hours of emotional support and crisis intervention for crime victims; four chaplains who donated 260 hours; 43 Explorers (young people invested in law enforcement, active members of Explorer Post 2024), who donated 6,883 hours in training and community service; and 152 Citizens Police Academy Alumni volunteers who donated 6,925 hours in support of police training and special community events throughout the year.

9.6 APD Volunteer Program Coordination

9.6.1 Supervision of the Volunteer Program

The department has one full-time civilian coordinator who completes all of the prescreening of volunteers and coordinates placement, recognition, tracking, evaluation, and, if necessary, termination of volunteers and interns. Also, the coordinator creates annual reports to include the statistics and compilation of hours from volunteer units.

9.6.2 Information Concerning the Selection, Orientation, Training, and Supervision of Volunteers

Each volunteer is selected through an interview process and a background check. Once a volunteer has been interviewed and qualified, he or she will go through an hour-long orientation with the volunteer coordinator. This interview and orientation process helps the coordinator match the volunteer's qualifications and interests to a unit or section to which they would best be suited. Each volunteer is trained according to the needs of the unit or section for which they are volunteering, as well as the needs of the department. The volunteers are supervised by the section supervisor to whom they are assigned as well as the volunteer coordinator. The volunteers are required to turn in a volunteer work record sheet once a month to the volunteer coordinator, which shows training, time worked, and duties performed.

The Victim Services Unit volunteers undergo an initial 40 hours of entry-level training and also attend quarterly one-day training updates in order to maintain on-call readiness.

9.7 Volunteer Commitment at the Scene of Horror: The Movie Theater Massacre

On July 20, 2012, a gunman entered the Century 16 movie theater during the midnight showing of a movie premier and opened fire, instantly changing the lives of the movie patrons and their loved ones. A total of 70 people were shot: 12 of them fatally and many more of them critically wounded and barely clinging to life. First responders came from all over during the first few minutes, hours, and days after the shots were fired to assist in a host of different capacities and in support roles. One group, however, responded not to secure the theater nor to investigate the crime, but to care for the victims and their families: The APD's Victim Services Unit (VSU) served as the victims' first line of contact with the law enforcement system. The unit was the primary source of information for victims in need of varied resources in the wake of the tragedy. Perhaps more importantly, they provided to the victims and their loved ones a familiar face, a shoulder to cry on, a hug, or a hand to hold onto when their world came crashing down. They have continued to be the victims' lifelines as they have transitioned through and even after the various stages of the painstaking court proceedings.

Incredibly, 75% of the VSU responders on that day were trained volunteers who chose to show up and work alongside the full-time VSU personnel. The VSU volunteers responded to a host of various locations throughout our city, and others covered the routine responsibilities of the unit. The VSU personnel and volunteers were recognized for their outstanding professionalism, strength, and compassion exhibited during the Century 16 shooting and its aftermath with certificates of appreciation during a formal awards ceremony.

Also on the morning of July 20, 2012, APD volunteers were summoned to handle a multitude of tasks that needed immediate attention. Responding volunteers used their own vehicles, coolers, and resources to pick up and deliver donations of water, ice, and food for officers posted on crime scene perimeters in over 90-degree heat. They assisted the property unit in logging, tagging, and releasing hundreds of personal items. Other volunteers answered countless phone calls and attended to hundreds of miscellaneous details. They set up tables for breakfasts, lunches, and dinners for department members working the shooting and cleaned up following each meal. Overall, APD volunteers selflessly gave an estimated 120 man-hours on July 20 and 21, assisting the police department as well as the Aurora community. In appreciation of their dedication, compassion, and tireless efforts in support of the APD and our community during the aftermath of the Century 16 shootings, they were all presented with a certificate of appreciation at a formal awards ceremony.

9.8 Conclusion

When an individual commits to becoming a community volunteer, no one can imagine the scenarios one could potentially face. It is doubtful that anyone could have foreseen nor anticipated the tragedy that would face the APD on that fateful day in July 2012. However, due to comprehensive training and personal commitment, all the members of the APD and the multitude of volunteers performed up to the task and actually exceeded expectations. Although police executives often examine the option to incorporate community volunteers into organizational operations from the primary perspective of law enforcement, it is imperative that police agencies analyze the specific and special talents inherent across the range of volunteers and be prepared to put them to use when duty calls as tragic or as challenging as that assignment may be.

Acknowledgments

The author is grateful for the contributions made by members of the Aurora Police Department command staff and agency volunteers who provided the detailed material included within this chapter. It should be noted that the professional and effective response to this tragic event was recognized by the International Association of Chiefs of Police, when agency volunteer personnel received the esteemed Volunteers in Police Service award as the top volunteer police program in North America.

"Doing More with Less" The Professional Model of the Los Angeles Police Department

10

MARK S. JOHNSON
MKAY BONNER
ROBERT D. HANSER

Contents

10.1 Introduction

The good times of the 1990s for law enforcement are gone. Police agencies, and the country in general, were enjoying some of the most prosperous economic times. With increased wages and a booming economy, revenues derived from taxes were available to improve public safety. One of the many improvements to public safety was to attract better applicants and retain the current personnel through raises and/or increased benefits. Retirements, incentive pay, and lower insurance payments led to the attraction of good recruits for law enforcement from a job pool that was competing for qualified personnel in every field.

For many years, law enforcement has been recognized as a profession with pay that did not rise to the level of the dangers faced by the officers (Peak, 2010). There was a component that did make up for the lower-than-desired pay: retirement and other benefits. Most law enforcement retirement systems across the country are separately funded and managed and not tied into other state retirement systems. These systems were able to make investments to bolster their portfolios and to keep increases for other parties, such as highway workers or teachers, from taking away from their assets. This worked well for many years. Law enforcement officers were retiring with good benefits and a bright future for life after police work.

In the mid 2000s, the great recession struck the country, and it became apparent that the promised guaranteed benefits and retirements could not be maintained. The increased payments to retirees could not be sustained by the current employees and their contributions to the system. Because these benefits were guaranteed by contracts and, in many cases, state amendments to constitutions, the money had to be dispersed even though not enough money was coming into the system. This dilemma led to the current but unpopular decision to cut current payrolls and benefits of working officers and employees to cover the cost of retirees (Ferguson, 2008). This has been no small undertaking. Many agencies across the nation have reduced their forces by as much as 50% in order to cover these costs (American Police Beat [APB], 2012, p. 3). Some agencies indicate that 85% of their budgets are dedicated to payroll, pension, and benefits, leaving 15% for equipment, training, supplies, vehicles, and other necessities to accomplish their law enforcement mission (H. Otwell, personal communication, November, 2011). Police administrators are forced to make adjustments and cutbacks in the only area they can, which is in personnel costs.

The phrases associated with meeting today's challenges include "do more with less" and "work smarter, not harder" (Ferguson, 2008). But the increased calls for service, insufficient manpower, and rising crime levels are proving hard to match. The public's perception that, when crime touches them, each police department should drop everything else and dedicate all of its resources into solving their problem first further aggravates the situation of insufficient manpower (Ferguson, 2008).

The backbone of any police agency is the patrol division (Peak, 2010). The public wants and needs to see uniformed police patrolling in marked police cars on the streets of our communities. Administrators know this and have to keep these positions filled. Furlough days and pay cuts have been forced upon many agencies. Layoffs of personnel are not unheard of these days (APB, 2012, p. 3). When chiefs and sheriffs are forced to make these layoffs, they pull officers from other areas of the departments to fill these slots. Specialized units and divisions, such as DARE, school resource officers, community relations, intelligence units, and so on, are eliminated or greatly reduced so that the officers can be put back on patrol duties. Officers in the patrol function serve mainly as a reactionary unit to crime fighting as opposed to a proactive approach, which is accomplished by specialized units (Peak, 2010). This has a serious effect on the fighting and prevention of crime and community relations.

Specific locations across the country that have faced laying off officers include Minneapolis, Minnesota, where 25 officers of the 850-man department were layed off in 2009 due to budget concerns (APB, 2012, p. 3). Recent studies by the U.S. Department of Justice indicate that cases pending before criminal courts are up by 10%, but these criminal justice agencies are also facing the same furloughs, layoffs, pay reductions, and freezes (APB, 2012, p. 15).

One of the biggest agencies in the county, the Los Angeles Police Department (LAPD), also faces the same challenges. This agency has taken the approach of maintaining just enough officers to cover losses due to attrition and retirements while not promoting supervisors within the department. This policy keeps more officers on the street but does not allow for senior officers ready for supervisory positions to advance within the department and their own career. Needed experience as a junior supervisor, which can later be expanded upon at senior management levels, is not gained (APB, 2012, p. 17). As a result, leadership and management capabilities suffer, and ultimately, newer officers are not properly led or trained. Debriefings of critical incidents find that ineffective supervision is the reason that policy and procedure violations occurred. This example of doing more with less has led to costly litigation for the agency. Morale issues are also becoming apparent within the agency because of the lack of officers to meet the challenges of increased crime.

The above actions are taken in order to meet the rising problem of doing more with less. Fewer officers at lower pay have to meet the same or often extraordinary challenges of law enforcement. A method of reducing some of this challenge is found from within the community itself. Reserve officers and deputies can and do make a real difference for law enforcement agencies (Williams, 2005).

10.2 Present State of Affairs: Budgetary Decisions

Budget proposals throughout the last decade in Los Angeles reflect the need to do more with less. Every mayor of the City of Los Angeles since the turn of the millennium has had to make many tough decisions related to public safety operations within the municipality (see Table 10.1). Among these decisions has been a push to consolidate security services provided through the city's department of general services with the LAPD as a means of providing a more efficient and coordinated patrol presence throughout the city. The result is a reduction in the hiring needs of LAPD by 37 officers, allowing that money to be reallocated elsewhere. This also eliminated the need for LAPD to have a July 2012 police academy class.

From this, it should be clear that this consolidation has, as its general goal, the intent to reduce the need for the city's most costly expenditure: personnel. Whether this will impair the operations of the department and, in the process, the safety of Los Angeles citizens, is yet to be seen. However, several points of observation can be made from moves such as these. First, if this does not impair operations and/or public safety, then one can presume that many positions in both the department of general services and the LAPD were, perhaps, not critical and were "fluff" positions that did not make

Table 10.1   LAPD Budget Modifications from the Mayor's Office

Budget Measure	Description of Modification
Replacement hires for police officers	During fiscal year 2012/13, LAPD expects to lose, through attrition, 320 sworn officers. Funding to maintain these positions will cover salaries, firearms, uniforms, and training but is expected to still be lower than the costs associated with higher paid and more senior officers on the police force.
Consolidation of Department of General Services Security Officers with LAPD	This modification combines the department of general services security staff with the LAPD. The intent is to save revenue through a more coordinated allocation of security staff. Reduces the need for 37 new sworn officer positions and also eliminates the need for the July 2012 Los Angeles Police Academy session.
Purchase of patrol and support vehicles	The funding for the replacement of 117 squad cars through short-term debt financing is expected to save revenue. Also, the increased use of asset forfeitures in criminal cases is expected to produce sufficient revenue to finance 200 other types of police vehicles, which includes more than 50 motorcycles.

Source: Villaraigosa, A. R., *Fiscal year 2012–2013 budget summary.* Los Angeles, CA: Los Angeles City Hall, Office of the Mayor, 2012.

Note: Table was created by authors of this chapter.

significant contributions to citizen protection. Whether such positions provided other important functions is unknown, but the fact that they are seen as expendable means that they were either not critical to public safety, or if they were, then public safety has been compromised by this decision. Either potential reality is not one that is desirable to discover.

Second, the morale of both departments as well as the morale of the citizenry will likely be impacted by these types of decisions. The less visibility that is provided, the more likely it will be that police–community relations are compromised. This is a particularly important point for Los Angeles to consider because it has been clear in the media that police–community relations in the 1990s and before have been strained in many neighborhoods. The opportunity for the LAPD to collaborate and partner with citizens is, on the face of it, compromised due to fewer officers on the street in general as well as fewer working community crime prevention programs in particular.

Further, the mayor's office has proposed that funding for the replacement of 117 black-and-white patrol vehicles be refinanced using short-term (as opposed to long-term) debt financing strategies. This is, from a purely accounting principle, a good move in one regard but a bad move in another. Short-term debt financing generally means that less interest will be paid on each police cruiser, which means that although the agency must pay for the cars more rapidly in the short term, it will save money in the long term by avoiding additional interest payments. On the other hand, motor vehicles (including police vehicles) depreciate in value almost immediately upon use.

Thus, this type of asset is a lose–lose investment in general net value terms. But, even more clever when using this strategy is the commonly understood benefit for agencies to count this depreciation against the total net worth of the agency and, thereby, meet the needs analysis for more funding.

In the end, this type of logic is simply negated by the fact that the city as a whole calculates these forms of depreciation into the overall budgetary scheme as do the agencies under its jurisdiction. This means that the depreciation process simply ends up being equivalent across agencies and throughout the city's budgetary structure. Further, the necessity of these expenditures is considered "fixed" within the actuarial process of accounting in the department, meaning that most of these costs are a routine liability that is automatically presumed simply by rote of having a police force; they are inevitable expenditures. On the other hand, the interest savings by the department are "real" savings for the city and provide an example of how smart budgeting can loosen money that does not initially seem to exist. Through a very methodical and careful calculation of interest savings, asset gain, and depreciation scheduling, dollars can be maximized.

Last, the City of Los Angeles has started to augment the funding for approximately 200 police vehicles (including 56 motorcycles) with revenue from its forfeited assets program. This is, of course, a common practice among many agencies but is one that is increasingly important for the LAPD for two key reasons. First, asset forfeiture has substantial potential in Los Angeles due to its proximity to the United States–Mexico border where drug trafficking from Mexican drug lords and a variety of street gangs, in tandem with organized criminal syndicates, operate. Second, income obtained from this source consists of dollar values that are essentially "invisible" within the larger and legitimate economy. Bringing these assets back into the circulation of the economy results in an immediate "boost" to the agency's net worth and is an unexpected net gain on the balance sheets that did not require a detectable investiture within those balance sheets. However, dangers can occur if agencies begin to calculate their potential budgets on likely future forfeitures. Such risks should be avoided among agencies and generally are discouraged in larger agencies.

10.3 Use of Reserve Police Officers

During the history of law enforcement, there have been many times when a disaster or event has left a police force overwhelmed with the duties of providing basic law enforcement services while mitigating or managing the special event occurring at the same time. With this thought in mind, agencies have bolstered their forces through the use of reserve forces (Williams, 2005). These reserve forces consist of citizens in the communities who volunteer to serve in law enforcement for no pay. Doctors, lawyers, plumbers, pastors, and others often volunteer their skills, services, and time to their local police departments. These people usually have full-time jobs yet have a special calling to serve their community as reserve police officers.

These men and women receive the same training, certification, and commissions that the full-time officers receive (Ferguson, 2008). Reserve officers usually have a minimum work requirement for their department that has to be met in order to maintain their reserve officer status. Examples vary from agency to agency, but most show an average of eight hours to 24 hours a month that has to fit into their already busy lives and schedules (Reserve Police Officer Program [RPOP], 2012). These officers perform various duties and functions from patrol duties to special events. Benefits to agencies are immediately recognized in reduced manpower costs. Reserve officers also allow the movement of full-time officers from these specialized events or disasters to continue regular patrol duties.

The presence of reserve officers during parades or other large gatherings are especially advantageous. The presence of these reserve officers provides a greater police presence, lowers the cost of overtime and other related expenses, and incorporates members of the public into the team while garnering greater community involvement (Williams, 2005).

Other areas in which reserve officers can benefit a department include directed patrols or stakeouts (Ferguson, 2008). If an area has a particularly high crime rate or rash of crimes, reserve officers can be placed at this location. These officers can serve as a uniformed presence to deter crimes from occurring just by their very presence. Or the reserve officers could blend in with the surroundings in the form of plainclothed surveillance, notify other units of activity, and call for the appropriate response.

Other added benefits of reserve officers in a police department relate to recruiting new officers. Many reserve officers find that law enforcement gets into "their blood," and they wish to pursue a full-time career in this position. Agencies then have the luxury of having an applicant that they have seen at work and have incredible insight into this person's work ethic, abilities, and experience (Ferguson, 2008).

One of the most successful reserve officer programs in the country is the LAPD's Reserve Corps. This agency is comprised of more than 650 active reserve officers and is the largest police department reserve unit in the state of California (RPOP, 2012). This unit is accredited by the California Peace Officer Standards and Training (POST). The reserve officers of the LAPD Reserve Corps unit receive the same training as regular full-time officers and work alongside them in every aspect of the department's functions (RPOP, 2012).

LAPD's Reserve Corps officers first have to attend an orientation meeting that is held on the first and third Thursday of every month. The standards, selection process, and the training program to join the Reserve Corps are the same for the full-time officers of the LAPD. This has made the acceptance of the reserve officers extremely favorable by the full-time officers. It is not uncommon for full-time officers to request a particular reserve officer to work alongside them during their tour of duty. Reserve officers have received numerous commendations for their actions in the field and are highly valued members of the LAPD team (RPOP, 2012).

The Reserve Corps of the LAPD is divided into three levels, which can be examined further in Table 10.2. A Level III officer is a uniformed officer who can be qualified to carry a firearm once he or she reaches the age of 21. These officers perform various administrative functions within the police department. Duties include front desk assignments, working with area detectives, and community relations assignments (RPOP, 2012). Requirements for Level III officers include the following: be a minimum of 18 years of age at time of application, be in good physical and mental health, possess a valid California driver's license, possess a U.S. high school diploma or GED equivalent, be a U.S. citizen or have applied for citizenship, and have no history of criminal or improper conduct.

Examinations for Level III officers include the following: preliminary background and job preview questionnaire, personal qualifications essay, initial background review, polygraph examination, departmental interview, medical evaluation/psychological evaluation, physical abilities tests, certification,

Table 10.2 Overview of LAPD Reserve Officer Corps

Reserve Officer Level	Requirements and Training	Common Duties
I	Must be 21 years of age. 340 hours of classroom instruction beyond training for Level III. Additional training in the area of tactics, firearms, and emergency vehicle operations. Includes 72 hours of basic self-defense on the higher end of the LAPD use-of-force scale.	Perform the same functions as regular, full-time police officers. They are armed and uniformed and work alongside full-time, salaried police officers.
II	Must be 21 years of age. 250 hours of classroom instruction beyond training for Level III. Additional training in the area of tactics, firearms, and emergency vehicle operations. Includes 72 hours of basic self-defense on the higher end of the LAPD use-of-force scale.	Perform the same functions as regular, full-time police officers. They are armed and uniformed and work alongside full-time, salaried police officers.
III	Same requirements as full-time salaried and sworn officers except for age requirement. 240 hours of instruction at recruit training center. Includes 26 hours of basic self-defense on the lower end of the LAPD use-of-force scale.	Perform many functions of full-time police. Must provide a minimum of 16 hours every month and attend mandatory reserve officer meetings.

and appointment. These are the same requirements for applicants applying for full-time officer positions (RPOP, 2012).

Training for Level III officers consist of approximately 240 hours of professional classroom instruction. Classes are held at the LAPD Ahmanson Recruit Training Center and consist of the following schedule: Every Tuesday and Wednesday night from 6:00 pm to 10:00 pm and every other weekend on Saturday and Sunday from 8:00 am to 6:00 pm. Academic subjects are normally taught in a standard classroom setting, and appropriate examinations are administered to ensure mastery of the subject matter. As training progresses, role-playing and practical field exercises are introduced. Level III officers receive approximately 26 hours of basic self-defense, which consists of wrist locks, twist locks, kicks, and other techniques at the lower end of the department's use-of-force scale. Physical fitness exercises are used to prepare recruits for self-defense training (RPOP, 2012).

Equipment and uniforms are provided to the officer at no cost. Level III officers, upon graduating from the academy, are required to work a minimum of 16 hours every month and attend mandatory monthly reserve officer meetings (RPOP, 2012).

Level I and II reserve officers perform the same functions as regular, full-time police officers. They are armed, uniformed peace officers and work in police vehicles along with full-time police officers. The requirements for Level I and II officers are the same as Level III officers except for the age requirement which mandates age 21 at the time of membership or application (RPOP, 2012).

Level I and II officers undergo the same examination testing as Level III officers. Additional training requirements exist for Level I and II reserve officers. Level II reserve officers undergo 250 hours of professional classroom instruction. Level I officers receive approximately 340 hours of professional classroom instruction. Training for Level I and II officers is held at the LAPD Ahmanson Recruit Training Center. Additional training in the areas of tactics, firearms, and emergency vehicle operations are conducted at the Davis Training Facility. The training schedule for Level I and II officers is the same for Level III officers, and it consists of every Tuesday and Wednesday night and every other weekend. The training presented for Level I and II officers is similar to those used in institutions of higher learning, and it also mirrors the curriculum of the LAPD academy for full-time officers. Level I and II officers also receive approximately 72 hours of self-defense training. This training includes techniques at the higher end of the department's use-of-force scale. Physical training includes weight training, calisthenics, and running. Level I and II reserve officers are required to pass a physical fitness and self-defense test prior to graduation (RPOP, 2012). As with Level III reserve officers, uniforms and equipment are provided at no cost to the reserve officer, and a mandatory monthly meeting along with 16 hours of work is required each month.

Another well-known agency that has established a reserve unit is the Los Angeles Sheriff's Department (LASD). This agency was established in 1850 and provides services to the most populous county in the nation. The Reserve Forces Bureau is the administrative headquarters for the department's reserve unit. The unit is comprised of the following programs: Reserve Deputy Program, Deputy Explorer Program, Mounted Patrol Programs, and Sheriff's Advisory Councils. The above programs consist of more than 800 reserve deputy sheriffs and 600 deputy explorers. The above programs provide the Los Angeles County Sheriff's Department with resources not available to most agencies (Reserve Forces Bureau [RFB], 2012).

Reserve deputy sheriffs serve their community by supplementing full-time deputies with additional manpower. Reserve deputies are professionally trained and duly sworn officers in the same manner as full-time deputies. California law requires reserve deputies to meet the same hiring, background, medical, and psychological standards as full-time deputies (RFB, 2012).

The sheriff's department recruits new reserve candidates and processes all pre-employment procedures to ensure all candidates are qualified to serve as reserve deputies. Upon being approved for admission to the agency, the candidate attends a reserve deputy sheriff's academy. Upon successful completion of the reserve academy, the reserve deputy will be given an assignment within the department that is suitable to his or her capabilities. The RFB is responsible for supervising and maintaining the program in relation to training, inspections, and coordination of reserve deputies at special events (RFB, 2012).

The LASD also maintains a deputy explorer program, which is designed for 16- to 21-year-old persons who are interested in a career in law enforcement. The program is associated with the Boy Scouts of America. Explorer recruits also attend an academy like reserve deputies and are eligible to have an assignment at various areas within the department (RFB, 2012).

Uniformed Reserve Forces perform law enforcement duties, such as traffic control, investigations, crime prevention, crowd control, special events, and patrol duties within the department. Each sheriff's station within the county has a reserve unit. Specialized units within the department are also open to those reserve deputies with certain skills and experience. These units include aero bureau, communications, custody, detectives, special victims unit, emergency operations, headquarters, narcotics, marine enforcement, jail operations, weapons training, and search and rescue (RFB, 2012).

10.4 A Significant Success Story

An example of the benefit of reserve officers is taken from the LASD. In January of 2013, Reserve Deputy Shervin Lalezary was on duty in the West

Hollywood station area when he was able to make a spectacular arrest and take a dangerous person off the street (APB, 2012, p. 34). Deputy Lalezary arrested Harry Burkhart, who was charged with setting more than 53 fires in a four-day period, which caused more than $3 million in damage. Burkhart has been described as the most dangerous arsonist in the county of Los Angeles in memory. Deputy Lalezary made the arrest after being vigilant and observant in his surroundings. Just hours before the arrest, video surveillance footage was released with a description of the suspect and his vehicle. Deputy Lalezary, who usually works part-time patrol on the weekends, was working his third full shift in four days as part of the arson task force. He observed the suspect vehicle in traffic ahead of him. The radio was busy with emergency traffic, and he was unable to summon assistance. He made the decision to stop the vehicle alone. Lalezary contacted the driver and placed him into custody after confirming the driver matched the description of the suspect. For this heroic action, Lalezary was highlighted in a press conference by Sheriff Lee Baca and LAPD Chief Charlie Beck. Lalezary was also named Reserve Officer of the Year for 2012 by the National Reserve Police Officer Association (National Reserve Law, 2013). Lalezary was only on his fourth shift of solo patrol after being promoted to Level I Reserve Deputy for completing the 1,064 hours of required training. LASD deputies are required to work 20 hours a month, but Lalezary usually works that amount each week. Lalezary is a real estate attorney who was born in Iran. Lalezary describes his work with the LASD as extremely fulfilling and effective because the reserve training program is a mirror image of the full-time program. The training may be held at different times, but everything is the same. Full-time deputies treat the reserve deputies and the job they do with respect. These deputies feel they have earned the right to be in the same car together because they have both had to earn their way (APB, 2012, p. 34).

10.5 Conclusions and Recommendations

In this time of shrinking budgets, law enforcement is forced to think creatively to utilize its resources and gain the maximum benefit of every asset. Reserve officers are often thought of as incapably being used for "real" police work. Many agencies have found this to be quite the opposite. A minimal investment can be made in the way of training, equipment, and uniforms to establish a well-trained force to supplement any agency (Williams, 2005).

With insufficient manpower to meet call demand, reserve officers are an inexpensive way to supplement personnel, stretch available resources, and provide additional assets in implementing the mission and goals of an agency. A well-managed reserve program can be just what agencies need in this tight fiscal climate (Ferguson, 2008). With this in mind, several potential recommendations can be provided as follows:

1. First and foremost, it is recommended to vigorously increase the use of reserve law enforcement personnel. As we have demonstrated, reserve officers provide a very tangible contribution to the LAPD and address the gap between affordability and the need for more officer saturation of problem areas throughout the city's jurisdiction.
2. The agency should continue to utilize methods of efficient financing to allow existing dollars to go further. In addition, the LAPD should, through public service announcements, demonstrate how they are stretching taxpayers' dollars to further gain citizen support amid hard financial times for the police agency.
3. Local media should showcase the impact that reserve police and reserve deputies have on crime-fighting efforts. This will help to further build morale and will also likely gain more interest among citizens for serving as reserve police and reserve deputies.
4. Reserve officers and reserve deputies should be specifically recruited from areas of Los Angeles that are underprivileged, areas that are identified as hot spots for criminal activity, or areas that have high calls for service. With added presence that is constant and from the immediate vicinity, the opportunity for deterring crime and for preventing criminal incidents is enhanced while these individuals are on or off duty.
5. Establish and maintain an evaluative data-driven system that can track the use of reserve officers and deputies, using appropriate research methodology, that can demonstrate through data the impact of reserve officers and also that can be used to further refine their use and placement throughout the city and its surroundings. Naturally, results should be highlighted in the local and regional media.

From the recommendations provided, it should be apparent that much of the challenge to optimizing the use of reservists in the LAPD and LASD comes through further showcasing of these programs. These programs have been shown, at least anecdotally, to work, and they undoubtedly alleviate many budgetary woes that face administrators. If this showcasing agenda were coupled with results obtained from evaluative data, LAPD and LASD could then provide demonstration that their programs are evidence-based and therefore sound from a scientific standpoint. This data-based evidence can also aid in securing funds from other sources when and if such sources should become available in the future. In short, this data would give law enforcement in and around Los Angeles the bragging rights that they most assuredly deserve.

References

Cops Get Jobs Back. (2012, February). *American Police Beat, XIX* (2), 3.

Ferguson, J. (2008, April). Auxiliary Police Officers…Just Add Training. *Law and Order Magazine.* Retrieved February 2, 2013, from http://www.hendonpub .com/resources/articlearchive/results/details?id=2749

Justice System Is a High-Value Target for Cuts. (2012, February). *American Police Beat, XIX* (2), 15.

Los Angeles County Sheriff Department Reserve Forces Bureau. (2012). Retrieved February 11, 2013, from http://www.lasdreserve.org/

National Reserve Law Officers Organization. (2013). Retrieved February 14, 2013 from https://nrlo.net/

Peak, K. J. (2010). *Justice Administration.* Upper Saddle River, NJ: Pearson Education.

Relieved City Lauds a Reluctant Hero. (2012, February). *American Police Beat, XIX* (2), 34.

Reserve Police Officer Program. (2012). Retrieved February 11, 2013, from http://www/lapdonline.org/join_the_team?content_basic_view/542

Supervisor Vacancies Putting Us at Risk of Lawsuits. (2012, February). *American Police Beat, XIX* (2), 17.

The Reserve Police Officers Association. (2011). Retrieved February 14, 2013 from www.reservepolice.org

Villaraigosa, A. R. (2012). Fiscal year 2012–2013 budget summary. Los Angeles, CA: Los Angeles City Hall, Office of the Mayor.

Williams, G. (2005, April). Reserve Officers on Bikes. *Law and Order Magazine,* Retrieved February 02, 2013, from http://hendonpub.com/resources /articlearchive/results/details?id-3933

Volunteering and Law Enforcement in the Carson City (Nevada) Sheriff's Office

11

COLLEEN MORIN
ROBERT MORIN

Contents

11.1 Introduction

The Carson City Sheriff's Office is located in Carson City, Nevada. Carson City is a consolidated city–county unit of local government, and Ken Furlong is the elected sheriff for Carson City. The Carson City Sheriff's Office formulated, adopted, and implemented a VIP program in 2002, and the VIP program has continuously been in operation since its inception. VIP is an acronym that stands for Volunteers in Police Service, and the acronym is employed by the Carson City Sheriff's Office in reference to the Volunteers in Partnership with the Sheriff Program. The VIP program consists of the use of volunteers in law enforcement agencies in order to provide law enforcement services.

VIP is a generic term employed throughout the United States to describe individuals in communities who volunteer their time and expertise with law enforcement agencies. Citizen involvement in policing has a long history and tradition in England and the United States. Citizens volunteered and performed policing duties until the establishment of formal police departments staffed by professional law enforcement officers. The first police department was established in London, England, in 1829 by Sir Robert Peel. Citizens continued to volunteer in policing in England subsequent to the establishment of the formal department in 1829. Citizen volunteerism in the provision of law enforcement services in the United States dates to the time of Colonial

America. Community night watches, staffed by community volunteers, performed policing functions in Boston in 1636 and in New York City in 1686 (Winright, 2001). During the 1980s, the concept of citizens serving as contributors in the delivery of public services became popular. The concepts of civic engagement and citizen participation in community-based collaborative partnerships with municipalities gained traction throughout the United States (Ren, Zhao, Loverich, & Gaffney, 2006).

The community-oriented policing movement gained traction and became a new paradigm in the field of policing during the 1980s and 1990s. The community-oriented policing paradigm was premised upon the establishment of a strong police–citizen partnership, and citizen volunteerism in policing was a foundational principle in the community-oriented policing movement. Citizen participation and volunteerism in policing was recognized as a necessity because it was acknowledged that the police were simply not able to control crime on their own. Additionally, community volunteerism in the establishment of the police–community partnership was perceived to be an effort to reduce the fear of crime and raise the level of collective efficacy in neighborhoods (Ren et al., 2006).

A national program in existence uses the acronym of VIPS, and this stands for Volunteers in Police Service. President Bush created the USA Freedom Corps in the aftermath of the September 11, 2001 tragedy at the Twin Towers in New York City and the Pentagon in Arlington, Virginia. President Bush called upon Americans to serve their country. Citizen Corps was created to help coordinate volunteer activities to make communities stronger, safer, and better prepared to respond to disaster situations. Five Citizen Corps partner programs were created in order to provide opportunities for citizens to engage in coproduction activities in their communities. The VIPS program is one of the five Citizen Corps partner programs. The International Association of Chiefs of Police implements and manages the VIPS program in a partnership arrangement with the Bureau of Justice Assistance, Office of Justice Programs, U.S. Department of Justice (Bureau of Justice Assistance, 2008).

Volunteerism in policing was further premised upon law enforcement agencies experiencing resource challenges during the period of time from 2001 to the present. Many law enforcement agencies experienced staffing shortages and were under pressure to supply the same levels or enhanced levels of policing services in their communities. Volunteerism in policing was a policy response to law enforcement staffing shortages in an attempt to maintain the existing levels of the provision of policing services to the community (Schmidt, 2006). A wide range of law enforcement functions may be performed by volunteers. Volunteers have performed law enforcement functions such as chaplaincy, code enforcement, crime prevention, public outreach, multicultural outreach, interpretation, translation, investigation, missing persons, patrol, property maintenance, traffic control, motorist assistance, DUI checkpoint assistance, victim services, domestic violence advocacy, sex offender management, clerical support, and warrant compliance (Bureau of Justice Assistance, 2010).

The last few years have presented law enforcement agencies with an additional resource issue. A poor economy has placed fiscal stress on all units of government, certainly including municipal and county law enforcement agencies. Law enforcement agencies have experienced budget reductions, decreased levels of funding, staff reductions, and the pressure of being asked to take on additional responsibilities. Accordingly, volunteerism in policing has become a need and not a luxury. Volunteerism is a method of coping with a declining budget and increasing service responsibilities. Many law enforcement agencies have responded to the fiscal stress environment by having volunteers from the community perform duties that were not previously performed by volunteers. Law enforcement agencies have discovered that it is beneficial to expand volunteer policing programs in an attempt to add value while there is a decrease in law enforcement budgets (Bureau of Justice Assistance, 2010).

11.2 History of Law Enforcement in Nevada and Carson City

In 1854, the Utah Territorial Legislature created Carson City, the first organized unit of local government in Nevada. In 1859, major deposits of gold and silver were discovered in the Gold Hill area, and in 1860, the Comstock Lode was discovered in the Virginia City area (Morin, 2009). The Gold Hill and Virginia City areas are located near Carson City. In March of 1861, lame duck President Buchanan signed legislation creating the Nevada Territory. Two days later, Abraham Lincoln became president, and Nevada secured statehood on October 31, 1864. Nevada structures and operates state and local government under the original 1864 Constitution. Carson City is the site of the state capitol of Nevada, which until 1969 was located in Ormsby County. The Nevada Constitution was amended in 1968 to allow the Nevada Legislature to consolidate Ormsby County and Carson City. On July 1, 1969, Ormsby County and Carson City consolidated with Carson City performing the functions of city and county governments (Morin, 2009; Morin & Herzik, 2001).

Nevada historically has been and continues to be a classic Dillon's rule state. County and city government delivers all authority from the state; no authority is directly conferred by the Nevada Constitution. Nevada's 17 counties are governed by similar multimember organizational structures that combine executive and legislative functions and are given the discretion to employ a professional manager. The state mandates the election of commissioners, clerk, treasurer, recorder, auditor, assessor district attorney, and sheriff at the county level. Each of Nevada's 17 counties is responsible for providing its citizens with law enforcement services. Each county has an elected sheriff who is charged with the responsibility of providing law enforcement functions and services within the geographic boundaries of the county. City governments are created by general or special charter. Generally, cities are granted broader powers than counties; legislative grants of power allow some autonomy and discretion within municipal boundaries. Depending on the nature of the charter, cities are governed by a mayor–council or commission form of government and may employ a professional city manager. The governing bodies of cities possess the authority under their charters to provide law enforcement functions and services within the geographic boundaries of their cities, and police departments are administered by chiefs of police that are appointed by city managers and the governing bodies of the cities (Morin, 2009).

On December 9, 1861, William L. Marley became the first official sheriff of Ormsby County by appointment of the territorial governor. From 1861 to 1890, the sheriff acted in the sole capacity of sheriff. From 1892 through 1918 and again from 1946 through 1958, the duties of sheriff were combined with the duties of the county assessor. The elected sheriff of Ormsby County held office for a two-year term of office until 1922 when the term of office became a four-year term of office. Sheriff Robert Humphrey was elected sheriff in 1966 and became the first sheriff of Carson City when Ormsby County and Carson City were consolidated. Upon consolidation, the office of sheriff was designated a nonpartisan office for electoral purposes, and the term of office currently for the office of sheriff is four years. There have been a total of 27 sheriffs in the history of Ormsby County and Carson City with six of the 27 sheriffs serving the Carson City consolidated city–county government. Ken Furlong is currently serving as Sheriff of Carson City and he began his service on January 6, 2003 (www.carson.org).

The State of Nevada Peace Officers' Standards and Training Commission (POST) is responsible as the state agency for the promulgation of rules and regulations regarding the training, education, and qualifications of peace officers. POST establishes minimum standards for the certification, decertification, recruitment, selection, and training of peace officers. POST has established three classes or categories of peace officers. Category I peace officers are traditional law enforcement officers, such as deputy sheriffs, city police officers, and Nevada Highway Patrol state troopers. Category II peace officers are specialists and include officers such as parole, probation, and bailiffs. Category III peace officers are officers that are solely assigned to corrections or detention responsibilities (www.en.wikipedia.org).

A complete outline of the different types of law enforcement agencies within Nevada is exhibited in Table 11.1.

Table 11.1 Law Enforcement Agencies in Nevada

State agencies	12 agencies
County agencies	16 sheriff's offices
	1 Clark County Constable
	1 Clark County Park Police
Educational agencies	6 agencies
Joint jurisdiction/ city–county agency	1 Las Vegas Metropolitan Police Department
City agencies	20 police departments, constables, court marshals, city marshals
Township agencies	11 township constables
Tribal agencies	3 tribal police agencies

Ken Furlong is currently serving as the Sheriff of Carson City. Sheriff Furlong has been a very community-focused sheriff and is committed to enhancing law enforcement in Carson City through educational opportunities, community involvement, and youth/senior citizen contacts. The foundation of the sheriff's programming is heavy community involvement. Some of Sheriff Furlong's most visible programs include VIP, chaplin's program, community resource officers, and a revitalized reserve program. The mission statement of the Carson City Sheriff's Office states, "The employees of the Carson City Sheriff's Office are committed to providing public safety services to the community while adhering to the highest professional and ethical standards. We are dedicated to building mutual trust and respect within our community intended to enhance the quality of life in Carson City" (www .carson.org). Agency and jurisdictional information regarding the Carson City Sheriff's Office are outlined in detail within Tables 11.2 and 11.3.

Table 11.2 Sheriff's Office Budget

Total FY 2014 department budget	$16,269,293
Total salaries and benefits	$14,410,521 (89%)
Total operating	$1,858,772 (11%)
Total full-time employees	136.16
Total sworn	93 (68%)
Total non-sworn	43.19 ($32%)

Source: www.carson.org

Table 11.3 Carson City Jurisdiction

Population	56,164
Landmass	153 square miles
Roadways	268 miles (average coverage = 53.6 miles per patrol coverage)
Ratio officer/population county	1.66 officers per 1,000
Ratio officer/population city	1.09 officers per 1,000

Source: www.carson.org

11.3 Carson City Sheriff's Office VIP Program

The Carson City Sheriff's Office VIP program began in 2002. The structure and conceptual framework guiding the program is simple and straightforward. The VIP program's existence is premised upon the basic idea that volunteers are invaluable to the sheriff's office in the provision of law enforcement services to the Carson City community. The Carson City Sheriff's Office VIP program is very much formulated and implemented in accordance with the literature that exists regarding the concept of volunteerism in policing. Many law enforcement agencies throughout the United States have formulated and implemented VIP programs. The concept of the coproduction of law enforcement services is the basic concept supporting the existence of the VIP program. In essence, the purpose of the program is to provide law enforcement services to the community. The VIP program allows the Carson City Sheriff's Office to provide levels of servicing that it could not otherwise provide to the community without the use of volunteers.

The purpose of the program is to enhance the ability of the Carson City Sheriff's Office to provide law enforcement services to the Carson City community. The stated purpose of the VIP program is to establish a partnership between the sheriff's office and the citizens of the Carson City community in order to make Carson City a safer and better place to live. The stated purpose of the VIP program is in alignment with the stated purpose of other VIP programs in operation throughout the United States. Additionally, an underlying purpose of the program is to allow for the better use of sworn law enforcement officers. The Carson City Sheriff's Office has provided a program description of its VIP program with the International Association of Chiefs of Police (www.carson.org). The International Association of Chiefs of Police maintains a listing of all VIP-type programs operated by law enforcement agencies in the United States. The program description for the Carson City Sheriff's Office clearly sets forth the underlying purpose of the program. The underlying purpose of the VIP program is to have the volunteers take over many mundane matters and allow the uniformed deputies to take care of the more important matters. This program allows uniformed deputies to protect and serve the community. Another underlying purpose of the program is economic. The Carson City Sheriff's Office has faced the same fiscal pressures that have been experienced by other law enforcement agencies around the country. The adoption and implementation of the VIP program in 2002 has allowed the Carson City Sheriff's Office to offer many services to the community that probably would not have been offered in the event paid employees were needed to perform those services (www.carson.org).

The Carson City VIP program provides volunteers with opportunities to learn new skills and assist the sheriff's office in a variety of ways. VIP program participants serve in clerical, technical, and community service volunteer jobs. VIP participants actually perform a variety of functions that are subcategorized. Volunteers are involved in Citizens on Patrol activities. The volunteers use a sheriff's office patrol vehicle and provide community patrol-based services. The volunteers patrol and issue citations for parking violations, such as violations of handicap parking restrictions and handicap sign displays. The volunteers also patrol and perform vacation house checks. Citizens who leave town on vacation or otherwise leave town for a period of time may contact the sheriff's office and request that their homes be watched while they are out of town. This has been a very popular service and has been provided exclusively through the use of volunteers in the VIP program (www.carson.org).

Volunteers also provide assistance with clerical and administrative processing of arrest warrants. These activities may include data entry; however, only sworn deputies will execute arrests in the field regarding outstanding arrest warrants. Volunteers also perform service regarding agency records and assist in the jail and with public safety dispatch. Volunteers also provide additional manpower for community events, such as the Nevada Day parade and other activities that are held in Carson City each October. Volunteers are engaged in the provision of services throughout the Carson City Sheriff's Office operation. Categories of participation include administrative, chaplains, citizen patrol, explorers, neighborhood watch, reserve officers, search and rescue, and mounted unit activities. The Carson City Sheriff's Office operates a Citizen Police Academy where interested citizens may attend a multisession, multiweek law enforcement academy in order to learn about law enforcement in general and the Carson City Sheriff's Office in particular. Students learn about patrol operations, arrest procedures, defensive tactics, units that specialize in everything from abatement of illegal drugs to reducing graffiti, to the important role that community policing plays in Carson City. The students tend to be very interested in performing volunteer activities for the law enforcement agency upon graduation. Although participation and graduation from the citizen police academy is not a prerequisite to joining the Carson City Sheriff's Office VIP program, academy participation is encouraged, and many VIP volunteers are graduates of the citizen police academy. The VIP program has extensive involvement in all aspects of the operation of the Carson City Sheriff's Office. The activities, duties, and responsibilities of the sworn personnel, non-sworn personnel, and volunteer citizen personnel are integrated and deeply interwoven in the fabric of the day-to-day operation of the Carson City Sheriff's Office (www.carson.org). The activities performed by volunteer citizen personnel, as seen in Table 11.4, illustrate the integration and scope of volunteer activities, duties, and responsibilities.

Table 11.4   Carson City Sheriff's Office Volunteer Activities

Civil records clerical	Sheriff's office reception	Citizen academy
Administration clerical	Traffic enforcement	Multijurisdiction support
Jail visitation	Tows	Search and rescue
Traffic control	Parking enforcement	Aerial support
DARE community service	VIN inspections	Nevada Day celebration
Property/evidence vault	Report taking	Parks and recreation support
Extradition	Inventory tracking	Homeless counts
Patrol services	Leave/vacation staffing	Crime scene protection
Prisoner transport	Chaplain services	Expanded law enforcement operations
Inmate hospitalization	Jail religious services	Vehicle maintenance
Tahoe beach patrol	SWAT support	Emergency response support
Safe graduation	DUI checkpoints	Home house watch
Community event details	Mail delivery	Mounted
False alarm reduction	Summons and subpoenas	

Source: Furlong, K. Personal Interview, Carson City, NV, February 7, 2014.

11.4 Carson City Sheriff's Office VIP Program Accomplishments

There have been many accomplishments over the past years for the Carson City Sheriff's Office VIP program. These accomplishments may be grouped into two major accomplishments. The first major accomplishment is successful implementation of law enforcement volunteerism as a cornerstone of the Carson City Sheriff's Office commitment to the philosophy of community-oriented policing. The Carson City Sheriff's Office has been extremely successful in its involvement of citizens and the community in its policing operations. Well over 150 citizens volunteer with the Carson City Sheriff's Office. Table 11.5 highlights a typical monthly commitment of citizen volunteer hours with the VIP Program of the Carson City Sheriff's Office.

Figure 11.1 sets forth the total manpower hours of volunteer service performed during the calendar year 2013.

The second major accomplishment is the successful coping with budgetary stress by the Carson City Sheriff's Office. The Carson City Sheriff's Office has, over the past few years, experienced budget reductions, decreased levels of funding, staff reductions, and the pressure of being asked to take on additional responsibilities. Citizen volunteerism is a method of coping with a declining budget and increasing service responsibilities. Every hour worked by a volunteer represents an hour of manpower that a law enforcement agency does not have to pay for and allows service provision to remain at an acceptable level. The Carson City Sheriff's Office VIP program has enabled the Carson City Sheriff's

Table 11.5   Typical Monthly Citizen Volunteer Commitment Hours

Administration	65 hours
Patrol	449 hours
Jail visitation	89 hours
Chaplains	110 hours
Evidence vault	94 hours
DARE	50 hours
Explorers	0 hours
Search and rescue	159 hours
Aero squadron	68 hours
Reserves	2,000 hours
Mounted	50 hours
Monthly total	3,137 hours

Source: Furlong, K. Personal Interview, Carson City, NV, February 7, 2014.

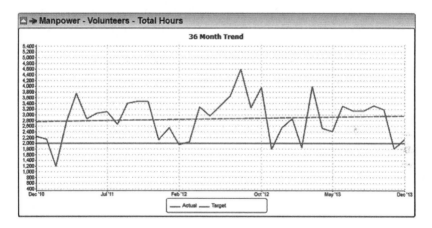

Figure 11.1 36 Month Volunteer Manpower Trends (2010–2013). (From Furlong, K. Personal Interview, Carson City, NV, February 7, 2014.)

Office to successfully provide law enforcement agency services that benefit the community at little to no cost from a personnel administration and budget perspective. The 2010 budget cut reductions sustained by the Carson City Sheriff's Office resulted in 13 full-time positions eliminated while volunteer labor hours increased by 20% during the same period of time (Furlong, 2014).

The economic value of the Carson City Sheriff's Office VIP program may be examined in a simple and straightforward fashion by employing a basic cost–benefit analysis method. If the Carson City Sheriff's Office receives an hour of volunteer service, then the Carson City Sheriff's Office receives a savings of one hour of personnel salary. The cost savings of the VIP program can be calculated. The hourly value of citizen volunteer time may be calculated.

The Bureau of Labor Statistics has determined that the hourly value of volunteer work, based upon the average hourly wage for all non-management, non-agricultural workers, was $20.25 per hour for the year 2008 (Bureau of Justice Assistance, 2008). The Carson City Sheriff's Office VIP program has collected data as to the number of citizen volunteer hours worked for the benefit of and dedicated to the Carson City Sheriff's Office. For the year 2012, the Carson City Sheriff's Office had received a total of 35,939 hours of citizen volunteer service, and 35,939 hours at the rate of $20.25 per hour equals $727,764.75 in volunteer personnel salary savings for the agency. The Carson City Sheriff's Office takes a more conservative approach in calculating volunteer personnel salary savings. The Carson City Sheriff's Office places a value of a Nevada volunteer hour in 2011 at $18.97. For the year 2012, 35,939 hours at the rate of $18.97 per hour equals $681,762.83 in volunteer personnel savings for the agency. The Carson City Sheriff's Office goes one step further in a more conservative approach in calculating volunteer personnel salary savings. The Carson City Sheriff's Office made an assumption that if only 50% of the total volunteer commitment in terms of hours worked were considered to be a necessary function of public safety, then the 2012 total volunteer hours would be reduced from 35,939 to 17,969 hours. For the year 2012, 17,969 hours at the rate of $18.97 per hour equals $340,881.41 in volunteer personnel salary savings for the agency. Based upon the cost–benefit analysis for the year 2012, the Carson City Sheriff's Office received a total of volunteer personnel salary savings ranging from $727,764.75 to $340,881.41 (Furlong, 2014). The Carson City Sheriff's Office calculated that it received a total of $719,629 in volunteer personnel salary savings for the year 2013 and has received a total of $3,297,445 in volunteer personnel salary savings from July 1, 2009 through the end of the year 2013 (Furlong, 2014). Figure 11.2 outlines the monthly

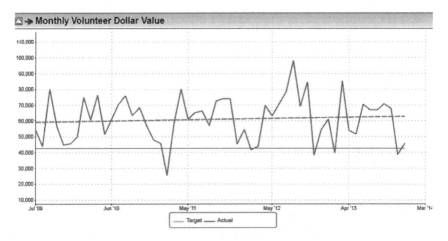

Figure 11.2 Monthly Volunteer Dollar Value (2009–2014). (From Furlong, K. Personal Interview, Carson City, NV, February 7, 2014.)

dollar value of volunteer efforts from July 1, 2009 through December 31, 2013, as calculated by the Carson City Sheriff's Office.

11.5 Conclusion

The Carson City Sheriff's Office has successfully implemented its VIP program. The two key components of the VIP program are community-oriented policing and budget management. Programs designed to encourage citizen volunteerism in law enforcement may be successfully formulated, adopted, and implemented. The Carson City Sheriff's Office VIP program represents an excellent example of successfully incorporating citizen volunteerism in a law enforcement agency. It would appear from the Carson City Sheriff's Office example that a sequenced set of steps is necessary in order to formulate a successful program. The first step is for an agency to have a sheriff or a chief of police who is truly committed to the philosophy of community-oriented policing. The chief executive officer of a law enforcement agency sets the tone for the agency from philosophy to mission to the day-to-day operations. The second step is for the agency to be creative in thinking about the various ways in which citizen volunteers may participate in law enforcement agency activities to serve the community and the agency. The third step is collecting data and calculating the citizen volunteer salary savings realized by the agency and the county or city. Cost–benefit discussions and analysis are simply a way of life in government, and law enforcement agencies must economically justify programs and operations to elected officials and the community. The ultimate goal is teamwork in that citizens volunteer in law enforcement agencies for coproduction purposes in order to provide law enforcement services for the community.

References

Bureau of Justice Assistance. (2008). *Volunteer programs: Enhancing public safety by leveraging resources.* Washington, DC: U.S. Department of Justice.

Bureau of Justice Assistance. (2010). *Volunteers in police service add value while budgets decrease.* Washington, DC: U.S. Department of Justice.

Furlong, K. (February 7, 2014). Personal Interview, Carson City, NV.

http://www.carson.org. Accessed June 1, 2016.

http://en.wikipedia.org. Accessed June 2, 2016.

Morin, R. P. (2009). Nevada. In D. P. Haider-Markel (Ed.), *Political Encyclopedia of U.S. States and Regions* (pp. 439–448). Washington, DC: CQ Press.

Morin, R. P., & Herzik, E. B. (2001). Nevada. In D. Krane, P. N. Riggos, & M. B. Hill (Eds.), *Home Rule in America: A Fifty-State Handbook* (pp. 269–276). Washington, DC: CQ Press.

Ren, L., Zhao, J. S., Lovrich, N. P., & Gaffney, M. J. (2006). Participation in community crime prevention: Who volunteers for police work? *Policing: An International Journal of Police Strategies & Management, 29*(3), 464–481.

Schmidt, C. (2006). Police volunteers and ethics. *FBI Law Enforcement Bulletin,* September 2006, 20–23.

Winright, T. (2001). Bowling alone but not patrolling alone. *FBI Law Enforcement Bulletin,* April 2001, 11–12.

Police Volunteer Programs

Global Perspectives

Auxiliary and Reserve Constables in Canada

12

Sixty Years of Community Service

RICK PARENT

Contents

12.1 Contemporary Canadian Policing

Policing is the largest component of the Canadian criminal justice system and, accordingly, receives the biggest slice of criminal justice funding at $12.6 billion annually in 2010 (Canadian Centre for Justice Statistics, 2011). There are 238 police services in Canada, and of those, 117 services have fewer than 25 staff. Five Canadian police services—the Royal Canadian Mounted Police (RCMP), the Toronto Police Service, the Ontario Provincial Police (OPP), the Sûreté du Québec (SQ), and the City of Montreal Police Service (Service de police de la Ville de Montréal, or SPVM)—account for just over 60% of all full-time police officers in Canada. Municipalities across the country, with the exception of those in the Yukon, the Northwest Territories, and Nunavut, have a choice as to whether to create and operate their own independent police service or to contract out to a provincial police service.

12.2 Quick Facts about Policing in Canada (2011)

1. Population of Canada: 34 million
2. Geographic area: (second largest country in the world)
3. Total number of full-time police officers: 69,438
4. Total number of civilian employees: 28,151
5. Police strength: 201 officers per 100,000 population (lower than United States [242] and England/Wales [252])
6. Visible minorities as a percentage of police officer positions: 4% (2001 data)
7. Aboriginal persons as a percentage of police officer positions: 4% (2,440 officers)*

12.3 Auxiliaries and Reserve Constables in Canada

It is within this setting that auxiliaries, also known as "reserve" police officers, have become a feature of Canadian police services for many years. These individuals are citizen volunteers who are provided with training, a police-like uniform, and "sworn peace officer" status while accompanied by a full-time police officer. The application process to become an auxiliary is competitive, and candidates must undergo a thorough background and security check. Often, people involved in auxiliaries are interested in a full-time career in Canadian policing and view the position as an opportunity to learn about the role and activities of the police. Others are motivated by a desire to contribute to the overall well-being of the community.

In the field, the tasks performed by auxiliaries may include accompanying a regular police officer on patrol and assisting with traffic duties at sporting events, parades, and other community events and in emergency situations when additional personnel are required. Auxiliaries generally do not have access to firearms while on duty. Rather, the primary role of the auxiliary is to serve as an additional pair of "eyes and ears" for regular police officers.

Many police auxiliaries have years of experience and an intimate knowledge of the community, especially in more rural settings. These auxiliary members are a particularly important source of information and assistance for police in regional and provincial services and for Federal RCMP officers who have recently been transferred into a local community. The newly posted RCMP officer will have likely come from a different area of the country,

* Statistics Canada, Canadian Centre for Justice Statistics, 2011.

possessing limited knowledge of the people who make up the community as well as the geographic landscape they are policing. In contrast, the police auxiliary officer may have been born and raised in the community, equipped with detailed knowledge pertaining to the layout of the land as well as the cast of characters that make up the township.

In some Canadian provinces, trained and certified auxiliary officers are additionally registered as "emergency services workers" within the local provincial emergency management program and may be called upon to assist the local police service or other government agency in an emergency. However, it is important to emphasize that auxiliary or reserve constables are not trained to the same level as regular police officers and do not possess special policing skills or intervention practices. Therefore, care and caution must be considered when the auxiliary or reserve officer is accompanying a regular officer to a dispatched report of violence in progress, including incidents involving weapons, or in attending any incident during which grievous bodily harm may be suffered.

12.4 Requirements for the Position of Auxiliary or Reserve Officer

For anyone considering an auxiliary or reserve position within the Canadian police service, there are certain basic qualifications, and although there is some variation around the country, generally an applicant must do the following:

- Be a Canadian citizen or permanent resident of Canada.
- Be between 18 and 65 years of age.
- Be a grade 12 graduate or equivalent, supplemented with accredited post-secondary education (most applicants have or are completing a college/university degree). This will typically include the passing of a police service intake examination, achieving a passing grade of 65% or better.
- Excellent verbal and written communication skills. This may include the passing of the Language Proficiency Index Examination.
- Not have been convicted of a criminal offense for which a pardon has not been granted.
- Be a fully licensed driver and meet the requirements of the graduated licensing system within the province of residence, having accumulated no more than six demerit points.
- Meet the vision standards, which include color, peripheral, and depth perception requirements and have uncorrected visual acuity of 20/40 and best corrected acuity of 20/20 with both eyes open (binocularly).

- Hearing loss in one ear not greater than 50 dB and the other ear not greater than 30 dB in the 500–3000 Hz range.
- Be physically able to perform the duties of the position with regard to personal safety and the safety of the public. This may include the passing of a medical examination.
- Meet the minimum fitness standards as set by the police service. This will typically involve the successful completion of the Police Officer's Physical Ability Test.
- Demonstrated sensitivity to people whose culture, lifestyle, or ethnicity is different than your own.
- Possess current certification in first aid and CPR (St. John's Ambulance Emergency First Aid with Level A CPR).
- Be of good character and have a historical background of proper conduct. This may include the passing of a polygraph examination.
- A history of demonstrated common sense and good judgment and a mature and responsible attitude. This may include the completion of a "lifestyle evaluation."
- Have no business or employment that may cause a conflict of interest with the police service.

Preferred qualifications may result in an applicant's ranking being raised; knowledge of a second language or culture, related volunteer experience, and post-secondary education may all serve to do this. For example, the applicant may have previous law enforcement experience from another agency or within another country.

12.5 Commitments and Required Training

There is a required commitment that, dependent upon the unique needs of the Canadian Police Service, may require the auxiliary officer to do the following:

- Volunteer a minimum of 10 to 12 hours a month.
- Minimum volunteer standards are to be met in 10 out of 12 months during the year.
- The hours may include, but are not limited to, training, ride-a-longs with patrol members, and participation in community events and programs.
- Attendance at monthly training meetings, typically 10 times per year.
- Successfully complete use-of-force recertification training days.

12.6 Code of Conduct Issues

Auxiliary constables are also subject to a code of conduct established by the chief constable or the commanding officer of the police service. Auxiliary constables are expected to demonstrate professionalism and ethical conduct at all times—both on and off duty. Although auxiliary constables do not have the same authority or duties as full-time police officers, the public expects the uniformed auxiliary or reserve constable to reflect the same standard of professional demeanor and ethical behavior. The ethical code serves as a guide to the auxiliary or reserve constable and also as a standard by which the public and the police service can measure the individual's level of performance.

Auxiliary constables meet many of Niederhoffer and Berkeley's requirements for being called a "professional." Past experience has certainly shown that the public has high expectations of those who volunteer in policing services. Auxiliary constables, regardless of their assignments, will be held accountable for their behavior in much the same way as regular police officers, and for this reason, it is important that auxiliary constables are aware of acceptable ethical boundaries and that their behavior may be held to a higher standard than other civilians who do not volunteer their time with the police. As a result, auxiliary constables are subject to a code of conduct established by the chief constable or the commanding officer of the police service (Whitelaw & Parent, 2013; Griffiths, Parent, & Whitelaw, 1999).

12.7 Training Program

Successful candidates must typically complete a basic auxiliary or reserve officer training program that is mandated and structured by the provincial Ministry of the Solicitor General's office. Training often occurs over a period of four months with classes held one to two evenings a week and one weekend day. Candidates are required to study legal issues, crime prevention, traffic, professionalism and ethics, communication tactics, and self-defense training. In addition, the auxiliary training will have a strong physical and team-building component.

In most instances, written exams are held for each of the classes of instruction by the local police service with one or more "certifying" provincial examinations conducted at the end of the four-month training session. Typically, there is a minimal grade of 70% for all exams as well as the successful completion of self-defense training. Successful completion of the intensive training program results in provincial certification as an auxiliary or reserve officer and being sworn in as a "peace officer" for the province.

In return for the successful completion of training and the volunteer hours that have been committed, the police service may provide direct benefits to the individual auxiliary officer that may include the following:

- Several months of intensive basic auxiliary police training
- Opportunities to participate in the delivery of crime prevention programs
- Opportunity to assist regular members in patrol and traffic enforcement
- Opportunity to assist with special events
- Access to the police service's HQ and support facilities, that is, the police services gym, the police library, and selected police training material
- Access to the Employee and Family Assistance Program (EFAP)
- Promotional opportunities within the auxiliary police program
- Uniforms and dry cleaning service

12.8 Duties of Auxiliary Police Officers in Canada

As stated, the auxiliary constable program is primarily a volunteer program intended to enhance community-based policing and provide an opportunity for citizens to participate in law enforcement on an organized basis. The primary duty of most auxiliary officers in Canada is to perform police duties when accompanied and supervised by a police officer. Auxiliary constables will typically complement municipal, provincial, and federal full-time police personnel by providing assistance in low-risk, nonemergency, and civil emergency operations.

Duties that an auxiliary constable may perform under direct supervision of a regular full-time police officer are widely varied and include, but are not limited to, the following:

- Community policing programs (i.e., neighborhood watch, bicycle safety, child identification)
- Guarding crime scenes to protect evidence
- Search for missing persons
- Routine crowd or traffic control at concerts, fairs, or events
- Perform proactive foot patrols
- Assist with large-scale special events (parades and other community events)
- Assist crime prevention officers in crime prevention initiatives and kiosk information booths

- Operational ride-a-longs with regular full-time officers
- Routine general duty patrols and traffic patrols
- Some activities for auxiliary constables depend on the geographical region or unique needs of the police service and may require that the auxiliary constables assist with marine activities or specialized sections, including training members of the dog squad (serving as a quarry for dog tracking) or emergency response team (serving as a hostage during a mock rescue operation)
- Office duties within police HQ or in a community policing storefront (i.e., computer queries, front desk duties, answering phones)
- Routine duties as assigned by the officer in charge

12.9 A Typical Tour of Duty

The following are examples of possible duties or issues that auxiliary constables may encounter when working with a police service during a tour of duty. The duties or issues will require specific competencies of the individual officer.

1. A request for service or assistance by a member of the public:
   a. The auxiliary officer will need to demonstrate patience as well as interest in learning of the individual's concern or issue.
   b. A need to remain impartial, polite, and professional.
   c. A need to communicate to the member of the public what can or will be done to assist them with his or her request.
2. Delivering a crime prevention seminar to the public:
   a. Attend the meeting on time and be well prepared.
   b. Demonstrate professional deportment and demeanor.
   c. If unaware of an answer to a question, be prepared to follow up after seeking advice from someone of knowledge in your police service.
3. A public demonstration:
   a. Demonstrate impartiality while attempting to determine the nature of the demonstration.
   b. Follow police agency policies and the direction of regular police officers.
   c. Do not offer personal opinions about the demonstration.
   d. Remain professional at all times.
4. The arrest of an individual:
   a. Follow the directions of the regular police officer who you are with.
   b. If you are alone and must arrest an individual, remember to attempt to use verbal communications in seeking peaceful compliance.
   c. Use only as much force as necessary to affect the arrest.

12.10 Examples of Canadian Auxiliary and Reserve Programs

In the western Canadian province of British Columbia, the auxiliary or reserve constable program was created in the early 1960s and is a volunteer program intended to enhance community-based policing and provide an opportunity for citizens to participate in law enforcement on an organized basis. The program serves to strengthen police and community partnerships, providing an opportunity for members of the community to perform authorized activities that address the cause of and/or reduce the fear of crime and disorder. Auxiliary constables within the province of British Columbia are volunteers under the command of the provincial police force (currently contracted to the RCMP) or an independent municipal police agency such as the Delta Municipal Police. Their primary purpose is to participate in community policing service activities related to public safety and crime prevention. They are unarmed and perform duties under the direct supervision of a police officer or under the general supervision of the police agency. In 1999, the attorney general in British Columbia determined that auxiliary members of the RCMP in that province could no longer wear sidearms—a practice that had been allowed under RCMP guidelines in the past. Auxiliary or reserve constables must complete a 92-hour basic training program conducted by their police agency prior to being eligible for an appointment. Topics include law, police procedure, professionalism, effective presentations, and public contact. Written and practical examinations are part of the training program. Each department or detachment may provide further training in addition to the 92-hour basic training (JIBC, 2013).

Similarly, in the eastern Canadian province of Ontario, the OPP auxiliary was originally formed in 1960 by an order-in-council when the program absorbed the emergency measures organization consisting of personnel who were trained in crowd control and first aid. The program was managed by the OPP, and its members in the early years helped at community events and patrolled with regular OPP members. The OPP continues to provide ongoing conferences and workshops for almost 900 auxiliary police members (OPP, 2016). OPP auxiliary members are expected to provide 120 hours of service annually, which amounted to 220,000 volunteered hours in 2015. The Ontario Provincial Auxiliary Program has also partnered with a postsecondary institution (Georgian College), which credits auxiliary constables for their volunteer time toward a criminal justice degree. Auxiliary constables accepted through this process must complete 1,000 hours of service over the course of four years to obtain their degree. The use of unpaid staff to perform a variety of police-related duties must be managed carefully as to not invite criticism or labor challenges from unionized police associations.

Auxiliary constables are not employees of the police service and do not hold employee status. In the case of the OPP, both the Ontario Provincial Police Association (OPPA) and the Commissioned Officers Association support the role of auxiliaries (Whitelaw & Parent, 2013).

12.11 Heroic Moments in Auxiliary Policing

12.11.1 Killed in the Line of Duty: Auxiliary Constable Glen Evely

(RCMP; End of Watch: Saturday, November 13, 2004)
RCMP Auxiliary Constable Evely was killed on Saturday, November 13, 2004, when his patrol car was struck by a stolen pickup truck following a police pursuit in Vernon, British Columbia. The initial police pursuit was commenced by other patrol units after receiving reports of a drunk driver. When they located the vehicle, they determined that it had been stolen the night before. As the officers attempted to stop the truck, the driver sped away. The pursuing officers broke off the chase shortly after it began as a result of the suspect's reckless driving. Even though the chase had been terminated, the driver continued to flee.

When the suspect's vehicle approached an intersection in the town area of Vernon, the driver ran a red light and struck the patrol car Auxiliary Constable Evely was riding in. Auxiliary Constable Evely was pronounced dead at the scene. His partner was transported to a local hospital in serious condition. Both suspects in the stolen vehicle were also taken into custody. Auxiliary Constable Evely and his partner were aware of the earlier pursuit but had not been involved with it and were not attempting to locate the vehicle at the time the incident occurred. Auxiliary Constable Evely had served with the RCMP for two years. He was survived by his wife and two children (ODMP, 2013).

12.11.2 Award of Valor: Nootka Sound RCMP Detachment

Auxiliary Constable Louis Mountain and Constable David Bezanson rescued seven passengers from a distressed and disabled fishing vessel during extreme weather conditions in the rough oceans of the Pacific Northwest in June 2003.

The two officers received commendations for saving the lives of seven people on June 7, 2003, from an eight-meter aluminum vessel being thrown against a reef by eight-meter seas off the west coast of Vancouver Island. The officers said the boat, which was anchored, was made to stand on its nose— almost vertically in the air—before being slammed stern-first onto the reef.

The vessel was on a halibut-fishing trip but had lost its power, and the operator had thrown out an anchor to stop it from being driven onto the reef. With its stern being tossed in the air, the occupants were ready to abandon ship, which likely would have resulted in their deaths due to the extreme weather.

Officers Mountain and Bezanson tried to get a towline to the disabled boat, but the sea was too rough, and there were times when they were in danger of crashing down onto its deck. In the end, they floated a line across to the charter boat using an empty plastic jug. Once they had secured that line, they attempted to pull the other vessel to create some slack on the anchor line so it could be released. Four hours after leaving their safe harbor, the two officers had managed to tow the disabled vessel into port. Due to their heroic efforts, the two officers received awards of valor at the prestigious Police Honors Night held by the Minister of Public Safety (PHN, 2006).

12.12 Conclusion

Police auxiliaries assist law enforcement agencies in developing partnerships with the community and provide an opportunity for the community to take ownership of problems. They are also a continual source of new energy and fresh ideas and help reduce the workload on patrol officers. In some instances, these individuals have risked their lives for the sake of others and with the goal of keeping their community safe. A major challenge for police services in Canada is retaining these volunteers, particularly in view of the competing demands on the time of community residents. In sum, police auxiliaries are a valuable component of Canadian policing, providing the necessary support for community safety and security in a strategic manner.

References

Canadian Centre for Justice Statistics. (2011). *Police Resources in Canada, 2011.* Cat. No. 85-225-X. Ottawa: Statistics Canada, Canadian Centre for Justice Statistics.

Griffiths, C., Parent, R., & Whitelaw, B. (1999). *Canadian police work.* Scarborough, Ontario, Canada: ITP Nelson.

Justice Institute of British Columbia. (2013). Retrieved from http://www.jibc.ca/programs-courses/schools-departments/school-public-safety-security/justice-public-safety-division/auxiliary/reserve-program

Officer Down Memorial Page. (2013). Retrieved from http://www.odmp.org

Ontario Provincial Police. (2016). *Annual Report of the Ontario Provincial Police—2015.* Ontario, Canada: Ontario Provincial Police.

Police Honours Night. (2006). *Police Honours Night Award Recipients: Awards of Valour.* Ministry of Public Safety and Solicitor General.

Whitelaw, B., & Parent, R. (2013). *Community-based strategic policing in Canada* (4th ed.). Toronto: Nelson Education.

Auxiliary Police in Hungary

13

PAL KARDOS
BEATA SZOKE

Contents

13.1 Introduction

In this chapter, we wish to reflect upon the past, present, and future of the Hungarian auxiliary police force. This extraordinary organization has played a vital role in the personal protection of Hungarian civilians for more than 20 years now. Therefore, this chapter aims to shed light on the history, establishment, structure, and functioning of the Nationwide Civil Self-Defense Organizations (Országos Polgárőr Szövetség, OPSZ). Furthermore, it is important to highlight the broad cooperation between the different Hungarian law enforcement agencies as well as the multidisciplinary international collaboration with other crime prevention associations. In doing so, we discuss the relevant legal provisions of the field, which, in turn, allow me to draw a comparison between the Hungarian auxiliary police and other foreign auxiliary forces. Following this overview, it will become clear how the social demand for a national auxiliary organization has allowed the Hungarian auxiliary police to branch out and prove themselves.

We have taken part in the administration, management, and day-to-day life of the Hungarian auxiliary police for more than two decades and have been members of the Civil Self-Defense Organization of Budapest and its Agglomeration (Budapest és Agglomerációs Polgárőr Szervezetek Szövetsége). Thus, we are able to present an objective approach to the national appreciation of the auxiliary police and its current position in Hungary. The study presented here is the result of personal correspondence with relevant associations and is further based upon Internet research in this field. We present the social perceptions surrounding the auxiliary forces and illustrate the possible areas of growth in the future. This may seem like a utopian outlook at the moment, but it is inevitable that we must elaborate on possible improvements if we wish to raise the efficiency of the Hungarian auxiliary police.

13.2 Historical Overview

Shortly prior to the change of political system in Hungary and directly after the leadership was overthrown, the transformation of the government and legislative background had a significant effect on the public security of the country. The social classes drifted apart from one another and existential uncertainty grew while crime levels escalated. The confusion of law enforcement offices and the sudden gaps in the law, regulation, and administrative provisions led to an incentive for criminal activity. Moreover, a new phenomenon arose as the borders were opened and an "influx" of foreign offenders began. These perpetrators committed crimes that Hungarian officials had never faced before, and within two years, the amount of criminal activity doubled. The new forms of illegal behavior that occurred were mostly related to organized crime, acts of terrorism, and contraband smuggling. The level of crime directly aimed toward civilians, such as property crimes and assault and battery, also grew considerably.

The police were dumbfounded at the turn of events, which evoked an urgent need for civilian intervention. Members of urban and suburban districts began forming their own groups to ensure the safety of the areas they lived in. These original cells were essentially spontaneous and unorganized; however, as time has progressed, the groups not only conducted neighborhood watches in their immediate surroundings, but expanded their patrols to various other places as well. Thanks to this effort, the levels of criminal activity decreased, and in many cases, the perpetrators were caught in the act. Yet the police departments were uneasy in regards to these civilian groups. They did not have an insight into the activities of these patrols, nor did they want to cooperate with them due to their negative bias toward civilian initiatives. Nevertheless, after changes in legal regulations, an official dialogue and partnership began between civilian self-defense groups from all around the country. The registered associations set up their mission statements with a clear goal of crime prevention, which resulted in regular independent patrols. They took on the responsibility of aiding law enforcement agencies, thus becoming an important part of the cleanup aimed toward reducing criminal tendencies.

In 1991, the police recognized that they could utilize the support of the 223 civil self-defense organizations that were operating at the time. The commissioner of the Budapest Police called together a conference to assess and discuss the possible basis for mutual cooperation and to acquaint himself with the organizations' accomplishments. It was during this spring consultation that the idea arose to forge a collaboration between civil self-defense agencies across the country so as to ensure a stronger presence and influence. On the 24th of August, 1991, the union was founded, taking on the name of Nationwide Civil Self-Defense Organization in November. Dr. Sándor Kopácsi, a retired major general, was selected as the president of the organization because he had come in contact with auxiliary police work during his years in Canada and the United States. By then, more than 20,000 auxiliary police were lending their services to the country.

Yet, like every beginning, the Nationwide Civil Self-Defense Organization had its own trials and tribulations as many politicians saw the organization as a reinstatement of the voluntary police force and the work guard. They suspected a political purpose behind these activities and could not believe that so many people would make such sacrifices purely for the sake of their communities. Even so, the organization eventually managed to prove itself as a legitimate keeper of peace and showed that it posed no threat to the government. Today in Budapest, the capital of Hungary, the auxiliary police perform an average of 3,500 citizen arrests a year by keeping criminals caught in the act of committing an offense on the scene of the crime until the police arrive.

In conclusion, the auxiliary police have been forced to stand their ground on more than one occasion. They have had to battle the police, who feared losing face in light of the auxiliary activities and the government, who misunderstood their efforts. They have also had hardships in living up to their own goals—that is, preventing crimes and making the streets a safer place. All the while, one must consider that the participants actually pay membership fees, use their own cars during patrols, and supply their own equipment. Since the establishment of the organization, the Nationwide Civil Self-Defense Organization has taken on several responsibilities, such as the following:

- Preventing traffic accidents
- Child and youth protection duties
- Building and strengthening the public safety of cities, villages, and communities, preventing crimes threatening the peace of the neighborhoods
- Helping the work of other national and local government-based law enforcement services

The auxiliary force is currently made up of almost 90,000 volunteers, who are members of 2,088 organizations in this field. To date, this is the largest auxiliary presence of all European countries.

13.3 Legal Background

The statute, Act II, Section 1, of 1989, allowed civil self-defense units to integrate into social organizations. Regarding the organizations' legal provisions, each separate association has the opportunity to specialize in different areas of work. For instance, some organizations place greater value on school-based prevention programs, and other groups aim their endeavors toward promoting healthy lifestyle choices and safety regulations. On February 13, 2006, act LII of the Hungarian Parliament entered into force regarding the activities of civil self-defense forces. The eight sections of the law were later modified in 2009 when act LXXXIV came into effect, including revisions of the cooperation of auxiliary police and non-self-defense organization members.

Moreover, 2011 resulted in further developments as the newly approved laws meant a profound shift in the way auxiliary police worked. Following these changes the civil self-defense units operate in the area in which their headquarters are registered, meaning that auxiliary police can only exercise their powers in their direct district or suburban area. However, an exception to this regulation is possible in cases in which a mutual written agreement is reached between the auxiliaries and other national or local authorities, such as police departments, public safety organizations, environmental offices, or tax administrations. In addition, the auxiliary police can only conduct their patrols if a written contract is drafted between them and other relevant authorities. Members of the auxiliary police must be 18 years of age or above, they must have a clean record sheet, and must wear appropriate clothing and uniforms. The auxiliary police are composed of civic-minded residents of the community, who are dedicated to improving the level of safety and security in their community during their free time. Finally, to become a member of the Hungarian auxiliary forces, one must be a Hungarian citizen or must possess valid residence permits as a foreigner. One must also meet the basic knowledge requirements, which include passing a mandatory written test.

13.4 Work of the Hungarian Auxiliary Police

Since the Nationwide Civil Self-Defense Organization was founded, one specific issue has been the cause of great concern: the protection of auxiliary police. The auxiliaries do not qualify as authorized officials in terms of general provisions, regulatory power, and individual levels of protection. This, in turn, means that auxiliary police can only receive higher levels of protection if they are on patrol with a member of the national police force. According to the Criminal Code of the Republic of Hungary, a person who assaults, stalks, harasses, or intimidates a police officer while in the execution of the officer's duty is liable for imprisonment. This, in turn, means that, if an auxiliary is assaulted while assisting the work of a police officer, then the perpetrator must expect the same punishment as if the action had been carried out against a police officer.

The conceptual background of the auxiliary police work is that of many definitions, seeing as auxiliaries generally focus their energy on crime prevention propaganda, and more specifically speaking, they conduct their watches and patrols to ensure and enhance the safety of their communities. In terms of the neighborhood watch, the activities may be related to moving or standing targets, and it may be a wide-scale area watch, an object observation, or the monitoring of an individual. In addition, the patrol may take place on foot or in a vehicle, either in the presence of other law enforcement officers or with the help of public domain superintendents. The core difference between an auxiliary and a civilian is the fact that the auxiliary pays specific attention to certain details, concentrates on filtering potential perpetrators, and examines suspicious circumstances. Moreover, the auxiliary police play a vital role in ensuring the safety of individuals with important duties and obligations, such as mailmen, fee collectors, agricultural guards, or even policemen.

In their efforts to reach their goals, the Nationwide Civil Self-Defense Organization's line of work includes the following:

- Basic crime prevention training for auxiliary police
- Regular consultations, focus discussions, and exhibitions regarding public safety issues
- Briefings on the civic rights and obligations in connection with social order
- Distributing pamphlets about crime prevention, road safety, environmental protection, and catastrophe prevention
- Public debate opportunities in order to discover how the members of certain communities view their current public safety situation and law enforcement regulations
- Holding presentations in schools about crime prevention
- Supporting and elevating physical fitness levels of auxiliary police and promoting a healthy lifestyle
- Carrying out neighborhood watches and patrols
- Assisting other self-defense groups in their activities
- Ensuring and monitoring the cleanliness of public domains, the levels of public health care, utilization of public areas, and amount of environmental consciousness
- Lending a hand to police officers or other members of law enforcement on duty
- Directing and organizing local government-based or national events

An auxiliary police officer may only commit him- or herself to these tasks if he or she is not under the influence of alcohol or other intoxicating substances. What's more, an auxiliary may not consume alcohol while being on duty and may not carry particularly dangerous tools or weapons. Also, an auxiliary, like any other Hungarian citizen, may only own a firearm for self-defense purposes with the necessary permits. However, effective since the first of September 2009, act LXXXIV allows members to carry police-issue pepper spray as well as to direct traffic collision sites and pedestrian crossings in front of kindergartens and primary schools. The auxiliaries must set an example with their behavior and must be law-abiding individuals who do not abuse their power. Finally, an auxiliary police officer must always identify him- or herself before taking any measures.

A member of the Nationwide Civil Self-Defense Organization must always conduct patrols in the standardized uniform with an indication of his or her unit and name unless, of course, the individual is taking part in an undercover operation. Nonetheless, in all cases, the auxiliaries must carry their identity card and papers with them. For their own safety, auxiliary police are always on duty with a partner and keep in touch with one another and the police through a radio connection. Although many times people expect the auxiliary police to intervene in certain situations, it is still wise for the auxiliaries to avoid this, if possible, because they do not possess the necessary equipment, training, and authority to perform the same actions that professional police are capable of doing.

In addition, the Nationwide Civil Self-Defense Organization is a member of the International Auxiliary Police Association (IAPA), which encompasses auxiliary and police reserve officers from around the world, allowing members from different cultural backgrounds to learn from one another. Hence, the members are able to discuss global issues as well as being able to discover the specific functions of each individual country. Furthermore, the association holds regular conferences, one of which took place in Hungary in February of 2011. The Hungarian auxiliary police forces have formed a particularly close partnership with the special constables of the United Kingdom, the auxiliary police of the United States and Canada, and the civil self-defense groups from its neighboring countries, such as Romania, Croatia, and Slovakia.

Using Police Reserves to Support the South African Police Service

14

CHRISTIAAN BEZUIDENHOUT

Contents

14.1 Introduction

The South African Police (SAP; as they were known before democratization in 1994) and the South African Police Service (SAPS, the new name after 1994) have always relied on civil society for support in its actions and crime prevention efforts. The government at that time was known for its apartheid regime and segregation practices. After outbursts of resistance by mainly the Black population of South Africa to government suppression and segregation in the 1960s, the then Minister of Justice B. J. Vorster created a reserve police force to assist the police in their regular duties when officers had to take care of other essential services. Legislation to cover this was soon passed, and recruiting began in earnest. During 1961, the police reserve was officially introduced. By 1963, they had to reorganize the reserve to ensure more effective use of the available volunteers and manpower. During these years, the reserves was predominantly White, but eventually and after special requests were made, a few Colored,* Indian, and, later in 1967, Black reservists were also accommodated in certain areas. They were given a six-month theoretical training, after which they started to work with a permanent police member. When on duty, reservists were viewed as "permanent" members of the police,

---

* In South Africa, the term "Colored" refers to persons who have mixed ethnic origins.

and had they been injured or killed in the line of duty, they were given the same medical benefits as a permanent member (Dippenaar, 1988, pp. 322–323, 421, 480–481, 486–487, 497, 539, 557, 634, 637).

A reservist is a member of the community who volunteers his or her services to perform policing functions or activities for the police without being remunerated for such a service. Any member of the community may become a police reservist who has a passion to make a difference in the community and would like to combat crime (www.saps.gov.za, www.sahistory.org.za).

The need to introduce a police reserve in South Africa can only be explained against the backdrop of the unique history of the country and, more specifically, the development and transformation of the justice system up until now. The police were dramatically restructured and reformed since 1994. Even today, the police are still being transformed. This, of course, impacted on the police reserve. With most of the major changes "completed" in the police, the reserve is now being targeted for change. The SAPS has recently revised the National Instruction 1/2002, which was the South African reserve police service regulation that regulated reservists from the date of this contribution. The revision of the regulating framework was necessary because several challenges and problems have been identified in the current system. This chapter briefly focuses on the history of the police in South Africa, the changes that were introduced in the police, the past outlook of the reserve, and current challenges as well as the envisaged new changes for the police reserve in South Africa.

14.2 Historic Overview of the Justice System in South Africa

Before 1652, when the Dutch Commander Jan van Riebeeck and his 90-man crew settled in South Africa, the earliest representatives of South Africa's diversity, at least the earliest that is identifiable, were the San and Khoekhoe people (otherwise known as the Bushmen and Hottentots or Khoikhoi). They were residents of the southern tip of the continent for thousands of years before its written history began with the arrival of European seafarers. Other long-term inhabitants of the area now known as South Africa were the Bantu-speaking or Black people who had gradually moved into the southern tip of the continent from the far north (Congo) many years before the arrival of the Europeans. Several different ethnic groups with their own unique languages and informal indigenous legal as well as cultural practices settled in South Africa over time.

Jan van Riebeeck landed in 1652 at the Cape of Good Hope under instructions from the Dutch East India Company to build a fort and develop a vegetable garden for the benefit of ships on the Eastern trade route. The traditional and indigenous practices of law were of little concern to the Europeans, and they immediately introduced and adhered to Roman Dutch law. By the end of the 18th century, the Dutch interest in the Cape of Good Hope faded, and the British used this opportunity to seize the Cape in 1795. British sovereignty of the area was recognized at the Congress of Vienna in 1815. The British introduced British law into the Cape after the seizure of the Cape Colony. In the meantime, at the beginning of the 19th century, the Zulu-speaking Black ethnic group started with an offensive known as Difaqane ("the crushing"). The Zulu group forced other Black ethnic groups to migrate to other areas by means of forced migration practices. The Zulu group, under the reign of Shaka, a well-known Zulu leader, evolved within two decades from a typical Bantu-speaking decentralized pastoral society into a highly centralized and organized nation-state with a large and powerful standing army.

At the same time, the Boer settlers of European descent as well as prospectors who were already settled in the Cape Colony decided to break away from British rule and started moving out of the Cape Colony into the inland area of South Africa. Those settlers that moved out of the Cape Colony were called "voortrekkers." Over time, the tensions between the voortrekkers (farmers and settlers), the different Bantu groupings, and the British increased. After many battles and wars, the formation of the Union of South Africa followed because the British defeated the farmers who were against British rule in the Anglo-Boer War (1899–1902). The farmers eventually negotiated independence from British rule, and the controlling National Party (NP) introduced a new system of rule, which lasted from 1948 to 1993. This system is now notoriously known as the system of apartheid (Bezuidenhout & Little, 2012, p. 369; Dippenaar, 1988, pp. 322–323, 421, 480–481, 486–487, 497, 539, 557, 634, 637; Official South Africa Yearbook, 1993, pp. 9–20; South Africa Yearbook, 1995, pp. 27–35).

14.3 South African Law Is Multicultural

The current South African law is grounded in the customs, traditions, and laws of the peoples of many cultures. Those who clash with the authorities in South Africa are not always dealt with in the same specific manner as indigenous law still plays an important part in the legal processes of South Africa. The different Black groups had for centuries their own unique indigenous methods to deal with transgressors. The Bushmen and Hottentots had their own unique ways to discipline wrongdoers. The farmers or settlers from different European countries also had their own views with regard to the disciplining of a lawbreaker. For the authorities of the time, indigenous laws often clashed with Roman Dutch law and later British law. Therefore, many influences shaped and impacted on the development of policing in South Africa.

Table 14.1   Population Distribution of South Africa in 2011

Population Group	Subtotal
Black	41,000,938
Colored	4,615,401
Indian or Asian	1,286,930
Other	280,454
White	4,586,838
Total	**51,770,560**

Source: www.statssa.gov.za/Census2011

The apartheid system also had a molding influence on the policing system in South Africa.

In South Africa, as well as in other countries that were previously under British colonial control, Eurocentric influence played a fundamental role in shaping the way in which the policing system was developed. The "New World" that was exported from Europe to Africa via the settlers and the colonial administrators resulted in an acculturation process in which Black people found themselves caught in between their traditional culture and Western culture. As a result, certain Blacks adopted some of the Western views regarding criminal justice processes and punishment for misbehavior, and the majority at that time rejected other Western views of policing and discipline (Bezuidenhout & Little, 2012, pp. 369–371). This challenge is further compounded by the fact that the majority of South Africans are Black. The challenge to juggle between indigenous beliefs and an ever-changing Westernized criminal justice landscape currently poses different challenges to Black individuals and their cultural heritage. The ethnic breakdown of the South African population in 2011 can be observed in Table 14.1.

14.4 Early Initial Stages: A Brief Overview of the SAP

The SAP traces its origin to the Dutch Watch, a paramilitary organization formed by settlers in the Cape in 1655, initially to protect civilians against attack and later to maintain law and order. In 1795, British officials assumed control over the Dutch Watch, and in 1825, they organized the Cape Constabulary, which became the Cape Town Police Force in 1840. In 1854, a police force was established in Durban, which became the Durban Borough Police. Act 3 of 1855 established the Frontier Armed and Mounted Police Force in the Eastern Cape, restyled as the Cape Mounted Riflemen in 1878. Eventually, the Mounted Riflemen's Association relinquished its civilian responsibilities to the SAP as most of its riflemen left to serve in World

War I. With the outbreak of the war in 1899, the Transvaal and Orange Free State police forces were called to active service in the Boer ("voortrekker") army, and the Cape Mounted Riflemen and Mounted Police and the Natal Mounted Police were called to support the British. In 1911, General J. B. M. Hertzog, the Minister of Justice, took the police bill to its second reading. It was passed to the following year as it was closely tied with the defense bill that was still being prepared. In 1913, the Defense Act was passed, and on December 31 of the same year, authorization for the establishment of a police force was given.

The SAP was therefore eventually officially created after the Union of South Africa was established in 1913. The SAP was the successor to the police forces of the Cape Colony, the Natal Colony, the Orange River Colony, and the Transvaal Colony. The entire force had to be restructured, and for a short period, the South African Defense Force's (SADF) military police assisted the SAP when necessary. The SAP and the military maintained their close relationship even after the SAP assumed permanent responsibility for domestic law and order in 1926. Police officials often called on the army for support in emergencies. In World War II, one SAP brigade served with the 2nd Infantry Division of the South African Army in North Africa (Potgieter, 1974, p. 632).

When the NP edged out its more liberal opponents in nationwide elections in 1948, the new government enacted legislation strengthening the relationship between the police and the military. Although racial segregation in South Africa began in colonial times under Dutch and British rule, apartheid as an official policy was introduced following the general election of 1948. New legislation classified inhabitants into four racial groups ("Native," "White," "Colored," and "Asian"), and residential areas were segregated, sometimes by means of forced removals. This system of racial segregation and the enforcement thereof through legislation by the NP government (the ruling party from 1948 to 1994) caused many frustrations and grievances. Under this system, the rights of the majority Black inhabitants of South Africa were curtailed, and White supremacy and Afrikaner minority rule was maintained. The police also focused their intentions predominantly on the protection of the White minority. Apartheid was therefore cultivated after World War II by the White Afrikaner-dominated NP and "Broederbond" (brotherhood) organizations. The police were heavily armed after that, especially when facing unruly or hostile Black crowds. During the apartheid regime, the police were used mainly for the protection of the White minority and the furtherance of the unequal political climate. The police were tasked with the function of guaranteeing the success of segregation in South Africa, which resulted in general crime prevention mainly being allocated to the White minority (apparently a 70%:30% distribution). The policing skills needed to perform the above functions, although effective under apartheid, would later probably be deemed ineffective against the background of a newly democratic country in the future developments of South Africa (later more about this). Due to the different priorities of the SAP during apartheid, widespread clashes occurred with mainly Black protesters. The police were cut thin, and during this time, a countrywide needs assessment was undertaken to ascertain whether a recognized official reserve force could be justified. Thousands of White males indicated their willingness to assist the police as reservists or volunteers. The then Minster of Justice B. J. Vorster immediately introduced a reserve police force to assist the police in their regular duties. Legislation to envelop this was soon passed, and recruiting began in earnest. During 1961, the police reserve was officially introduced in South Africa. The Police Act (No. 7) of 1958 was amended to accommodate the changes pertaining to the reserve force and to broaden the mission of the SAP beyond conventional police functions, such as maintaining law and order and investigating and preventing crime, and gave the police extraordinary powers to suppress unrest and to conduct counterinsurgency activities.

The newly established reserve was divided into four groups: The A-group reservists could be called up for short periods of time to assist police in their normal police duties. They were also remunerated during these times. Later on, the remuneration of reservists was revoked (currently one of the reasons why the reserve police were completely overhauled in South Africa). B-group reservists only served as "homebound" guards. They guarded and patrolled their neighborhoods during a state of emergency or when crime was rife. The C-group reservists were employed by local government or key industries. They were to guard these companies and departments (who employed them) when needed. D-group reservists operated in the rural areas and assisted the police during riots and uprisings in the rural areas. They all underwent training of four to six months and were issued with police uniforms and firearms. They could also be promoted to constable–laborer, constable, sergeant, noncommissioned officer, or lieutenant by the commissioner of the police. In 1965, ministerial approval was given to add and recruit scuba divers from different diving clubs to assist the police in the water (e.g., recover a body after a drowning; recovering evidence in criminal cases from the sea, dams, and rivers). In 1972, amateur radio operators (radio amateurs) were also allowed into the reservists to assist the police to better their radio communication (Beeld, 1981; Cillié, 1983, p. 12; Hoofstad, 1969; Transvaler, 1984; van Zyl, 1985, p. 20).

During 1981, the then Minister of Police, Mr. Louis le Grange, announced that schoolboys aged 16 years and older could qualify to be employed as police reservists. The idea to recruit schoolboys originally came about when the sons of senior policemen volunteered to help with "minor police activities" during school holidays. The stock theft unit in Natal used schoolboys to identify and help destroy dagga (cannabis or marijuana) plantations. The plan was only to use the boys during school holidays and only if they did not have school activities during the holiday period. They would be unarmed, and their lives were not to be put in danger. A permanent member of the police was to escort them at all times. After they completed school, the boys would be released from duty, and the South American Defense Force (i.e., the South African National Army) would have priority to call them up for military training (Potgieter, 1974, p. 395; van Zyl, 1985, p. 20). The recruiting of schoolboys eventually dissipated after the eventual excitement about the prospect of using them as reservists.*

In 1982, ministerial approval was given to appoint females to the police reserve. Ladies of 21 years and older could apply, and the first female reservist, Mrs. Hester Fouché, was appointed on February 17, 1982. Their duties included serving as clerks, switchboard operators, or any other duties relevant to the charge office milieu (Citizen, 1982; van Zyl, 1985, p. 20).

In addition to the new addition of reservists, the Police Amendment Act (No. 70) of 1965 empowered the police to search without warrant any person, receptacle, vehicle, aircraft, or premise within one mile of any national border and to seize anything found during such a search. This search-and-seize zone was extended to within eight miles of any border in 1979 and to the entire country in 1983.

At that stage, political unrest was rife, and the majority Black population regularly staged different uprisings. The government used announcements to declare a state of emergency whenever uprisings threatened the stability of the country. They used this tactic to crack down against their Black political opponents at times of heightened resistance. Police could detain anyone for reasons of public safety. Also, meetings and gatherings could be banned by the police. The first state of emergency was declared in 1960 after the Sharpeville Massacre when the African National Congress (ANC) and Pan Africanist Congress (PAC) also were declared illegal political parties. The Sharpeville incident occurred on March 21, 1960, at the police station in the South African township of Sharpeville in the Transvaal (today the Gauteng province). After a day of demonstrations at which a crowd of Black protesters far outnumbered the police, the South African police opened fire on the crowd, killing 69 people. Some sources state that the crowd was peaceful,

---

* For a very long time, military training was compulsory for all White boys in South Africa. Compulsory conscription took place to either assist the police or to fight in the border war of South Africa. South Africa has been involved in several wars since 1652, namely WWI, WWII, and local wars between the inhabitants (e.g., the Boer war for independence) as well as wars in South West Africa and other parts of the South African border. Later a "war" in the rural and urban areas had to be fought by the apartheid government, known as the urban and rural war against the uprising of the Black masses. In 1977, compulsory national service had been increased from one to two years, followed by a series of annual compulsory "citizen force" camps, ranging from one to three months long. Legislation provided stringent sentences for White boys who refused to do compulsory national army service; usually prison terms of up to six years were handed out.

and others state that the crowd had been throwing stones at the police the whole day long. The shooting started when the crowd advanced purposefully toward the perimeter or cordon around the police station. The policemen were apparently skittish after nine policemen had been shot during a protest in a event that had occurred recently in Durban (www.sahistory.org.za).

The pinnacle was the 1976 uprising by school-going children who protested against the Afrikaans Medium Decree of 1974, which forced all Black schools to use Afrikaans and English in a 50:50 mix as languages of instruction. This introduced a wave of uprisings and strikes against the White minority government as many Blacks have their own unique indigenous language and refused to be educated in a second language. In those days, indigenous languages would only be used for religion tutoring, music, and instructions about a healthy way of life. This and many other frustrations caused by apartheid set the stage for violent protests, which dragged on for more than a decade. On June 17, heavily armed police officers were deployed to Soweto (a predominantly Black district adjacent to Johannesburg). They drove around in armored vehicles and monitored the area from the sky with helicopters. The South African Army was also on standby as a tactical measure to show military force. Crowd control methods used by South African police at the time included mainly dispersal techniques (e.g., spraying with water cannons, tear gas, rubber bullets, etc.). The aftermath of the Soweto uprising was harsh as live ammunition was also used. However, it most likely introduced the cycle of change toward the new democracy that was established in 1994.

By the mid-1980s, Black militants endeavored to make South Africa "ungovernable." A state of emergency once again had to be declared whereby organizations as well as meetings could be banned. Thousands of people were arrested and detained. On June 12, 1986, just before the 10th anniversary of the student uprising of 1976 that started in Soweto, a state of emergency was declared throughout the country. The provisions of this state of emergency were broader than any previous ones, but antiapartheid mobilization continued. The government restricted political funerals, imposed curfews, and banned certain indoor gatherings. Television cameras were banned from "unrest areas," preventing international as well as national coverage of the growing tension and police repression. Many violent clashes followed, and international pressure on the NP increased. On January 31, 1985, State President P. W. Botha offered Nelson Mandela (who later became the first Black president of the newfound democracy) conditional release from prison if he could renounce the violence and uprisings. Similar offers were made in 1987 and 1988. When P. W. Botha resigned as leader of the NP in February 1989, F. W. De Klerk succeeded him. In September 1989, De Klerk was elected as the new state president (the last president of the apartheid regime). He probably should be hailed as the key figure in the development of the South African democracy as he soon announced his policy of reform. He wanted to create a suitable climate for negotiations that would end apartheid and bring about a new constitutional dispensation for South Africa.

In December 1989, De Klerk met with the imprisoned leader of the ANC, Nelson Mandela. On February 2, 1990, De Klerk lifted the ban on the ANC, the South African Communist Party (SACP), and the PAC. On February 11, Mandela was unconditionally released from prison after 27 years of imprisonment. Negotiations with Mandela and other party leaders were held for the peaceful end of apartheid and the transition to democratic rule. In 1993, De Klerk and Mandela were awarded the Nobel Peace Prize for their efforts to reform South Africa peacefully. After the 1994 elections, Mr. De Klerk was appointed the position of second vice president in President Mandela's cabinet but retired from all politics in 1997 (Kalley, Schoeman, & Andor, 1999; www.saps.gov.za; www.sahistory.org.za).

14.5 South African Police Service

The current SAPS has undergone a paradigm shift since the abolishment of the apartheid regime in 1994. Before 1994, the SAP employed a paramilitaristic approach to policing, which was based on limited community involvement in policing matters. Since then, the "force" has changed into a "service" with the emphasis on merged police–community partnerships. South Africa became an internationally accepted democracy in 1994 when President Nelson Mandela was elected as the first president of the new South Africa, bringing the era of apartheid to an end. This new democratic order brought about many changes in the country and also had a substantial impact on policing (Bezuidenhout, 2011b, p. 11; www.saps.gov.za; www.sahistory.org.za).

After the end of apartheid, the SAP was renamed to the SAPS, and the Ministry of Law and Order was renamed the Ministry of Safety and Security in keeping with these symbolic reforms. The new Minister of Safety and Security, Sydney Mufamadi, obtained police training assistance from Zimbabwe, Britain, and Canada and proclaimed that racial tolerance and human rights would be central to police training programs in the future. By the end of 1995, the SAPS had incorporated the 10 police agencies from the former homelands and had reorganized at both the national level and at the level of South Africa's nine new provinces. These so-called homelands were the following: Transkei, Bophuthatswana, Venda and Ciskei (i.e. the four TBVC states), Gazankulu, Kangwane, Kwandebele, Kwazulu, Lebowa, and Qwaqwa. Each had their own policing agency, bringing the total number of policing agencies in the country to 11 (10 homelands plus the old SAP). All 11 policing agencies had different uniforms, rank structures, and conditions of service and were established under different pieces of legislation. They also used diverse recording techniques for the documenting of reported crimes.

With the adoption of the interim constitution in 1994, the Homelands and old development regions were abolished and integrated into a united South Africa with nine provinces. The new constitution established a single National Police Service for South Africa under the executive command and control of a national commissioner who is appointed by the president (Official South Africa Yearbook, 1993, pp. 9–20; Rauch, 2001, p. 121; Rauch & van der Spuy, 2006; South Africa Yearbook, 1995, pp. 27–35; www.saps.gov .za; www.sahistory.org.za).

In 1995, the development of the SAP Service Act (Act 68 of 1995) implemented the changes envisaged into a legal framework. The restructuring of the police was now going to form part of the constitution, and a more accountable and civilian-based police service would be utilized. A clean break with the past of policing in South Africa was needed and envisaged. With an emphasis on creating better relationships between the police and the community and adopting a new mindset within policing, the changes were well underway that would send South African policing into the realm of a democratic state (Rauch, 2001, pp. 120–121).

The new service-oriented approach adopted by the SAPS aligned itself rather with a vision-driven and not a rule-driven approach (Rauch & van der Spuy, 2006, p. 55). Community cooperation (community policing and sector policing) was seen as a vital part of policing the country (Roelofse, 2007). It is the belief that by being more readily involved in the community, the problems faced by the community could be recognized instantly and could be prioritized by the police. It is believed that closer ties with the community increase the level of accountability of the police because they are not only accountable to the individuals who are in command, but they are accountable to the community in which they work (Berning & Masiolane, 2011, p. 66). Greater interaction with the community as well as higher levels of accountability in the police was envisaged as an expected outcome of this approach.

On January 29, 1995, General George Fivaz was appointed by President Nelson Mandela as the first national commissioner of the new SAPS. George Fivaz had the immediate responsibility of amalgamating the 11 policing agencies into a single united SAPS to ensure more efficient community involvement and to align the new police service to new legislation as well as the process of transformation in South Africa.

South Africa held elections in 1999, and the country's new president, Thabo Mbeki, was appointed. National Commissioner George Fivaz's term of office expired during January 2000, and he was succeeded by Jackie Selebi. It was thought that policing in South Africa had entered a new era with the appointment of Jackie Selebi as the second national commissioner of the SAPS (the first Black commissioner of the police). Jacob (Jackie) Sello Selebi is also the former president of the ANC Youth League and a former president of Interpol. In January 2008, Selebi was put on extended leave as national police commissioner and resigned as president of Interpol after he was charged with corruption. He therefore had to be replaced as national commissioner in July 2009. During this time, Selebi was found guilty of corruption on July 2, 2010, and sentenced to 15 years imprisonment on August 3, 2010. His appeal against his sentence was rejected by the supreme court of appeal on December 2, 2011, after the court unanimously ruled against him. However, he was released on medical parole in July 2012.

A decade and a half after Nelson Rolihlahla Mandela was formally elected as the first president of a democratic South Africa and after President Mbeki took the oath of office as the second president of the republic in June 1999, Mr. Jacob Zuma became the next President of the Republic of South Africa on May 9, 2009. After his inauguration on May 10, 2009, he announced the appointment of a new cabinet. Minister Nathi Mthethwa was appointed as Minister of Police, and Deputy Minister Fikile Mbalula was appointed as Deputy Minister of Police. President Zuma stressed that he necessitated building cohesive, caring, and sustainable communities. During this time frame, the title of the Ministry for Safety and Security was changed to the Ministry of Police. After the spectacle of the disgraced National Police Commissioner Jackie Selebi, a new commissioner was identified by president Zuma. General Bheki Hamilton Cele was appointed by President Zuma as police commissioner of the SAPS on August 2, 2009. In contrast to the "service approach," General Bheke Cele opted for a more forceful approach to crime prevention in South Africa. His abrasive approach to crime fighting, namely, that he and the SAPS would get tough on criminals, was somewhat out of sorts with a service delivery approach of community and sector policing. Nonetheless, he received mixed support, and many opted for this new "tougher" militaristic approach as crime was and still is out of control in South Africa. Not long after his announcement of more vigilant abrasive policing, a group of eight policemen were shown on national and international television news channels while they were beating and shooting a protester, Andries Tatane, during a protest. Tatane and other civilians were protesting against poor service delivery by the local government in Ficksburg in the Free State Province. Although the tough stance was celebrated by some, others felt that Cele's "fight fire with fire" approach could increase, rather than diminish, police brutality by and against police. Criminals who believe that they are more likely to be killed than arrested by the police will probably arm themselves more heavily in response and will be more willing to shoot at the police in a bid to escape arrest. Law-abiding civilians who experience heavy-handedness will increasingly become afraid of police and will be unlikely to cooperate with them.

Since this incident of apparent unnecessary use of force, the police have been criticized in different forums for their brutality and poor relationships with the community. Then again, the SAPS insist that the community continues to show a lack of support. Furthermore, the police are often seen as poorly managed, poorly trained, and ruthless. To compound these challenges, Bheki Cele was also eventually suspended from duty as the national commissioner of the SAPS in October 2011 due to allegations of corruption. On June 12, 2012, the President of the Republic of South Africa, Mr. Jacob Zuma, announced the appointment of a new national commissioner of the SAPS, General (Mrs.) Mangwashi Victoria "Riah" Phiyega (the first female national police commissioner in South Africa). Soon after she was appointed, the world was shocked when 44 miners were killed by the police service during an industrial action. The shooting incident on August 16, 2012, referred to as the Marikana massacre, was the single most lethal use of force by South African police against civilians since 1960 during the apartheid era—the Sharpeville massacre. At least 78 additional workers were also injured on August 16, 2012. The total number of injuries during the strike remains unknown, and it appears as if these types of incidents are tarnishing the community's trust in the police. Controversy emerged after it was discovered that most of the victims were shot in the back, and many victims were shot far from police lines. The official investigation has revealed many interesting perspectives including that the mine workers who stood in the line of fire visited a traditional healer (Sangoma) before their strike and march at the mines to cover them with a special concoction to make them invisible to the police and also bulletproof.

Even so, this type of violence and police action resonates negatively against the constitution, calling for police in South Africa. The Constitution of the Republic of South Africa, 1996 (Act 108 of 1996) lays down that the SAPS has a responsibility to do the following:

- Prevent, combat, and investigate crime
- Maintain public order
- Protect and secure the inhabitants of the Republic and their property
- Uphold and enforce the law
- Create a safe and secure environment for all people in South Africa
- Prevent anything that may threaten the safety or security of any community
- Investigate any crimes that threaten the safety or security of any community
- Ensure that criminals are brought to justice
- Participate in efforts to address the causes of crime

To fulfill this and to adhere to the mission of the SAPS, all the members are subjected to a code of conduct. The official code of conduct of the SAPS was introduced on October 31, 1997. The code of conduct is a written undertaking, which each member of the SAPS is obliged to uphold in order to bring about a safe and secure environment for all people of South Africa. Every member of the SAPS must make the code of conduct part of their code of life, principles, and values. The Mission of the SAPS is to do the following:

- Prevent and combat anything that may threaten the safety and security of any community
- Investigate any crimes that threaten the safety and security of any community
- Ensure offenders are brought to justice
- Participate in efforts to address the causes of crime

In addition to all the changes, the police, although being demilitarized after 1994, have recently been remilitarized in some ways. Specific reference to the reintroduction of the military ranking system is applicable. The former military ranking system was reintroduced in an effort to garner respect and discipline. Many feel that this reversion to the old ranks simply instills fear and not respect (National Planning Commission, 2011, p. 355). It is understood that the police have been reverting to a paramilitary type of force since the year 2000, but the official changing of ranks only occurred in 2010. However, there is still the belief that the SAPS has continued to view itself more as a "force" than as a "service" (Police revert to military ranks in April, 2010).

The changing of the ranks was done in order to create more respect for the police and within the policing ranks. This argument has, however, been questioned as police brutality rates have increased since the military ranks have been reintroduced. A general understanding is that effective and efficient policing will harness more public respect than military ranks (National Planning Commission, 2011, p. 355).

A general consensus has been gained in that, although the remilitarization was supposed to decrease crime rates, it has, in effect, increased police violence toward the public. The sentiment is shared by the National Planning Commission as well as Berning and Masiolane (2011). A report conducted by the Independent Complaints Directorate in 2011 found an increase of 800% in the torture rate committed by police against civilians since the remilitarization (National Planning Commission, 2011, p. 356). Berning and Masiolane (2011) indicate that the rise in police shootings, police brutality, use of excess force, and a culture of questioning senior superior orders shows how South Africa once again now faces a militarized police.

The most important and serious duties of any police power are to uphold the law and to maintain law and order. The police have to investigate crimes, protect life and property, and take responsibility for the official duties assigned to them. In order to fulfill these duties, SAPS officers should have a comprehensive knowledge of the country's legal system and undergo thorough training in all aspects of the job, which is continued throughout their service. Recruits are supposed to be assigned to departments that suit their skills or talents. In addition, the police have been supported by the community in the form of reservists since the 1960s. A reservist function is extremely important in South Africa if the police-to-population ratio is considered. The total South African population is 51,770,560, and the total number of police officers (excluding permanent contractual civilians) is 157,518 (April 2013) (www.saps .gov.za). This calculates to an estimated national ratio of 1:329 (one permanent police official for every 329 citizens). This, therefore, clearly supports the need for additional support to the police in the form of a reserve grouping.

14.6 Contemporary Police Reservists in South Africa

The police reserve is currently regulated under the National Instruction 1/2002. This National Instruction was backed by additional regulations in the form of certain amendments that were made by the then Minister of Safety and Security Steve Tshwete. The most notable adjustments include issues pertaining to the nature of the services that must be rendered by a reservist appointed to a specific category, the training such a reservist should undergo, whether the reservist may wear a police uniform when on duty, and whether such a reservist could be called up for compulsory duty when needed (Government Gazette, 2004, p. GN1214). (Please note that several changes are in the pipeline, and they are discussed at the end of this section).

A reservist is a member of the community who voluntarily performs certain duties in the police service. They have similar powers as permanent police officials while they perform their duties as reservists. Thus, any member of the community may become a police reservist if they are the following:

- A permanent resident in South Africa
- Not younger than 18 years or older than 70 years of age
- Free of any mental or physical defect or visible tattoos when wearing uniform
- In possession of a senior certificate or equivalent qualification
- In possession of a driver's license although not a prerequisite
- Able to speak, read, and write English and one other language
- Free of any criminal offense
- Prepared to undergo training
- Prepared to complete a psychometric test
- Prepared to complete a medical questionnaire
- Prepared to take the oath of office
- Of a good character

Currently, reservists attend introduction, orientation, and basic training for SAPS members during periods as determined by management. Training is presented over a period of between three and six months, depending on the category of appointment, including the practical phase, which is usually presented by means of in-service training. During the training period, reservists work in the Community Service Centre (CSC; previously known as the charge office) as part of their in-service training. At the end of the training period, reservists are posted to vehicles or conduct patrols within their specific community or other duties as determined by the commander. Firearm training is included in the training program, and no reservists are allowed to perform functions with a firearm if this module is not successfully completed. Additional training, such as training in domestic violence, victim support, sector policing, and tactical policing, could also be incorporated in the curriculum, depending on the area of utilization. After successful training, the reservist is appointed as a constable. Promotion to a higher rank is subject to the provisions or any other conditions or exceptions that the national commissioner may determine. The promotion of a reservist to the rank of captain or higher must be approved by the national commissioner. Captain to superintendent/superintendent to senior superintendent/ senior superintendent to director (these ranks have recently been changed back to military style ranks of brigadier, etc.) requires a minimum of four year's service in each of the above ranks with a minimum of 576 hours of service rendered during each period of rank before promotion to the next rank will be considered. The above requirements may be deviated from in cases of previous members of the service who had held similar or higher ranks or who have sufficient applicable experience in the service. This is also the case when a reservist formerly held a similar rank in the Reserve Police Service and has had to forfeit it as a result of transfers and an absence of a need for reservists in that rank at the new station. A reservist may, however, not hold a rank above that of the commander under whose command he or she is serving. Also, a reservist is supplied at no charge with a full police uniform after having successfully completed the training. There are no insignia to distinguish between a permanent member's uniform and those of a reservist. Uniforms and equipment may only be worn by a reservist while on duty. If a reservist makes unauthorized use of the police uniform or equipment, disciplinary steps will immediately be taken against the reservist (Kempen, 2004a, pp. 25–26; www.saps.gov.za).

At this time, there are four categories of reservists in the SAPS:

a. Category A reservists: Functional policing
b. Category B reservists: Support services
c. Category C reservists: Specialized functional policing
d. Category D reservists: Rural and urban safety

Category A reservists perform functions in all operational facets of policing. They must wear a uniform except if they are placed with the detective service or crime intelligence section. They must undergo basic training and in-service training in the relevant aspects of functional policing, such as firearm training. They may be called up by the national or provincial commissioner to perform duties at specific places or during certain times (e.g., to man a ballot station during the general election period). They perform functions on any operational level of policing. They can wear a uniform and should have completed the entire training on operational policing.

Category B reservists usually perform specific support functions and may not be utilized to perform functional or operational policing functions. B reservists may not wear a uniform and may not be issued with a firearm. They may only perform duties as predetermined by the relevant commander. When necessary, they should also be trained in relevant legal aspects, policy, and relevant instructions from the head office. They may be called up by the national or provincial commissioner to perform duties at specific places or during certain times (e.g., to assist at the switchboard).

Category C reservists must have a particular skill or expertise that can be utilized by the police service. C reservists may, with prior approval by the commander, wear a uniform. They should also be trained in relevant legal aspects, policy, and relevant instructions from the head office. With the approval of the relevant commander, they may wear a uniform. They may be called up by the national or provincial commissioner to perform certain duties at specific places or during certain times pertaining to their expertise or in line with their proficiency (e.g., a pilot, a social worker, a pastor, a lawyer for legal advice, or an animal expert to assist in the training of police dogs).

Category D reservists perform functions in operational facets of policing relating to rural and urban safety in a specific sector at the station or unit level. This excludes specialized functional duties. They may wear a uniform but can only perform such functions under the supervision of a permanent member of the police or a Category A reservist who completed their training. Furthermore, they should also be trained in relevant legal aspects, policy, and relevant instructions from the head office. Training on basic principles of functional policing is also advised. They may be called up by the national or provincial commissioner to perform certain duties at specific places or during certain times pertaining to sector policing in urban and rural areas (e.g., assist during a mega sporting event).

A reservist appointed to one category may be transferred to any other category if he or she complies with all the requirements for the specific category and has undergone or is willing to undergo the required training relevant to the category. No reservist may perform general operational duties at the special task force, security or protection services, a national key point, an airport, or any intervention unit without written permission of the national commissioner.

Each commander of a station, unit, or department determines the establishment of reservists at his station or office in accordance with the specific needs and priorities at his or her station or office. The relevant commander should consider the available resources at his disposal, the proper training of the reservists, and whether he or she will be able to equip each reservist once they finish their training. This sometimes hinders proper training as a shortage of ammunition may prevent proper firearm training in the case of A-category reservists (National Instruction 1/2002; www.saps.gov.za; Van Niekerk, 2002, p. 14).

The following individuals will *not* be considered for a reservist position or can only be appointed if they comply with certain conditions:

- A person who has been discharged as medically unfit from a previous employer provided that such a person may be appointed as a category B reservist
- A former member of the service whose application for reenlistment was rejected due to negative considerations
- A member of the regular force of the SADF referred to in section 52 of the Defense Act, 2002 (Act No. 42 of 2002)
- A person in a key position as determined by the department of labor
- A person who holds any post or office in a political party, organization, movement, or body
- A person who is actively involved in politics or who is an outspoken supporter of a political party and who may violate the nonpartisan nature of the service
- A full-time journalist
- A person who does not have a fixed residential address
- A scholar
- A security officer or guard or a person attached to a private security organization (whether as director, partner, or employee)
- A member of a municipal police service (including a local law enforcement officer), a sheriff or deputy sheriff

The following persons may, *subject to* the condition or conditions stated in each case, be appointed as reservists:

- An official or employee of Transnet, with the written approval of his or her head of department
- A member of the Department of Correctional Services
  - If his or her duties as reservist will not interfere with his or her normal work activities
  - If the interests of the department of correctional services will at all times be served first

- May not be called up in terms of regulation 5 of the regulations without the permission of the department of correctional services
- Public Service Act personnel employed by the service if they perform their duties as reservists outside their normal working hours
- An employee of a municipality, including a member of the emergency services
  - If his or her duties as reservist will not interfere with his or her normal work activities
  - If the interests of the municipality will at all times be served first
  - May not be called up in terms of regulation 5 of the regulations without the permission of the said municipality
- A reserve member of the SADF
  - If his or her duties as reservist will not interfere with his or her normal work activities
  - If the interests of the SADF will at all times be served first
  - May not be called up in terms of regulation 5 of the regulations without the permission of the SADF

A person who previously served in the SAPS may reenlist as a reservist provided that he or she meets the requirements. They should also undergo a refresher course if they have been inactive in policing duties for more than two years. In addition, a service record should accompany their application (National Instruction 1/2002; www.saps.gov.za).

The general selection and recruitment requirements are as follows:

- The applicant must have grade 12 (12 years of schooling) or an equivalent qualification excluding category D reservists when it is not a requirement.
- The reservist must be a permanent resident of the Republic of South Africa.
- He or she may not be younger than 18 and not older than 70 years.
- He or she must complete a medical questionnaire.
- Psychometric assessment, especially with regard to category A reservists. The assessment is not necessary if it is not a requirement in the specific units for category B, C, and D reservists.
- The person must be proficient in English and one other official language of the country.
- He or she may not have a previous criminal conviction.
- No visible tattoo should be able to be seen when they wear a uniform.
- They must be willing to undergo the necessary training.

- They must be willing to take the oath.
- Fingerprints will be taken.
- Although a driver's license is not a prerequisite, a reservist with at least a learner's driver's license will be favored over those without any knowledge of driving a vehicle.

14.7 Reservists in Action

In view of the above theoretical framework, one wonders how these reservists are actually utilized in the field. Table 14.2 contains two examples of accomplishments by reservists in the field.

Table 14.2   Reservists in Action

Reservists and the Soccer World Cup in South Africa 2010

A reservists opinion:

It's a little-known fact that if it wasn't for the reservist component of the SAPS the 2010 Soccer World Cup would have gone very differently. A big problem the SAPS faced during this time was manpower in securing the various soccer stadiums around South Africa. Many foreigners who attended the matches were impressed by the police presence at the stadiums. They would frequently voice their approval, saying "how comforting it was to have so many police members guarding them, especially after all the terrifying crime stories they had heard before coming to SA." What they did not realize though is that it was an extremely delicate balancing act to bring so many police members out of the areas they normally worked in. Many police stations around the country were faced with operating with skeleton staff because of this month-long tournament. As such, permanent police members would typically only supplement the stadium numbers on their off days (and also typically only on match days). But for the rest of the time, a large number of reservists were called up to secure the stadiums. These reservists were paid, but only half of what the permanent members were paid (and were also not provided with daily food vouchers), and had to work much longer hours than most permanent police officers. For example, at Cape Town stadium, a group of reservists with a minimal permanent member component (particularly commanders and members on management level) were responsible for establishing perimeter security around the stadium well in advance of the first matches. Reservists typically worked a 2-day shift—this is the 2-day 2-night on and 2 days off pattern, which is more intensive than the usual police shift schedule during this time which has 4 rest days in their schedule. While the safe and successful hosting of the World Cup plans was certainly a team effort between the specialized units, permanent police members and other role players, the pivotal quiet role reservists played in the success story of the Soccer World Cup in South Africa is unimaginable.

(Continued)

Table 14.2 (Continued)   Reservists in Action

Satisfying Account of a Reservist in Action

Interview with Bernard Allen (police reservist):

Question by author: Share one "feel good" story with me that you consider a highlight in your career as reservist?

Answer: I'll use an example of my own, despite it not being a "guns blazing" glamour story. But it is reflective of the kind of thing that happens often in serving the community in this country, thanks to reservists, and is a good example of how reservists literally step in when nobody else can.

A few years back, over an Easter weekend, I received a last-minute call (either on the Saturday or Sunday) saying that the day shift for the Easter Weekend Monday would be running on skeleton staff at the police station thanks to various factors and asking if it would be possible for me to assist in any way. So I did what reservists all over often do and canceled a chunk of my family time to go assist when it was needed most.

As it happened, when I went in that morning, my permanent partner was highly occupied within the Client Service Centre (CSC) because of the low staff numbers that day, so it took a while before we could get out on the road to patrol. While waiting for him, I saw a man entering the CSC, and I offered to assist him. The man wanted to open a case docket for housebreaking and theft. Upon talking to him, I found out he'd just moved to the area, and I expressed my dismay that he'd had such a bad welcome to the area so shortly after his arrival, and that we'd do our best to assist him, but obviously also told him honestly that there was no guarantee we'd be able to get his possessions back.

Shortly after completing his docket and saying goodbye, my partner and I were able to get out on the road to patrol. Within about ten minutes of being on the road, a call came through over the radio for police assistance at a particular address, with a woman there "having found some credit cards," and no further details were given. We made our way to the address and discovered that it was actually a guesthouse, and that the credit cards found were left in a dustbin by a guest who had just left the premises a few minutes earlier (the cleaning staff had gone in to his room immediately after he left). Along with the credit cards, there was a flat screen computer monitor and the ID books of various people also left behind in the room. We asked the guesthouse owner which way the man had gone and immediately went searching for him in the area as we realized the situation was a lot more immediate than the initial radio call had implied.

A few street blocks away from the guesthouse we found a man matching the description of the one who'd left the goods behind in the room. He was on his phone and had a bunch of suitcases with him. I apprehended him with my partner and began searching his bags and person. The very first suitcase I opened gave me a huge smile. I recognized virtually every item in the bag as having been mentioned in the statement for the man whose docket I'd taken back at the station earlier. Here, within perhaps not even twenty minutes, we'd recovered his stolen possessions, including his laptop and other valuable items.

We phoned the complainant as soon as possible to tell him to come identify and collect his things. I'll never forget that although the man was grateful he gave me the remark "that's good work...for a reservist" with such a dismissive attitude that I felt he had the impression that reservists were somehow inferior police members by default, when in actuality the only difference between them and permanent members can often be the number of hours worked.

Upon further investigation, we discovered that the suspect's modus operandi was to stay in the guesthouse over the Easter weekend and walk with his partner from house to house while people were away and help themselves to their belongings. We also discovered that he was wanted for separate cases in about 3 other towns close by. So all in all, a very rewarding arrest, despite not being action packed like some other things one encounter in the course of policing as a reservist, and something that would not have happened if it hadn't been for the unique contribution of reservists—free of charge.

14.8 Future Prospects and Concluding Thoughts

South Africa covers a vast geographical area and is currently divided into nine provinces. The land surface of 1,219,090 km^2 must be serviced by 1,125 police stations and 157,518 permanent police members and 41,873 civilian police members in contractual obligation of the police (not reservists). The national ratio of 1:329 (one permanent police member to 329 civilians) clearly shows that additional help is needed in the form of a reserve group of volunteers (www.saps.gov.za). During August 2003, the Component: Visible Policing held a national strategic work session on the effective utilization of the South African Reserve Police Service. The workshop was to pave the way for reservists to be utilized in a more productive manner by addressing issues such as sector policing, area crime combating units, and the National Instruction 1/2002. The work session further aimed to determine a strategic direction for reservists, and representatives from each province attended the session (Kempen, 2004b, p. 55; National Instruction 1/2002). The Division: Crime Prevention continues to revisit the National Instruction 1/2002 for the South African Reserve Police Service with the goal of developing a strategy to ensure an enhanced reservist environment. However, a specific National Instruction has not yet been introduced. Nonetheless, the SAPS are engaged to completely revise the National Instruction 1/2002 due to certain challenges. Some of these challenges are as follows:

- Some reservists no longer view the system as voluntary due to the occasional remuneration that some reservists were given when they were officially called up to perform operational duties. Many reservists now demand payment whenever they perform reservist duties that are fundamentally voluntary.
- Many reservists view the current reservist system as a means to obtain access to permanent employment in the police even in cases in which they do not meet the set selection and recruitment requirements. Reservists often "volunteer" with the idea that this will act as a "foot in the door" to be permanently incorporated into the police. Even if they do not qualify to be recruited for permanent police duty, many demand to be permanently employed.
- In many cases, "reservists" who purely joined as volunteers started to demand all the benefits available to permanent members (e.g., salary, medical scheme, pension, etc.). Apparently, this idea was nurtured by the fact that reservists were seen as and treated as "police members" when they were on duty.

- In recent times, ill discipline increased among the reserve group, and several reservists have been found guilty of crime and corruption on and off duty.
- Many reservists are unhappy about the fact that they are "disarmed" because all police members are targets of ruthless criminals, irrespective if they are permanent members or reservists. A category A reservist is trusted enough to do his or her work as a reservist but not to have a state-issued firearm in their possession when they sign off from duty.

Based on the above, the SAPS management decided to review the existing standards and quality of reservists. The hope is that this envisaged enhancement will protect the integrity of the police and reestablish a professional, more effective, reservist system (Mothiba, 2013). Although some challenges exist, an active reserve is still in place. The strength of the South African Police Reserve on May 6, 2013 is outlined in Table 14.3.

The author of this chapter also wrote a letter to the SAPS to ascertain how the new envisaged reserve system will function to address the above challenges. SAPS was willing to share some broad principles of the envisaged system with me in an official letter from the Divisional Commissioner: Visible Policing. A detailed description of some of the significant changes to the reservist system in South Africa is outlined in Table 14.4.

The South African Reserve Police Service serves as an important force multiplier and is an essential part of the police service. These men and women, also known as "weekend warriors," should be seen as key elements in the police, and with the emphasis shifting to cooperative police–community partnerships, the reserve can even be used more effectively in the "policing" of localized crime areas. Furthermore, the role of the reservist in the community can be of incalculable value in intelligence-led policing (Bezuidenhout, 2011a). The community policing approach and the involvement of high-quality reservists can only work if everyone buys into the presumption that the police alone cannot effectively control crime or address

Table 14.3 Strength of the South African Police Reserve

Male	Female	Total Reservists
1,352 White males	263 White females	
315 Indian males	27 Indian females	
1,455 Colored males	1,121 Colored females	
6,159 African males	8,545 African females	
Subtotal 9,281	**Subtotal 9,956**	**19,237**

Source: Colonel Nicolene Mostert: Section Commander: Reservists' Division: visible policing—provided in writing on 06 May 2013.

Table 14.4   Envisaged Changes to the Reservist Service

It is envisaged that
- Community members who join as reservists will be appointed in terms of the South African Police Service Act, 1995 (Act No. 68 of 1995) with full policing powers and authority equal to a constable when officially on duty. When a reservist is not on duty, they will not have any policing powers or authority.
- The revised system will be managed in the true spirit of volunteerism and will serve as a voluntary system without any remuneration.
- Only two categories of reservists are envisaged, namely
  - **Category 1** – Functional Policing. Reservists appointed in this category will perform the following duties: Functional policing duties in the sector where they reside, Community Service Centre (CSC) duties based on a specific need that exists at police station level (the station commander's discretion and prior approval from the relevant Provincial Commissioner is important here), specific operational duties identified to be performed at National or Unit level after approval is given by the Divisional or Unit Commander (e.g., Detective Services).
  - **Category 2** – Specialized Functional Policing. A reservist appointed in this category must be someone with specific skills or expertise that the police can utilize operationally (e.g., a pilot). They will perform all duties under the command and control of the permanent existing police structures; they will perform their duty in the same uniform as permanent members; they will be clearly distinguishable since they will not be allocated any rank insignia.
- The police endeavor to draw and recruit good quality reservists. They want to establish a professional environment with high standards:
- **General Requirements**
  - The number of reservists to be recruited will be determined against a set criteria and communicated to each province annually.
  - Biannual recruitment drives will be launched to ensure high-quality applications. These structured recruitment drives will be based on the operational needs of and demands of the police and the required number of recruits that are needed.
  - The selection and recruitment requirements of reservists will be aligned with that of permanent police members.
  - Only the National Commissioner may condone any of the determined requirements.
  - The recruitment of reservists will be aligned with the available training capacity and availability of equipment to advance applicants immediately after recruitment and to properly equip them to ensure their safety.
  - Communities will be involved in identifying suitable applicants through accepted structures.
  - Community members will be encouraged to get involved in other community initiatives if they cannot be accommodated as reservist (e.g., community policing, sector policing, neighborhood watch).
- **Specific Requirements**
  - Must be a South African Citizen by birth.

(Continued)

Table 14.4 (Continued)　Envisaged Changes to the Reservist Service

- Must be 18 years and shall retire when reaching the age of 60 years.
- Must be medically, mentally, and physically fit.
- Must have a health questionnaire completed by a registered medical practitioner at their own cost.
- Must be of good sound character (positive background enquiries must be obtained).
- Must fit the psychometric profile as determined by SAPS.
- Must complete an assessment questionnaire as determined by SAPS.
- Must undergo a vetting/background screening process.
- Must be employed, and proof of employment must be provided. This requirement may be condoned in rural areas.
- Must have a senior certificate (Grade 12—completed the required 12 years primary and secondary schooling) or have an equivalent qualification.
- Must be able to speak, read, and write two of the 11 official languages of South Africa of which one must be English.
- Must allow his or her fingerprints to be taken.
- Must not have a criminal record or departmental case pending against them or should declare any such case.
- Must not have any visible tattoos.
- Must be willing to undergo such training as may be determined from time to time.
- Must be prepared to take the prescribed oath of office.
- Although it is not prerequisite, an official driving license will count in the applicant's favor.
- **Who will not qualify to become reservists?** The revised system prohibits the following individuals to be appointed as reservists based on their position or association, namely a person who
  - Was discharged as medically unfit from a previous employer.
  - A former member of the police whose application for reenlistment was rejected due to negative considerations.
  - Is a member of the regular Force of the National Defense Force.
  - Holds a key position (as determined by the Department of Labor).
  - Holds a post in a political party.
  - Is actively involved in politics and political organizations or is outspoken about his political interest. It is believed that this may violate the nonpartisan nature of SAPS.
  - Is a full-time or part-time journalist.
  - Has no fixed residential address.
  - Is a scholar.
  - Is a bouncer or chucker-out.
  - Is a member of the municipal police.
  - Is a sheriff or deputy sheriff.
  - Is in any way connected to a brothel, escort agency, or any undertaking involved in sexual acts, striptease activities, the making and or selling of pornographic material.

(Continued)

Table 14.4 (Continued)   Envisaged Changes to the Reservist Service

- Is in any way connected to a business that has a contract with the police or submitted a tender to the State to render a service or to supply a product to the SAPS.
- Is involved in the private security industry, the taxi industry, the trade of liquor or keeps a tavern or shebeen (informal pub), the preparation or completion of applications for liquor licenses, private investigation services, the operation of a scrap yard, micro lending services, trading in secondhand goods, the tow-in or breakdown services, the gambling industry, the preparation or completion of applications for firearm licenses, the rendering of physical security services, insurance investigations and investigations on behalf of agencies handling claims against the Road Accident Fund, serving of court processes excluding serving summonses in civil cases, trading in livestock excluding such trading as part of bona fide farming activities, and finally those individuals involved in funeral undertaking.
- **Certain individuals who could qualify subject to certain conditions (Note: Very similar to the previous requirements in the National Instruction 1/2002)**
  - A Community Police Forum member while he or she does not serve on a Community Police Board or on the Executive Committee of a Community Police Forum
  - An official or employee from Transnet with written approval from the head of the specific department
  - An official from the Department of Correctional Services
    - If his or her duties as reservist will not interfere with his or her normal work activities
    - If the interests of the Department of Correctional Services will at all times be served first
    - May not be called up in terms of regulation 5 of the regulations without the permission of the Department of Correctional Services
  - Public Service Act personnel employed by the service, if they perform their duties as reservists outside their normal working hours
  - An employee of a municipality including a member of the emergency services
    - If his or her duties as reservist will not interfere with his or her normal work activities
    - If the interests of the municipality will at all times be served first
    - May not be called up in terms of regulation 5 of the regulations without the permission of the said municipality
  - A reserve member of the South African National Defense Force
    - If his or her duties as reservist will not interfere with his or her normal work activities
    - If the interests of the South African National Defense Force will at all times be served first; and may not be called-up in terms of regulation 5 of the regulations without the permission of the South African National Defense Force (Mothiba, 2013)

the causes thereof. This envisaged refreshed approach to the reserve grouping and the platform that community policing provides citizens allows the community to share responsibility in the combatting of crime and to endeavor that all people in South Africa are and feel safe (Annual report of the South African Police Service, 2011/2012).

References

Annual Report of the South African Police Service. (2011/2012). Pretoria: South African Government Printers.

Beeld newspaper. (1981). Reserviste leer in bittere koue [Reservists learn in freezing weather]. September 15, 1981.

Berning, J., & Masiolane, D. (2011). Police militarisation: Is South Africa disproving or failing to learn from police history? *South African Journal of Criminology*, 24(3): 60–71.

Bezuidenhout, C. (2011a). Sector Policing in South Africa—Case Closed—Or Not? *Pakistan Journal of Criminology*, 3(2 & 3): 11–25.

Bezuidenhout, C. (2011b). Explaining the implications of intelligence-led policing on human rights in South Africa. In J. F. Albrecht & D. K. Das (Eds.), *Effective crime reduction strategies: International perspectives*. Boca Raton, FL: CRC Press (Taylor & Francis Group).

Bezuidenhout, C., & Little, K. (2012). Juvenile justice in South Africa: Challenges and existing processes. In P. C. Kratcoski (Ed.), *Juvenile justice administration*. Boca Raton, FL: CRC Press (Taylor & Francis Group).

Cillié, P. (1983). Reservistemag vervul 'n belangrike rol [Reservist force fulfill an important role]. Servamus. February 1983.

Citizen newspaper. (1982). Hester—SA's first woman reservist. February 18, 1982.

Dippenaar, M. D. (1988). *SA Police Commemorative Album 1913–1988*. (1st ed.). South Africa: Promedia Publications.

Government Gazette. (2004, GN1214). GNR. 334 of March 22, 2002: South African Reserve Police Service Regulations: Department of Safety and Security as amended by: Notice GN 1214; Governement Gazette; October 22, 2004.

Hoofstad newspaper. (1969). S.A. kan trots wees op reserviste [S.A. can be proud of reservists]. December 4, 1969.

Kalley, J. A., Schoeman, E., & Andor, L. E. (1999). *Southern African political history: A chronology of key political events from independence to mid-1997*. Westport: Greenwood.

Kempen, A. (2004a). Reservists: Lending a hand to build a better life for all (Part I). Servamus. June 2004.

Kempen, A. (2004b). Reservists: Lending a hand to build a better life for all (Final). Servamus. September 2004.

Mothiba, L. M. (2013). Request for information regarding police reservists. Official letter from the Divisional Commissioner Visible Policing [Ref. 3/1/5/1/191; Col Mostert]. March 28, 2013.

National Planning Commission: National Development Plan Vision for 2030. (2011). Available: http://www.npconline.co.za (Accessed 12/04/2013).

Official South Africa Yearbook. (1993). Cape Town: CTP Book Printers (on behalf of the Government Printer).

Police revert to military ranks in April. (2010). Available: http://www.defenceweb .co.za (Accessed 12/04/2013).

Potgieter, D. J. (Ed.) (1974). *Standard Encyclopaedia of Southern Africa* Vol. 8, Cape Town: Nasou.

Rauch, J. (2001). Police Reform and South Africa's Transition. Available: http:// www.csvr.org.za (Accessed 26/03/2013).

Rauch, J. & van der Spuy, E. (2006). Police reform in post-conflict Africa: A review. Available: http://www.idasa.org (Accessed 26/03/2013).

Roelofse, C. J. (2007). *The challenges of community policing: A management perspective*. Durban: LexisNexis.

South Africa Yearbook. (1995). Cape Town: CTP Book Printers (on behalf of the Governement Printer).

Transvaler newspaper. (1984). SAP-Reserwemag brei uit [SAP- Reserve force increases]. March 16, 1984.

Van Niekerk, S. (2002). Reserviste staan polisie by: Hulle word in verskillende kategorieë ingedeel [Reservists assist the police: They are divided into different categories]. Beeld newspaper. Tuesday November 26, 2002.

van Zyl, H. J. P. (1985). Die reserwe polisiemag [The reservist police force]. Servamus. January 1985.

A special word of thanks to:

1. The Section Head Brigadier S. Govender and all the ladies at the Corporate Image and Information Corporate Communication Heritage Services (The police archive), Pretoria, who assisted me in collecting official historic documents and newspaper articles of yesteryear pertaining to the history of police reservists in South Africa.

2. Brigadier J. C. Le Roux, Section Head: Proactive Policing and Crime Reduction as well as Major General S. Pienaar and coworkers who forwarded the latest information on the new envisaged reservist police to me in a form of an official letter on behalf of Lieutenant General L. J. Mothiba, Divisional Commissioner: Visible Policing.

3. Colonel N. Mostert: Section Commander: Reservists' Division: visible policing who provided me with the exact number of the SAPS Reserve strength.

Reserve Police Force in the Netherlands

15

From a "Reserve" to a "Volunteer" Police Force

PAULA TORN
RONALD VERBIEST

Contents

15.1 Introduction

In 1931, the Netherlands set up a reserve police force to support the regular police. In this chapter, I give my impression of the way the reserve police force has developed into a volunteer one in the Netherlands. This concerns volunteers in uniform ranking as officers on the beat and constables who, together with the regular police force, carry out duties aimed at maintaining public order. A new category of volunteers has meanwhile been developed, namely "volontairs," that is, special police constables who work in various different ways both on the streets and at police station computers to support professional police officers.

Within the police force in the Netherlands, Haaglanden* is one of the regions with long experience working with volunteers. Burgersamenwerking† (citizen cooperation) is an office in the region that matches volunteer demand and supply. There are now approximately 550 volunteers actively working for Haaglanden Regional Police. After giving a short history of the volunteers in the Netherlands, I go on to look more closely at the organization and mission of the Burgersamenwerking office and cite a few examples of the dedication of volunteers and special constables in the Haaglanden region.

15.2 Origins of the Reserve Police Force

Taking England as the model, a decision was made at the start of the 1930s to create a reserve police force in the Netherlands. Operating alongside the regular police force, the organization rapidly developed in a relatively short period. In World War II, by mid-1942, there was a reserve force of 2,200 officers and assistant officers. In about 1948, the Dutch government decided to greatly increase the use of volunteers in the already existing Rijks-en Gemeentepolitiekorpsen, i.e., the state and municipal police departments (Vermathen, 2000).

The intention was to bolster government authority at a time when supporters and opponents of emerging communism were causing a great deal of unrest. Reserve police force volunteers were seen as a pair of extra hands, especially during extreme circumstances. The Reserve Police (Legal Status) Decree of 1964 is a particularly good example of this. It states the following:

> Reservists can be taken on in time of war, threat of war, related exceptional circumstances or due to disaster, with the permission of ministers involved, during serious disturbances of the peace or serious concern this might occur to assist the professional police force in carrying out its general duties.

In 1968, the Reserve Police Remuneration Order appeared. The element banning employers from firing their employees for not being able to carry out their normal job because of their reservist commitment is of great significance here. So now reservists could allow their commitment to the reserve police force to prevail over and above that to their normal profession. As the political and economic situation in the Netherlands became more stable

---

* A national police force has been in existence in the Netherlands since January 1, 2013. This entailed running individual police forces together, such as those of the regional police force at Hollands-Midden (Mid Holland) with that of Haaglanden that now operates under the name Eenheid Den Haag (The Hague Unit).
† Was begun as Bureau Vrijwilligers (i.e., the office of volunteers), and in 2011, the name was changed to Bureau Burgersamenwerking (i.e., the Office of Public Cooperation). This will be explained more thoroughly later in this chapter.

during the 1960s, people no longer regarded as acceptable deploying the reserve police force for the original purpose for which it had been set up.

Despite an interdepartmental reserve police committee in 1973 concluding that under normal circumstances reservists must not be deployed, in practice they were still needed here. In addition, under the guise of going on "exercises," the reservists were brought in for ordinary police work, especially when numbers of professional police officers were lacking due to it being the weekend, the evening, or the night and due to seasonal variations in pressure of work.

Regular police officers and their trade unions, however, were highly critical of any such deployment, seeing it as posing a threat not only to the quality of police work, but also to the strength of the regulars as the reservists were less experienced and less well trained. Meanwhile, the reservists' own lobby argued that, on the contrary, it was not the intention to usurp the role of the regulars but that their work should be seen as complementing that of the professional police force. In the early 1980s, to go some way toward meeting the criticism of their opponents, a more demanding course and examination criteria were established for reservists.

15.3 Volunteer Police Force

In February 1987, a committee of inquiry came up with a number of recommendations aimed at making savings within the Dutch Police Force across the board. One of the subjects discussed was the relatively "expensive" nature of the reserve police force, particularly in terms of the costs of deployment. The decision was made to abolish the reserve police force, and a voluntary police force was set up in its place. The 1993 Police Act incorporated the option of engaging volunteer police officers to carry out police duties (Vermathen, 2008).

In contrast to the reserve police force, the voluntary police force is not an organization operating in parallel to the regular police organization; rather it is integrated into it. Originally, the reserve police force was formed to do "normal" police work in exceptional circumstances while volunteer police officers contributed their support to basic policing in terms of carrying out simple police duties during peak hours.

Volunteer police officers wear a police uniform and have at their disposal a pair of handcuffs, a truncheon, and pepper spray. Volunteer police officers are thus not equipped with a firearm as the reservists had been. Although the range of duties, the arming of the police, and reimbursement for being deployed is limited in comparison to the reservists, the demands of training have been greatly increased. Volunteer police officers attend the same training program as professional police officers on the beat. This is linked to an extensive selection process, sports, and a medical checkup. In recent years, because of the extent and length of time this training program involves, the need to create a short program arose so that volunteers could be deployed more quickly for a defined range of duties. The aim was to train the volunteers in a focused way for duties that would, in practice, need them most, such as beat officers in the public domain, carrying out traffic surveillance, supervising events, and so on.

In addition to this, there appeared to be a need for greater opportunities for career advancement for the volunteers. In 2010, the Police Chiefs Council established the Framework Memorandum for Police Volunteers. This contains principles setting out how to develop new policy for volunteers, including deciding to differentiate the training on offer so that those in both the lower and the higher ranks of volunteers can be trained and deployed for a wide range of duties. In certain cases and after a specific program of training, volunteer police officers can carry a firearm. This means they can also be deployed for emergencies (112, comparable to the United Kingdom's 999 or 911 in the United States). Training volunteers more quickly for specific duties means they remain motivated and are less likely to drop out during training. Moreover, deployment needs of individual police stations are better matched with volunteers who, in turn, are placed where they are properly equipped for the duties they have to perform. Volunteers are never there instead of professional forces but always as a complement to them. This goes some way to answering the concerns of a number of professional colleagues that their own work is being supplanted by the deployment of a cheap workforce made up of volunteers. Present day volunteer police officers can be deployed in many areas of policing, such as traffic surveillance and alcohol testing, as officers on the beat, and as counter and reception staff, but they can also be deployed during events, including sports events and large-scale events, such as Prinsjesdag (the state opening of parliament on the third Tuesday in September). Volunteers from all across the country are deployed for national events such as Prinsjesdag in The Hague.

15.4 Special Constables ("Volontairs")

A new category of volunteer was formed within the Dutch Police Force in the year 2000 referred to using the French term "volontairs" (special constables). In particular, their duties cover operations for which no tracing authorization is required. This could involve not only practical support on the streets, such as preventive and descriptive work, but also special duties at the police station. Some special constables work as male or female hosts, running facilities, minding dogs and horses, as custody officers, community mediators, providing judicial support, advising on media relations, and so on. They perform a number of these duties in uniform, a different one from that of the regular police. However, special constables have no police rank and are not armed. Later in this chapter, I sketch a number of examples of the way in which special constables are deployed in the Haaglanden region.

Some metropolitan police regions, such as Amsterdam-Amstelland and Rotterdam-Rijnmond, have become experienced in the use of special constables as special investigating officers for specific duties with tracing authorization.

Despite those involved experiencing the pilot scheme as positive, this has not yet led to it being rolled out countrywide as this would entail a change in the law. In addition, this concept of "volunteer administrative technical personnel" (ATP) was recently introduced into the new police act. This creates the legal basis for providing volunteers with greater powers.

15.5 Flexible Deployment

In addition to time spent on training, both volunteer police officers and special constables are deployed in such a way as to work an average of eight hours a week. Most volunteers are placed with a particular police station as a matter of course. In addition, flexible volunteers are placed at a variety of sites. In the Haaglanden region, the so-called "Flexploeg" (flexible team) has been set up, consisting of both volunteer police officers and special constables. Team volunteers carry out project-based assignments that can vary in length from no more than a single day to no less than three months. Local police stations, detective agencies, and support offices can all submit such requests. Here we can think of, for example, preventive action to frustrate property crime, maintaining surveillance at shopping centers, providing support for door-to-door inquiries, tackling hot spots systematically, big festivals and marches, large traffic control operations, alcohol testing, joint operations with customs, border police, and other countrywide inspections. Other volunteers still are deployed in helping professional police officers to collect unpaid fines and settle final judgments.

15.6 Haaglanden Regional Volunteers Organization

Set up in 2004, the primary duty of the volunteers office in the Haaglanden region is to match up the demand in the Haaglanden region for deployment of volunteer police officers or special constables on the one hand and the supply of such personnel on the other hand. Related duties could include recruiting and selecting volunteers, professional development in the form of tailor-made training courses, relationship building, developing and implementing regional volunteer policy and new volunteer jobs and projects, arranging preconditions and facilities, financial management, planning and control, and so on. The central service line of the volunteers office operates like a walking encyclopedia for members of the public, volunteers, police colleagues, network partners, potential new volunteers, and trainees.

In 2011, Bureau Vrijwilligers (i.e., the office of Volunteers) changed its name to Bureau Burgersamenwerking (i.e., the Office for Public Cooperation). The reason for this was that the office no longer focused on volunteers but on a variety of topics related to public participation. The title "Public Cooperation" therefore better covers the entire range of products the office has to offer (Boele & Stijfhoorn, 2010).

Local police stations are responsible for the actual management of volunteers' duties. Included among such duties at these devolved police stations is that of developing public participation in their catchment areas and using such things as town hall meetings, neighborhood watch teams, and so on, to supercharge people by stimulating, supporting, and enabling them.

15.7 National Police Force

Due to the formation of a single national police agency in January 2013, the formerly independent 25 police forces have been reorganized into a single Korps Landelijke Politiediensten (KLPD; Netherlands Police Agency). There are now 10 regional units set up according to a single national blueprint. This development has led to less ambiguity in the Netherlands in terms of volunteer deployment, organization, and management. In all 10 regional units the coordination of volunteers and special constables has been brought under the regional coordination of the Police Duties Unit.

The new collective bargaining agreement for the police (Terms and Conditions of Employment Agreement Police Sector 2012 to 2014) states that the Minister for Security and Justice will consult with the Netherlands Police Force to establish a countrywide policy for the management of volunteers. This meets the Police Chiefs Council's wishes mentioned earlier. Training courses for volunteers are set up as modules and shortened to make them better fit the duties volunteers carry out. In addition, training courses for higher levels are being developed and offered so that volunteers can gain broader and deeper experience in the field of policing. At the end of their careers, professional staff will have the opportunity to work as volunteers to maintain their police connections. To be able to decide if they would like to do this, they are educated about the options on offer for doing voluntary work. The Minister for Security and Justice continues to strive to attain the goal established in 2015 that 10% of the operational strength of the Netherlands Police

Force consist of volunteers. In this region, the 550 volunteers currently working at Haaglanden Police Force more than meet this aim.

15.8 Mission

When formulating a countrywide strategy for the Netherlands Police Force on how to tackle crime, great importance is attached to working together with members of the public. Even public participation that goes as far as "co-creation" is regarded as a desirable development—that is, the police, the public, and the social partners acting together to decide what ought to happen. The countrywide implementation plan for the formation of the Netherlands Police Force (2012) states that cooperation with the public would be more intense if public participation, including volunteer work, was encouraged and facilitated. Within the Haaglanden region, voluntary work is seen as the ultimate form of public participation.

The Netherlands Police Force's mission statement is working to uphold the values of the constitutional state "waakzaam en dienstbaar" (watchful and helpful). This the Netherlands Police Force does by protecting people and goods; curbing unlawful, possibly violent behavior; and endorsing and supporting desirable behavior. In doing so, police staff are incorruptible, reliable, brave, and unifying, and this applies to volunteers as well. Volunteer work contributes to the mission of being "watchful and helpful" and to working on security and trust. This emerges from the following diverse ideas of what voluntary work might mean:

- Involving the public in policing, that is, public participation to enhance security and trust.
- Volunteer work can help specific groups currently underrepresented within the police, for example, women, young people, and people with an immigrant background, to become more involved with police work.
- Volunteers gain an accurate picture of policing, working as ambassadors for the police organization and forming a bridge between it and the wider society, thus reducing the current feeling of "them and us."
- The police organization can use volunteer know-how and experience to its own advantage, that is, creating a fresh look.
- Volunteers can do work that regular police officers hardly ever get around to, if at all.
- Volunteers can move on to higher levels, taking on regular policing jobs according to their availability, training, and experience. Volunteering acts as an incubator for new police personnel (Baardewijk, Brink, & Os, 2007).

15.9 Example 1: Special Constables "MOE-Landers" (CEE Countrymen and –Women)

Criminal nuisance that Central and Eastern European country nationals cause in the Netherlands as migrant workers, that is, so-called "MOE-landers," is on the increase. The Hague has begun a volunteer-run project intended to build bridges between the police and the Polish and Bulgarian communities. Volunteers, that is, special constables, working on the project originally come from Central and Eastern Europe. All of them have been living in the Netherlands for a long time and can speak Dutch. Deploying such volunteers can result in one of two things. On the one hand, thanks to the volunteers, the police get to learn about the cultural backgrounds of Poles and Bulgarians. On the other hand, volunteers offer the police practical support as they think alongside them about solutions to social problems in local neighborhoods.

15.10 Example 2: Volunteer Neighborhood Investigators

At the back end of 2012, Haaglanden region started to deploy volunteers as neighborhood investigators. Once briefed, the volunteers go out to the immediate vicinity of the scene of the crime. These could be door-to-door operations and operations in the public domain. Volunteers gather information about the crime committed in the neighborhood and provide tips for local residents on crime prevention and police aftercare for those reporting criminal activity. In addition, volunteers stimulate members of the public to report any suspicious circumstances. This is intended to increase the chance of catching the perpetrators of the crime.

15.11 Example 3: Using Volunteers to Enhance the Ability to Catch Criminals Red-Handed

Tracing criminals is a difficult assignment without the active and alert assistance of members of the public. Research in the Netherlands in particular has found that about 85% of all arrests result from something discovered while the crime was being committed and the subsequent action taken. This often entails the police communicating directly with an alert member of the public. In addition, it appeared that only a small portion, that is, one in nine of the red-handed detections, was reported to the police, and this means that in a great many cases the police are unable to follow up what members of the public, entrepreneurs, and social partners detect.

Increasing reporting of red-handed crime by the public is an important means of enhancing the results of detection. It is more difficult to detect crime after the event, and it costs a lot more time and money and results in a greatly reduced chance of being caught. This is why increasing the strength of the red-handed units has become an important spear point in the strategy of the Netherlands Police Force. The Minister of Security and Justice has referred to this as a countrywide priority.

In the Haaglanden region, the "Samen Meer" (Together More) Project has developed a red-handed unit to combat the deterioration of the Leyweg shopping center in The Hague located in a neighborhood within a police catchment area where problems in the areas of work, social cohesion, quality of life, and security are reinforcing one another. The center is afflicted with young people who are causing a nuisance and repeat offenders suffering from addictions, such as alcoholism. Ongoing high levels of shoplifting and cycle theft, pickpocketing, vandalism, and threatening behavior made customers stay away and more businesspeople had to shut up shop. Shopkeepers hardly ever reported any of the criminal activity partly because they were afraid of reprisals and partly because they were not confident that this would break the negative spiral. In addition, they invested little if anything in the security of their businesses inside the shopping center.

The Haaglanden Police have been deploying volunteers in this area in particular on market days, during late-night shopping, and on the weekends. They carry out surveillance duties in and around the shopping center, build up relationships with the shopkeepers, call those causing a nuisance to account, and establish contact with the shopping public. Having been briefed beforehand, the volunteers then go out to work; briefings are held in advance of every assignment. On completing their tour of duty, they are debriefed, and the information they have gathered is shared with the regular police and entered into the police computer.

Besides the police, other partners, such as the head of the Retail Trades Industry Board and the municipality, play an active role as well. A great deal of effort has been spent on reinforcing the shopkeepers' association and stimulating measures aimed at crime prevention. Taken together, these joint efforts have led to a sharp rise in the number of arrests of criminals caught red-handed and a parallel drop in the numbers of complaints about loitering youths and alcohol-related nuisance. In addition, confidence has clearly improved, and once again, the police, the municipality, the property developer, the retail chains, the shopkeepers, and the members of the public are all working together. Businesspeople and the public once again experience the shopping center as a place of safety, and this has led to longer opening hours, less empty shop premises, and people being increasingly prepared to invest in the shopping center.

This project was in line with Haaglanden Police Force's strategy to be both well briefed and problem-oriented in advance and to work together with the public in tackling crime. Choosing specific crimes, locations, and times and conducting a thorough analysis of potential groups of perpetrators and victims has led to the most efficient use of human resources and financial means. The project was nominated in 2012 for the Hein Roethof Prize: an annual award in the Netherlands presented to anyone with the best initiative for promoting crime prevention or public safety.

References

Baardewijk, J. van, Brink, G. J. M. van den, & Os, P. (2007). van *Meer heterdaadkracht: aanhoudend in de buurt, de rol van burgers bij de directe opsporing*. Politieacademie.

Boele, W., & Stijfhoorn, D (2010). *Vijf jaar Bureau Vrijwilligers. De burger als partner*. Den Haag: Politie Haaglanden.

Vermathen, E. (2000). *De geschiedenis van de reserve- en vrijwillige politie in Nederland: Een korte historische schets*. Venlo: Politie Limburg-Noord.

Vermathen, E. (2008). *VP Journaal. Het blad van de vrijwillige politie en volontairs*. Venlo: LOPV.

Effectively Using Police Volunteers in the "Little Red Dot" Singapore

16

WAYNE KOO
DESMOND TAN

Contents

16.1 Introduction

Singapore is known as the "Little Red Dot" on the world map, Asia's safest city with the highest quality of living, according to the 2016 results of the quality of living survey by Global Human Resources consulting firm Mercer. Its survey recognized Singapore as the top Asian city in the world for quality living and 26th worldwide (Mercer, 2016). Crime in Singapore is generally lower than other comparable cities.

16.2 Modern History of Singapore

The modern history of Singapore began in 1819. British statesman Sir Stamford Raffles founded Singapore and established a British port on the island. Under British colonial rule, it grew exponentially and grew in importance as the entrepôt trade in Southeast Asia, rapidly becoming a major port city.

During World War II, Singapore was under the occupation of the Japanese Empire from 1942 to 1945. When the Japanese occupancy ended in 1945, Singapore reverted to British control with increasing levels of self-government being granted, culminating in Singapore's merger with the Federation of Malaya to form Malaysia in 1963. Singapore became an independent republic on August 9, 1965, after some social unrest and disputes between Singapore's ruling People's Action Party and Malaysia's Alliance Party.

16.3 Volunteer Special Constabulary in Singapore

The Volunteer Special Constabulary (VSC) started before Singapore became an independent republic. The VSC was formed in 1946 to augment the slender ranks of the regulars immediately after the war when manpower was badly needed to restore law and order. About 150 men responded to appeals made in the press and formed the pioneers of the VSC. The part-time Police National Service was introduced in 1967, soon after Singapore gained independence. The VSC's strength was absorbed as part of the part-time national service scheme until it disbanded in 1981 (Singapore Police Force, 2016c).

The VSC has since grown and contributed significantly to maintaining law and order in Singapore. The VSC aims to play an essential role in the safety and security of Singapore, striving to become a leading police volunteer organization in the world. Recent manpower statistics reveal the VSC strength to stand around 1,250 officers, including more than 300 honorary VSCs who have been appointed to deal with disciplinary issues within the local schools.

With the discontinuation of the part-time police scheme, the VSC now consists exclusively of Singaporean and Singapore permanent resident volunteers from all walks of life, from white-collar directors of companies, civil servants, and other professionals to blue-collar employees, such as technicians, drivers, and even homemakers, all with a common passion and aspiration to serve the nation by maintaining law and order within their respective communities.

16.4 Requirements for the Volunteer Special Constabulary

VSC officers are required to faithfully serve a minimum of 16 hours each month for police officers below the rank of inspector, serving until the age of 50, and senior officers with the rank of inspector and above must serve at least 24 hours each month until the age of 55, but most of the VSC officers have served an average of more than 40 hours per month. They are permitted to claim an allowance of S$3.60 per hour (approximately $3.00 U.S. dollars) while on duty regardless of rank or number of years served (Singapore Police Force, 2016b).

Aspiring volunteers are screened at the entry level for physical and psychological fitness before going through a panel of interviews to ensure that only good fit, ethical, and passionate VSC officers are selected as once they are deployed in their communities, there is no differentiation between VSC officers and regular officers. As such, all new VSC recruits have to undergo a nine-month basic VSC course at the SPF Training Command (referred to in Singapore as "TRACOM") twice weekly in the evenings to ensure that they are equipped with adequate knowledge needed for their positions, including law, police procedure, hard and soft self-defense, and tactical skills, among other topics. They are required to pass all exams and achieve a designated level of proficiency before graduating. To ensure that officers are physically fit and up to date in their skills, such as shooting and police defense tactics, each VSC officer is required to pass the individual physical proficiency test and shooting and defensive tactics proficiency tests on an annual basis.

16.5 Early Years (1950s to 1970s)

The first challenge for the VSC took place during the Maria Hertogh riots in 1950 when VSC officers performed duties alongside the regular forces in suppressing these disturbances. Other achievements include the arrest of a communist arsonist, the arrest of a terrorist suspected of grenade attacks in the central part of Singapore, and the quelling of the Hock Lee Bus Riots in 1955.

On May 12, 1955, later known as "Black Thursday," a major riot broke out in the streets of Alexandra and Tiong Bahru in central Singapore. The police tried to break up the 2,000 students and strikers using water cannons and tear gas, but the crowd retaliated by stoning the police officers and buses. Two police officers died as a result, including Detective Corporal Yuen Yau Phang, who was burned to death when the car he was in was set alight by rioters, and VSC Constable Teo Bock Lan Andrew, who was fatally injured during the Hock Lee Bus Riot.

In 1956, the new headquarters for the VSC was formed. The VSC sought to maintain if not improve its performance by moving into its new and better-equipped headquarters at the Police Training School at Whitley Road. The VSC in 1958 was headed by a volunteer commandant holding the rank of superintendent ("SUPT").

Part-time National Service was introduced in Singapore in 1967. The total force of the special constabulary, including volunteers and national service officers, stood at approximately 10,000 by 1977. The National Servicemen were required to serve 12 years on a part-time basis. Up to 70% of them were deployed for patrol duties in neighborhood policing units and in the coast guard, radio, and traffic divisions. A small number were also attached to field services to help in crowd-control situations. The part-time Special Constabulary National Service was discontinued in 1981. However, some of them remain in the force as volunteers up to this day.

The VSC was reorganized following the introduction of National Service in 1967 and the establishment of the Police National Service Command. The VSC merged with the first batch of 2,055 part-time National Service police-men to form the Singapore Special Constabulary. VSC officers came to be known as Special Constabulary Volunteers, and their National Service coun-terparts were called Special Constabulary National Servicemen.

16.6 Changing the Face of the Volunteer Special Constabulary (1980s to 1990s)

The part-time National Service program was discontinued in 1981, and the VSC became a full-fledged volunteer force. Deployment of VSC offi-cers became more flexible, and officers were also given opportunities for short-term or long-term postings of up to six months to a year in a crime unit. Changes were made to the VSC uniform, for example, the red lan-yard on the uniform of the VSC officers was replaced by the blue lanyard worn by regular officers. The VSC first volunteer commander was Assistant Commissioner Chao Hick Tin. Prior to 1981, the highest rank a volunteer police officer could hold was that of superintendent. Commander Chao was assisted by two deputy commanders, holding the rank of deputy assistant commissioner, individually responsible for operations command and head-quarters command.

To ensure that VSC officers were operationally competent, the VSC initi-ated its own in-service training in 1983. The first assistant superintendent of police course was held twice weekly for six weeks at the police academy for senior officers holding the acting ranks of inspector and above. Subjects covered were law, police procedures, and drill.

The VSC's first recruitment drive attracted 223 recruits, and the VSC ladies scheme, introduced in December 1981, attracted seven applicants. By 1984, morale had risen, and the strength of the VSC grew to 1,250.

In 1982, a number of VSC constables were deployed within the Central Narcotic Bureau, the premier drug enforcement agency in Singapore. In 1985, VSC officers were deployed for duty in the Marine Police (now known as the Police Coast Guard) for the first time. At the Police Coast Guard, where VSCs are deployed at all four marine bases, they take part in coastal patrol duties. They are responsible for deterring illegal immigrants and smuggling, and this involves boat patrols and searches through forested areas for illegal encampments.

In 1995, as part of the VSC restructuring to adopt the same staff and line structure of the Singapore Police Force and to support the integration with the regular and Police National Service officers, a pilot project was initiated within the Bedok Police Division to provide integrated deployment of VSC officers with their regular counterparts.

A number of VSC officers have also been deployed within the Airport Police Division, where they have played an important part in maintaining the safe reputation of Changi International Airport since 1997.

An interesting development occurred in 1997 with the introduction of the Honorary VSC School Scheme. The scheme was initiated to train school discipline masters and teachers as police officers in an effort to tackle youth crimes. These "teacher–cops" play the role of law enforcers within the school context and provide advice on matters pertaining to delinquency and police procedures. They also provide counseling to delinquent students and work with stakeholders to address youth crimes. Currently, more than 90% of the schools have participated in this program.

Following the full integration of volunteer officers with career police personnel, VSC officers replaced their "V" collar insignia (symbolizing vol-unteer) with the police crest (worn by career officers) in January 1999. With a common uniform code and accoutrement, VSC officers had finally inte-grated into the mainstream police force with total uniformity with the regu-lar and Police National Service officers.

16.7 Staying Relevant in the 21st Century (2000 to Present)

The VSC is now routinely mobilized to participate in large-scale events, often working alongside regular forces to maintain law and order. VSC officers also have the opportunity to attend developmental and advanced courses to improve their leadership skills and police operational and tactical knowledge.

The first accomplishment of the new century involved the mobilization of VSC officers in full force as part of the 4,000-member Singapore Police Force task force to handle any public law and order issues that may have resulted from the Y2K bug on the night of December 31, 1999. On December 31, 1999, Singapore saw a big millennium party called Millennium Swing, which was held in the main shopping belt of Singapore, called Orchard Road. More than 750,000 people celebrated at six different venues across the island, from Serangoon Gardens to Orchard Road. For the Millennium Swing at Orchard Road alone, VSC officers supported the 3,000 police officer contingent to maintain order for a crowd of 500,000 in the event of any contingency affecting traffic and transportation operations.

In 2001, VSC headquarters was relocated from Toa Payoh to the Police Cantonment Complex as part of ongoing efforts to improve its operational and administrative efficiency. This new office serves as a convenient and centralized location for command and staff personnel to meet regularly.

In September 2006, Singapore held the Annual Meetings of the Boards of Governors of the World Bank Group and the International Monetary Fund, locally referred to as the S2006 ("Singapore 2006"). This was the largest police deployment in history with more than 10,000 police officers deployed for the event. More than 750 VSC officers supported various public order task groups, 12 command posts, and six event locations around the Singapore International Convention and Exhibition Center.

As part of the revised VSC training and promotion road map, the VSC conducted its first senior officers developmental course at the Police Training Command, located at the Home Team Academy. Twenty-two VSC senior officers attended the course from October to December 2006. To date, three groups of VSC senior officers have graduated from this course.

In 2007, the VSC identified a pioneer group of seven VSC officers to support the SPF Public Transport Security Command. Deployed with career police officers to perform transportation patrols and security profiling, these police officers now wear the gray beret.

The 13th ASEAN Summit hosted more than 2,000 delegates from 43 countries in November 2007. Many VSC officers, as part of a 2,500-member Singapore Police Force detail, provided security coverage and traffic arrangements for the more than 70 heads of state, heads of government, and ministers from ASEAN and East Asia countries amid the threat of activist and supporter protests.

The staging of the inaugural Formula One Singapore Grand Prix night race in Singapore in September 2008 required extensive security coverage and support from police officers from all units and other home front agencies. More than 500 VSC officers rallied behind all land and specialized divisions to deliver the world-class racing events to a crowd of 110,000 at the newly built Marina Bay Street Circuit in the Marina Bay area and to millions of viewers worldwide. This was also the first time Singapore hosted a Formula One Grand Prix race as the last Singapore Grand Prix was a Formula Libre event in 1973.

In October 2009, Singapore hosted the 78th INTERPOL General Assembly. The annual event brought together the chiefs of law enforcement agencies from INTERPOL's 187 member countries. VSC officers were strategically deployed for frontline duties and special roles as ambassadors at the Changi Airport VIP complex to assist the Singapore Police Force during a series of high-level conferences and meetings spanning four days. This event has been recognized as a resounding success.

In November 2009, the Asia-Pacific Economic Cooperation 2009 Leaders' Week was held at Marina Bay and Istana, and about 450 VSC officers were deployed to support their national police colleagues with the security coverage of more than 10,000 delegates, business executives, and visitors, including 21 world leaders and 63 ministers from the 21 APEC member economies. This is also the first major event conducted after the introduction of the Public Order Act.

In addition to the world's first night Formula One Grand Prix race being held in Singapore, Singapore also hosted the first inaugural Singapore Youth Olympic Games in August 2010. During this event, 500 VSC officers worked closely with the regulars, full-time and reserve national servicemen and auxiliary police officers. They covered duties such as management of security screening points at hotels, sports venues, the Olympic Village, and the opening and closing ceremonies. The VSC displayed the biggest support on August 14, 2010, during the SYOG 2010 Opening Ceremony, at which 237 VSC officers were deployed for frontline duties on the ground. The VSCs' enthusiasm was so strong that 123 of them took leave from their day jobs to support the SYOG 2010 Closing Ceremony duties on August 26, 2010.

16.8 VSC Today: An Indispensable Part of the National Police Force

The VSC has supported the national police in its fight against crime and the maintenance of peace and order in Singapore for more than 65 years. As part of the integration program, the VSC officers today wear the same uniform, undergo the same homogenous training, patrol on the same beats, and serve with equal passion and dedication.

The VSC presence is felt in all the vanguard departments, divisions, and units of the Singapore Police Force as VSC officers are now deployed in all land divisions and neighborhood police centers. Together with their regular counterparts, they man the front counters, patrol the streets in the "fast response cars," and take part in surveillances and plainclothes operations with the crime control unit and compliance management unit. The VSC clearly contributes to the operational needs of the national police beyond the day-to-day policing duties.

16.9 Some Impressive Volunteer Commitments

In Rochor, a number of VSC officers have been conducting the "Rochor Special" anticrime patrol from Friday to Saturday, 9 pm to 6 am every week since the year 2000. To combat street corner gangs, a team of VSC officers from Marina Bay NPC continue to conduct Operation "Bay Beat" every weekend evening since July 2009. To reduce fighting and disturbances at Boat Quay, the VSCs have performed Operation "Night Watch" and Operation "Iron Hammer" from midnight to 7 am regularly on Saturday nights. Together with their regular counterparts, the VSCs from the Tanglin Police Division perform Operation "Eagle Sweep" on Friday and Saturday nights from 10 pm to 4 am with duties such as checking on entertainment outlets and streetwalkers in Orchard Road and Clark Quay. Indeed, with such persistence, crime and disorderliness have dropped significantly.

On the counterterrorism front, many VSC officers have contributed to Red Teaming exercises in various land divisions, where the officers are tasked with acting as role players to "intrude" on protected areas. It is a win–win situation for all stakeholders as such exercises are conducted in the qualified hands of VSC officers. In addition, many VSC officers are given exposure and opportunities to volunteer beyond the normal police duties. To reach a higher level of professionalism, five VSC officers have attended the Red Teaming Officers course conducted by the Ministry of Home Affairs since 2010. These specially trained officers are appointed by the Permanent Secretary of Home Affairs and have often been activated by police divisions.

16.10 Volunteering in Action (2010 to Present)

True to the spirit of volunteerism, Singapore VSC officers have volunteered passionately with career police officers to provide security coverage at major events and incidents. Many of the volunteers routinely take their own personal leave from work during the weekdays and have sacrificed family time over the weekends to promote safety and security throughout Singapore.

In 2011, the VSC became part of the Singapore's Home Team Volunteer Network. The network is an entity that promotes the implementation of volunteer management best practices for the benefit of Home Team volunteers. Other Home Team volunteers include agencies such as the Civil Defense Force and the Singapore Prisons Service. The network is also the key channel through which the Home Team seeks to maximize the engagement with the volunteers through multiple means. Singapore's Home Team Volunteer Network, which now includes the VSC, has about 60,000 volunteers, who fall under the domain of the Ministry of Home Affairs (Singapore Police Force, 2016a).

The Singapore General Election in 2011 saw fierce competition in almost all the Group Representative Constituencies. This meant that more manpower was needed to ensure law and order, both during the rally speeches and on Election Day from April 28 to May 7, 2011. Bearing in mind the limited manpower and resources of the national police, 545 VSC officers volunteered their services to serve alongside the regulars at rally sites, such as stadiums and open fields, all over Singapore. They began their duties in the late afternoon and continued often until after midnight to ensure that the crowd dispersed in an orderly manner. Despite having to work sometimes on muddy grounds and having to wake up early to go back to their own jobs the next morning, the morale of VSC officers continues to remain high. Likewise, there was a turnout of 254 VSC officers during the Singapore Presidential Election 2011 on August 27, 2011, many performing duties at the various polling centers. Many VSC officers showed their commitment by staying until the early hours of the morning as the final vote tally resulted in a recount.

Since 2008, the VSC headquarters has been testing the operational readiness of the VSC officers during emergencies and national disasters. The Singapore National Police has conducted four agency-wide silent recalls involving all active VSC officers. They were required to report within four hours to their reporting centers once they were activated by their respective divisions or units via the Short Message Service (SMS) or phone calls. This means that these officers had to excuse themselves from their work or family commitments to report immediately. The VSCs' responsiveness has always been outstanding with more than 90% of recallable officers reporting within the targeted time frame during the 5th VSC Silent Recall in November 2012. In fact, the results have improved as most of the officers were able to report within three hours.

With the acceptance of Singapore permanent residents into the VSC, the VSC now includes volunteers from all over the world, including Holland, Japan, China, Canada, and India. They have the same passion and dedication as their VSC colleagues, but they bring with them new international perspectives to this critical volunteer work. They can also be counted on to bridge the language and cultural gaps between the Singapore Police Force and visiting foreigners when the need arises.

The VSC is on a constant learning journey and has conducted study visits to regular and volunteer police forces in Malaysia, Hong Kong, Macau, the People's Republic of China, United Kingdom, and the United States in order to network, learn, and adopt best practices from foreign counterparts. Feasibility studies are routinely conducted before any of these best practices are assimilated into the VSC system.

With the launch of the VSC Commitment Awards in 2011, the VSC has set out to revitalize volunteer commitment and dedication by motivating them to contribute beyond the standard 200-man hours per VSC officer per annum to a target of 300 hours per year or more. Such deserving officers will be rewarded with attractive medallions and opportunities, such as local and overseas study visits.

Under the guidance of our current VSC commander and VSC senior leaders, coupled with the strong support of the Singapore Police Force, the VSC is looking at growing its strength and building quality officers. This is to ensure constantly professional manpower support. At the same time, the VSC will continue to upgrade and evolve with the national police in order to keep up with operational development over time. This will help the VSC to realize its vision to be a reliable and premiere volunteer police organization.

16.11 Conclusion

In today's challenging environment in which the Singapore Police Force operates, VSC officers have to stay ahead of the game. The VSC will continue to stay relevant by equipping VSC officers with the latest skills and knowledge through training and professional development. As civilians by day and police officers by night, VSC officers will continue to play an important role in supplementing the national police in major operational duties in both land divisions and specialized units while playing an even bigger role in the maintenance of law and order. The leadership of the VSC will continue recruitment efforts to attract more volunteers and encourage VSC officers to perform more hours in an effort to support their regular counterparts.

Singapore VSCs are clearly proud of their past achievements but will not rest upon their laurels. They will continue to strive to be a reliable and dependable partner in preventing, deterring, and detecting crime and serving their local communities when called upon.

16.12 Volunteer Special Constabulary in Action

16.12.1 Criminal Investigation Department: On the Cutting Edge

The Criminal Investigation Department (CID) is the leading crime-fighting agency in Singapore, which has been tasked with solving major crimes. CID Director Senior Assistant Commissioner of Police Hoong Wee Teck has had many experiences working with VSC officers during his stint as commander of the Bedok Police Division. To quote him: "The professionalism and integrity displayed by the VSC officers has left a deep impression on me. This has led me to believe that the skills of VSC officers in policing could be highly effective and a valuable resource to CID." As a result of this idea, a VSC unit within the CID to tackle hardcore criminals has been hatched. The formation was officially approved by the commissioner of police in May 2012. With the endorsement, recruitment work to join CID began, which generated very encouraging responses by the VSC officers.

Due to the seriousness of offenses that CID officers deal with, the importance being placed on officers' integrity and character cannot be emphasized more. There is zero tolerance for any misconduct or misuse of power. After rounds of stringent checks and screenings, the pioneer batch of 24 officers was finalized and was posted to the CID in September 2012.

The nature of CID operations will be a new frontier for the VSC officers. With their passion and commitment to the Singapore Police Force, all are confident that the newly minted CID VSC officers will continue to uphold the trust and reputation painstakingly established by the CID over the years so that Singapore remains a safe and secure nation for many years to come.

16.12.2 Traffic Police Special Operations Team

The VSC Traffic Police was formed in 1974, working hand in hand with the Traffic Police career officers. They are often called upon to assist in traffic duties during national events, such as the annual National Day Parade, the S2006 World Bank meetings, the ASEAN Summit 2007, APEC 2009, and the Singapore Youth Olympic Games (S2010).

A special group of VSCs also formed the VSC Special Operations Team (SOT). The SOT provides police outriders to escort local and foreign head of states and high-risk dignitaries for their official and private visits so as to ensure an uninterrupted and safe journey while in Singapore. The SOT duties involve the prestigious honor of escorting very important people, such as the Singapore President, President of the United States, and many other foreign heads of state.

16.13 Some Impressive Volunteer Special Constabulary Members

16.13.1 Volunteer Special Constable Janet Lim

Some would have given up. But long-time VSC officer Janet Lim, 53, persevered. She found herself a single mother of a nine-year-old boy overnight when her husband Seah Ben Hur, like her, a VSC officer with the Traffic Police, died in a tragic accident while on duty in 2005.

Although the incident still haunts her to this day, she has no regrets remaining with the VSC. If anything, she credits her friends and colleagues in the force for helping her overcome this painful period in her life and for being a constant source of support for her.

For Janet, who currently holds the rank of station inspector, the VSC has always held a special allure that sets it apart from other uniformed groups. "I can't explain it," she says, "but the feeling is different. Putting on the uniform makes me very proud and passionate, and it reminds me that I'm responsible for maintaining law and order."

It was in 1989 that Janet experienced a vicarious taste of this when she watched a popular local Chinese action drama about the lives of police officers, produced by the Singapore Broadcasting Corporation. Her husband, a driving instructor, followed suit and signed up a year later.

There was never any question about which division she wanted to be posted to when she signed up to be a VSC volunteer. Indeed, so intent was she on joining the Traffic Police that she even learned to ride a motorcycle. Janet eventually got her wish after spending a stint with the Police Academy, and she jokes that the experience of riding a police bike was a true eye-opening experience.

"No one will give way to you when you're riding your own bike, but when you're on a police bike, everyone avoids you. You're like a ghost—all the other drivers just follow behind you," she says, as she recalls her experience of patrolling the roads.

As a volunteer traffic police officer, she learned to operate revolvers, participated in car chases, and conducted roadblock inspections, among other duties. However, her greatest sense of satisfaction comes from helping others stay safe on the roads. "I get a sense of relief after talking to the driver and explaining why we're stopping them," she says. For her, making sure they understand the offense they have committed is important so they can observe better road safety in future.

16.13.2 Volunteer Special Constable Sergeant Stijn Welkers

In 2008, the VSC started recruiting permanent residents of Singapore. It has taken VSC Sergeant Stijn Welkers, 42, many rounds of patrolling the Toa

Payoh heartland, the central part of Singapore, as a VSC officer before he finally earned public recognition as a "real police officer" and a genuine law enforcer. Sergeant Stijn has grown accustomed to people "literally staring in disbelief, looking around for hidden cameras, because it's obviously not a real police officer on duty."

Today, residents' reactions center on "Oh, it's that guy, the 'angmo.'* He's walking around again." Shopkeepers exchange greetings with him, kids gravitate toward him, and parents stop to have a conversation. Sergeant Stijn was born and raised in Hoorn, the Netherlands. He worked for an American software distribution company and moved to Singapore. He volunteered in a small martial arts school, which was owned by a senior VSC officer, who encouraged him to join VSC.

16.14 Critical Insight and Opinion

16.14.1 Assistant Commissioner of Police Lakshmanan†: Commander VSC (2005–2014), Justice of Peace

"Someone told me volunteers are seldom paid; not because they are worthless, but because they are priceless! I am proud to be a volunteer police officer."

16.14.2 Former Singapore Police Force Commissioner of Police Khoo Boon Hui

"Thank you for the tremendous and unwavering support that the Volunteer Special Constabulary has provided me and Singapore Police Force to enable the national police to be a Force for the Nation; one that inspires the world.

---

* "Red-haired" in local dialect, a Singapore colloquial term used to describe Caucasians.
† Served as a career police officer for 14 years and a VSC officer for the last 18 years since 1994.

Through the dedication and sacrifice of volunteers from all walks of life, you have helped keep Singapore safe and secure for all of us. The many major events would not have been successfully organized if not for your contributions. Indeed the public cannot tell the difference between a volunteer and a regular from the professional manner you discharge your responsibilities. I am proud of you, exemplars of the finest spirit of volunteerism."

16.14.3 Singapore National Police Commissioner of Police Ng Joo Hee

"Not everyone gets to become a police officer. We are very selective and choose carefully who we bring into the force. We set high standards for ourselves, demanding that every police officer live up to the core values of courage, loyalty, integrity, and fairness.

"As officers, whether regulars, national servicemen, or volunteers of the Singapore Police Force, our work is to help make Singapore a safer place for all and to protect Singaporeans from disorder and criminal harm. I remind my officers, at every opportunity, that we should be obsessed with this outcome.

"Policing is exceedingly difficult work. Police officers don't get paid a lot of money and work unforgiving hours. Many of us have no life outside the office, and our families often suffer unfairly. When we do really well, bad things do not happen, and people take the resulting safety and security for granted. When bad things do occasionally happen, we invariably take the blame, rightly or wrongly.

"We love our jobs because, above all, it is a noble and a significant one.

"There is really nothing else quite like being a police officer. Singaporeans count on us to shield them from all manner of criminal harm and to hunt down the crooked, who prey on the innocent, the vulnerable, the helpless, and the ignorant.

"We are truly the 10 thousand that protect the 5 million.

"We are Singapore's finest!"

Extracted from the Singapore Police Force Commissioner of Police Speech at the Police Annual Dinner June 13, 2011

References

Mercer. (2016). Mercer's 18th Annual Quality of Living Survey. London: Mercer.

Singapore Police Force. (2016a). *The Home Team Volunteer Network Fact Sheet*. Singapore: Singapore Police Force.

Singapore Police Force. (2016b). *The Volunteer Special Constabulary Headquarters Fact Sheet*. Singapore: Singapore Police Force.

Singapore Police Force. (2016c). *The Volunteer Special Constabulary Headquarters Heritage*. Singapore: Singapore Police Force.

Volunteer Policing in Israel

17

CHARLES A. LIEBERMAN

Contents

17.1 Introduction

Throughout the world, many law enforcement or police agencies are augmented by civilians who serve as volunteer or auxiliary police. For some of these regions, the resources necessary to train, equip, and fund additional police are not available. Other regions have an existential threat that necessitates additional service from members of the public. Israel is a unique country in that it is an island of democracy surrounded by unstable governments and hostile populations, some of which have clearly expressed their desire to eradicate the small country from the map and return its lands to what they believe to be the rightful owners. Although the premise of this perspective—that Israel is not a legitimate country or that it stole the land from Arab Muslims—may be argued with varying degrees of validity, Israel is part of a region with a rich history that has been a source of conflict for thousands of years.

17.2 Israel: A Brief History

The history of Israel dates back more than 3,000 years to around 1000 BCE when David ruled Judea in the area now known as Israel. David was followed by one of the most famous of historical Jewish figures, King Solomon. The region was subsequently invaded, conquered, and/or governed by Assyrians, Babylonians, Persians, Greeks, Romans, Turks, Arabs, Crusaders, Ottomans, and the British. Israel has been under the control of numerous empires under various forms of government for much of its history with very little of its history during which the local population was under self-rule. Some would argue that due to the control over the occupied territories, which comprise the West Bank and Gaza Strip, and a comparatively large population considering the size of the territories, the country is not a true democracy. Some even compare Israel to apartheid, a system of government employed by the South African National Party from 1948 to 1994 that repressed the indigenous population. However, Israel was not formed by the occupation of foreign lands by a European nation in an attempt to colonize or expand the resources available. Israel was formed after World War II after the withdrawal of British forces and after which the region was split into Arab and Jewish states. The Arab population in the region, primarily those in Israel, Egypt, Syria, Iraq, and Lebanon, rejected the formation of a Jewish state and attempted to take control of the former British colony through military force. This led to a war between the Arab populations and the Jews, who were overwhelmingly outnumbered by the Arabs in the region. Israel's Independence War and subsequent conflicts over the course of the following decades led to the formation of the current state of Israel, the only Jewish state in the world.

Although internal and external threats to the stability of a state are in a constant state of transformation due to environmental factors, police organizations are required to adapt in order to effectively and efficiently respond both proactively and reactively. The utilization of the community has always been an effective method of expanding the operational and intelligence-gathering capabilities of an organization. Furthermore, inclusion of the community in maintaining safety and security increases the perception of legitimacy of the organization by allowing members of the public to gain a greater understanding of the role and responsibility of the organization and its members. As perception of legitimacy is an integral factor in the level of cooperation and collaboration with the public, the cyclical nature provides a logical foundation for providing support and structure for continued police–public interaction and community policing. Organizational support for civilian volunteers, such as auxiliary police, within policing provides the interaction and opportunity for the necessary support and structure.

Subsequent to and concurrent with the wars, battles, and skirmishes between Israel and its neighbors, another threat rose to prominence. Terrorism, guerilla warfare, and bombings became a normal course of business for the population of Israel and its police. The 1972 Munich Olympics were the first Olympic games held in Germany since the Nazis hosted the games in 1936. Many Israeli athletes, coaches, and trainers had family members who had been killed during the Nazi regime. On September 4, eight members of the Palestinian terrorist organization Black September took the Israeli team hostage, which led to the death of 11 members of the Israeli team. The constant reporting by international media, which acted as a force multiplier with regard to the impact of the attack, captivated audiences worldwide, leading to a polarization regarding this relatively local issue. The notoriety of this terrorist attack led to vast increases in the international support, funding, and operational capability for these types of organizations worldwide. The 1970s was a decade of significant change worldwide with regard to "revolutionary" organizations that engaged in terroristic tactics to promote their ideologies, including numerous UN resolutions to address these tactics. In addition, many public and private structures adopted new strategies and procedures to counteract their vulnerabilities. However, many of these strategies are more of a deterrent than an effective countermeasure as shown by the success of the September 11, 2001 attacks in the United States.

Israel has been targeted for a disproportionate number of terroristic attacks, both nationally and internationally. As a result, Israelis are more vigilant about safety and security. The First and Second Intifadas organized violence, riots, and protests by the Muslim population in Israel, including numerous bombings of transportation, shopping centers, and restaurants targeting civilians, enhanced the already present perception of the importance of civilians taking an active role in taking responsibility for public safety and security. Most Israeli civilians are required to serve in the military (the exemption for religious scholars was revoked, but new policy has not yet been implemented, and there is great public outcry from the orthodox community), which provides basic training in weapons, allowing for a qualified pool of volunteer police that have many of the skills necessary for the police profession.

17.3 Israel Police

The Israel Police is a national police force responsible for public security, law enforcement, maintaining order, fighting crime, and ensuring the smooth flow of traffic.*

- Policing and law enforcement in Israel are the sole responsibility of the Israel Police.

---

* http://www.police.gov.il/English_contentPage.aspx

- As a national force, the Israel Police is responsible for all aspects of policing, including crime prevention and law enforcement.
- The work of the Israel Police takes on a whole new dimension when operating in such a sensitive area as Israel.

The Israel Police operates in compliance with the Police Act of 1971 and additional articles of legislation. In the context of those powers, the Israel Police is responsible for the following areas.*

17.3.1 Public Security

- Prevention of acts of terror: The police conduct patrols and raids and work to increase public awareness.
- Response to calls from citizens requesting examination of suspicious objects and dismantling of explosive devices.
- Deployment in terrorist incidents: Rescue of citizens, evacuation of casualties, searching for additional bombs, distancing of curious bystanders, directing traffic to alternative routes, arresting of suspects.
- Arrangement of security procedures in cities, towns, and rural communities.
- Organization of volunteers in the context of the Civil Guard for routine and emergency functions.

17.3.2 Maintaining Law and Order

- Response to reports of public disturbances
- Response to demonstrations, unlawful gatherings, and delinquency
- Responsibility for detainees in detention centers and escorting of detainees to and from the courthouse
- Implementation of court orders
- Responsibility for security and maintenance of public order in government agencies, public institutions, foreign embassies and consulates, and so on.
- Responsibility for security and maintenance of public order at official ceremonies
- Responsibility for security at official installations, including seaports and airports

* http://mops.gov.il/ENGLISH/POLICINGENG/POLICE/Pages/default.aspx

17.3.3 Fighting Crime

- Investigation of crimes and apprehension of offenders
- Detection and exposure of unreported crimes, such as drug trafficking, extortion of "protection" money, and trafficking of stolen goods
- Crime prevention: Instructing the public how to protect themselves and their property and how to make it more difficult for criminals to attain their objectives
- Unique response to juvenile delinquency

17.3.4 Traffic Enforcement

- Directing traffic and working to ensure smooth traffic flow
- Enforcement of traffic laws
- Investigation of traffic accidents and apprehension of traffic offenders
- Instructing the public, especially young people, on traffic safety
- Participation in the decision-making process in such matters as the planning and construction of roads and the placement of road signs and traffic lights with the goal of increasing traffic safety

17.4 Israel National Police Structure

17.4.1 National Headquarters

The Israel Police is headed by an inspector general. The role of the national headquarters, located in Jerusalem, is to assist the inspector general in formulating policy, allocating resources, developing relationships with external agencies, providing professional guidance, promoting research and development, providing management services, and public relations. The eight divisions of the national headquarters are provided below:*

1. Policing and security
2. Investigations and the war on crime
3. Intelligence
4. Traffic
5. Community and Civilian Guard
6. Planning and organization
7. Support and logistics
8. Human resources

* http://www.police.gov.il/english_contentPage.aspx?pid=4&menuid=5

17.4.2 Israel Police Districts

The Israel Police has six territorial districts:

1. Northern
2. Central
3. Tel Aviv
4. Jerusalem
5. Southern
6. Judea and Samaria

17.4.3 Ministry of Public Security

The Ministry of Public Security supervises the Israel Police, the Israel Prison Service, and the Israel Fire and Rescue Services. The Ministry's functions are to formulate public security policy, determine and monitor the allocation of resources, initiate projects, work with other Ministries, and more.*

17.4.4 Civil Guard and Community Policing

The Civil Guard was established in 1974 following a number of severe terrorist attacks that occurred that year. Today, the Civil Guard is the largest volunteer body in Israel, which has participation from 100,000 volunteers—a significant percentage of the total population of the small country with a population of less than 8 million. Civil Guard personnel are trained to provide the initial response to a security situation until the police arrive. The history of the Civil Guard is provided in more detail below.

17.4.5 Volunteer Police

The Israeli Auxiliary Police is called the Mishmar Ezrachi, which translates from Hebrew to English as Civil Guard. The Mishmar Ezrachi, hereto forward to be referred to as the Civil Guard, includes uniformed and nonuniformed civilians who take part in police work in various fields, including the following:

- Neighborhood watch
- Regular patrol with marked cars
- Traffic city police
- Highway police
- Bomb squad assistants

* http://www.mops.gov.il/english/pages/homepage.aspx

- Youth crime prevention unit
- Police coast guard
- Sniper units
- Border patrol
- Police diving unit

The Israel Police provides the Civil Guard, a part of the police and community division, with weapons, equipment, and training. Each community will have one or more local bases, depending on the size of the community. Civil Guard volunteers are generally armed with M1 Carbines; however, those who have civilian gun licenses may also carry a sidearm. After basic training, most Civil Guard volunteers perform their service in uniform to augment the full-time police. Civil Guard volunteers have limited police powers while on duty and are authorized to apprehend and arrest suspects when necessary. Volunteers in the Civil Guard are generally equipped with a fluorescent yellow police vest, flashlight, radio, firearm, and handcuffs; however, some units may have additional equipment depending on the specialized role of that unit. Although the minimum requirement is 12 hours a month, many Civil Guard volunteers will work at least one shift each week, exceeding the minimum requirement.

In contrast to the full-time police, volunteers do not have the authority to perform police duties outside of the hours performing Civil Guard volunteer duty. Volunteers are not authorized to take any official police action while off duty (including assistance to other law enforcement officers); however, volunteers have the same right to take action as any civilian upon encountering criminal activity and may do what they deem necessary to protect members of the public. The primary difference is that they will not be protected, as a full-time police officer would be, upon review of the incident by governmental authorities. Therefore, volunteers are discouraged from taking action while off duty unless there is a threat that requires immediate action to save lives, such as in the case of a terrorist attack.

17.5 History of the Civil Guard

In April 1974, about six months after the end of the Yom Kippur War, the responsibility for the safety and security of the general population within the borders of Israel was transferred from the Israel Defense Force (IDF) to the Israel National Police via Knesset resolution 411. During this time, an increasing number of terrorist attacks led to public advocacy for the creation of a volunteer police force to bolster the capacity of the small nation to enhance internal security. One of the most notorious attacks that occurred on May 15, 1974, referred to as the Ma'a lot Massacre, led to the death of

21 Israeli children and six adults that were taken hostage by three Palestinian terrorists armed with assault rifles, explosives, and grenades at a school. In addition, there were nearly 100 injuries of other victims at the school. Soon after, on July 10, 1974, the Civil Guard was established to augment the operational capability of the Israel Police. The Civil Guard, operating within the community and civilian guard division of the police, plays an important role in improving domestic safety and security in Israel.

In 1977, in preparation for the late Egyptian president Anwar Sadat's historic visit to Israel, Civil Guard volunteers were integrated into the planned activities of the Israel Police in one of the largest and most complicated public security operations at that time. Operation Gate was the first significant operation in which Civil Guard volunteers were integrated into the activities of local police stations, which were almost completely vacant of police officers, who had been deployed for the Sadat visit. In 1981, in the wake of the close collaboration of the Israel Police and Civil Guard volunteers, an experimental pilot project incorporated special uniformed Civil Guard units. The concept was formally adopted in 1982, and units of uniformed Civil Guard volunteers began to operate in regular police activities, such as patrols, detective work, traffic enforcement, and crime prevention.*

In January 1989, Israel's parliament, the Knesset, enacted an amendment establishing the powers of Civil Guard volunteers, which allows Israel Police to enlist the assistance of the Civil Guard in police activities related to the protection of the lives and property of citizens. In the 1990s, the Civil Guard was Israel's largest volunteer organization in Israel with tens of thousands of volunteers representing a vast spectrum of religious affiliations, ethnic communities, and age brackets. In 1998, Civil Guard was incorporated as an integral part of the Israel Police, which allowed volunteers to take a more active role in the Israel Police's community and civil guard division. The community outreach division established a successful, cost-effective community policing center program. In addition, police officers specializing in community policing, together with Civil Guard volunteers, increased efficacy of the organization, specifically with regard to reducing crime, addressing traffic conditions, and responding to vehicular accidents and road conditions.†

17.6 Conclusion

Throughout the world, many law enforcement or police agencies are augmented by civilians who serve as volunteer or auxiliary police. For some of these regions, the resources necessary to train, equip, and fund additional

---

* http://mops.gov.il/English/PolicingENG/Police/Pages/CivilGuard35.aspx
† http://mops.gov.il/ENGLISH/POLICINGENG/POLICE/Pages/CivilGuard35.aspx

police are not available. Other regions have an existential threat that necessitates additional service from members of the public. Israel, an island of democracy surrounded by unstable governments and hostile populations, does not have the resources and funding to maintain its security needs. Therefore, Israel requires members of the public to volunteer their time to effectively augment the capability of the government to maintain internal safety and security. Since its establishment nearly 40 years ago, the Civil Guard has continued to evolve, developing into its current state of existence, a highly effective and significant force that has had a major impact on police work and has helped to improve the quality of life in Israel. The Civil Guard provides a functional and effective model that could be employed by other nations to augment the operational capability of police, improve community relations, and enhance the perception of police legitimacy.

"Special" Kind of Policing
Volunteer Policing in England and Wales

18

CAROL BORLAND JONES
ROSS WOLF

Contents

18.1 Introduction

Volunteering within the criminal justice system in England and Wales has a long history, and its relevance continues. Magistrates, prison visitors, and special constables provide services that reduce the costs to government and therefore the public while also empowering community residents who may feel disengaged or disenfranchised. Special constables, in particular, are a very visual entity whose presence in locations where police are rarely seen can provide confidence and reassurance as well as reducing fear of crime.

The role of special constables continues to be an increasingly important element of crime prevention and community safety throughout England and Wales through routine patrolling, attendance at large gatherings, and engaging with communities. Progressively, volunteers are being sought to provide specialist services.

However, it should be noted that, at times, the life of some special constables has been made uncomfortable by some of their full-time colleagues and members of the public who have variously called them "hobby bobbies" or "policing on the cheap."

18.2 Using Volunteers in Policing in the United Kingdom

In 2009, Baroness Neuberger's review of volunteering across the criminal justice system in the United Kingdom identified that a "lack of investment in volunteer management inevitably results in volunteers having a bad experience" (Neuberger, 2009, p. 19).

Volunteering is not about getting public services on the cheap; it requires investment but can reap multiple benefits. In the United Kingdom, there is a long history of volunteering in the criminal justice system, including magistrates, prison visitors, and special constables.

A brief outline of volunteer policing in England and Wales and, more specifically, the role of special constables (SCs) in the 21st century, is now more closely examined. Many authors have attempted to provide an extensive history of the Special Constabulary in the United Kingdom (Gill & Mawby, 1990; Seth, 2006), but the focus shifts to the demographics of SCs with regard to gender, ethnicity, and the present state of affairs within the organization.

18.3 Brief Overview of the Special Constabulary in England and Wales

There are distinct differences between criminal justice practices across the United Kingdom. Although the United Kingdom constitutes the political union between Scotland, Wales, England, and Northern Ireland, each is also a nation state in its own right. Although England and Wales follow the same criminal justice system, Scotland and Northern Ireland differ. Therefore, although SCs exist in Scotland and Northern Ireland, historically their implementation has differed from that in England and Wales. In the first instance, Scotland's criminal justice system and laws vary from those in England and Wales (Donnelly & Scott, 2010), and in Northern Ireland, historically an area of political and religious disharmony, their criminal justice system has been organized along military lines (Farrell, 1983).

In England and Wales, the way that SCs are utilized also varies in each constabulary, and specific representations are outlined to reflect that diversity. Although in the United States reserve or auxiliary policing covers a diverse miscellany of agencies and voluntary officer roles, in England and Wales the profile of SCs is somewhat less complicated. This is because effectively "the police" in England and Wales are all members of a national police service currently divided into 43 "localized" forces. Each individual force is under the direction of a chief constable who is accountable to the office of the police and crime commissioner who is the holder of that force's finances. Every force must adhere to the laws of the land, the same laws across England

and Wales, although each police force may have different priorities and operational policies, dependent upon localized issues.

SCs generally wear uniforms the same as or similar to those worn by regular officers, and the equipment they carry is likewise provided. In 2015, however, the College of Policing stated that "(t)he agreed view of the Association of Chief Police Officers (ACPO) is that special constables should not be issued with Tasers or firearms." That aside, members of the public are generally unaware of the status of an attending officer.

In March 2015, there were 5,647 authorized firearm officers in England and Wales, only 2.7% of all regular officers (Home Office, 2016), and although Tasers are being issued to more and more officers each year, they are not carried by all regular officers.

With the creation of the first modern police force in London in 1829, Sir Robert Peel focused priorities on crime prevention and a model that was a civilian, rather than military, force. The Act for Improving the Police in and Near the Metropolis, also known as the Metropolitan Police Act, emphasized the preventative aspects of law enforcement. This reflected the notion that it is better to *prevent* crime than it is to respond to calls for help.

The police, and the criminal justice system itself, rely heavily on the public on many different levels, and "it is no exaggeration to state that the system is dependent upon both public involvement and co-operation" (Gill & Mawby, 1990, p. 5). It has historically been acknowledged that the police in England and Wales have policed "by consent." Reith (1956) maintained that British policing was unique around the world because its ethos was that of cooperation of the public rather than policing through fear.

Although the role of the Special Constabulary, first formally recognized in 1662 in Britain, was initially to enforce the law (Reay, 2012), in 1831 their role became more consistent with that of the British police with an emphasis on protecting the peace (Reay, 2012). Throughout England and Wales, special constables carry warrant cards giving them the same powers of arrest as their full-time colleagues, and these can be utilized at all times irrespective of whether the officer is off or on duty. In addition, since 2007 and in common with their full-time colleagues, warrant cards held by SCs allow them to work anywhere in England and Wales; prior to that, their cards allowed them to work only in their own constabulary or those that were coterminous.

The term "special" has been known to create confusion as many different police agencies tend to utilize the word in describing other police functions or units, such as special branch, special response, and special police patrol groups (Gill & Mawby, 1990). The term may also create confusion with those who work as "special police" or with private police forces. Modern SCs are volunteers who work under the direction of a chief constable and function as duly authorized members of a police force (Gill & Mawby, 1990). It is estimated that in September 2015 there were approximately 16,050 SCs in the

United Kingdom, something of a reduction from the 20,352 in March of 2012 (Allen & Dempsey, 2016).

18.4 Requirements and Training for SCs

Anyone wishing to become an SC must first satisfy the requirements as laid down in the initial application form as well as in interviews, background checks of the applicant and family members, and physical and psychological fitness. Applicants must be a European Economic Area citizen (or have an unrestricted right to remain in the country) and be at least 18 years of age. Applicants must be willing to donate at least 16 hours per month to the police force and are assessed on their interpersonal skills, their ability to work in a team, leadership potential, and initiative. Many police forces also use the police initial recruitment (PIR) test to screen candidates to judge the ability of the applicant to write clearly and accurately, solve numerical problems, and reason logically. If accepted, all SCs receive their warrant card, and after nationally recognized training, they will continue to receive training while accompanying a mentor.

Training for SCs is often provided on evenings and weekends as most have full-time jobs or other daily commitments. Training includes mandatory basic law and procedures courses, first aid, and dealing with conflict (including use of handcuffs, batons, and other protective equipment). Once training is complete, SCs must participate in "coached patrols" during which they are supported by regular police officers, who provide additional training and develop skills about policing.

18.5 Special Constabulary Staffing and Statistics

Statistics about the Special Constabulary are maintained by the United Kingdom's Office of National Statistics (ONS). This is "[t]he UK's largest independent producer of official statistics and the recognised national statistical institute of the UK."* That said, feedback from a number of constabularies suggest that levels of engagement by SCs can fluctuate with some forces acknowledging that they had lost track of the exact number of their volunteer officers; for example, media reports relating to officers in the Metropolitan Police showed that SCs (as well as full-time officers) have been disciplined or sacked for abusing the use of their warrant cards and free travel passes. In London, such passes are a valuable asset, which has cost the force (and

* https://www.ons.gov.uk/

therefore the public) significant amounts of money (Boyle, 2015). Such behavior, as well as a failure by some constabularies to regulate the number of hours served by each SC, leads to some question regarding the accuracy of the official national statistics.

Figure 18.1 clearly illustrates the increase and decline in SC numbers in the 10 years beginning 2006, two years before the global financial downturn, which resulted in deep and lasting economic cuts in both the public and private sectors. The increase in recruitment as illustrated in Figure 18.1 suggests that, as full-time officers were made redundant or moved on to retirement, SCs had been recruited to increase policing numbers. This is, however, a simplistic and often erroneous interpretation of events.

The number of SCs has historically fluctuated for a range of reasons. In 1995, there were 20,026 documented SCs, only 326 fewer than the recent peak number in 2012 (the year of the London Olympics), and in 2004, the number had dipped to 10,998 (Allen & Dempsey, 2016). These figures are far below the numbers who served during World War II, when some 130,000 reserve officers policed the streets while large numbers of regular officers were serving in the military.

As noted, the numbers of SCs in England and Wales have fluctuated throughout their history, and reasons given have been varied. For example, in preparation for the 2012 Olympics in London, many forces attempted and in part succeeded in increasing the numbers of SCs to help patrol and police their communities as regular officers were sent to Olympic sites for the duration of the games. When the games were over and the full-time officers returned to

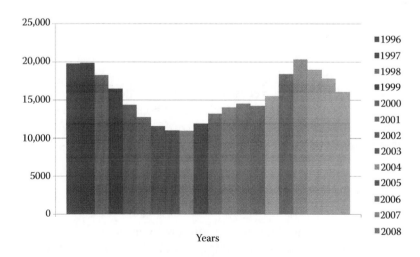

Figure 18.1 Number of special constables in England and Wales from 1996 to 2008. (From Office of National Statistics, *Police Workforce England and Wales, 31 March 2015*, London, Home Office, 2015.)

their home stations, SCs were often no longer utilized for the sorts of frontline policing that they had routinely undertaken in the absence of their full-time colleagues. In informal discussion with a number of former SCs, many cited this factor as a reason for stepping down, and others felt that they had, in the words of one special constable, been "put on the back burner."

18.6 Special Constabulary Gender and Ethnicity

The disparity with regard to gender in the police profession is similar in both the United States and the United Kingdom. According to the national census of 2011, females made up 50.8% of the population of England and Wales (ONS, 2012), and in March 2015, female police officers in England and Wales accounted for 28.2% of police staffing levels and 30.7% of the total number of SCs. These percentages, however, vary from force to force with only 16.5% of SCs in Kent being female, and in North Wales the percentage was 41.2 (ONS, 2015).

Following the death of Stephen Lawrence in 1993, the Macpherson Report concluded that the Metropolitan Police force was "institutionally racist."[*] As a consequence, police forces were required to engage minority ethnic officers, both within the Special Constabulary and in the full-time staff, to reflect the ethnic demographics of their communities. In spite of this, according to the ONS in 2015, ethnic minority SCs accounted for 11.2% of the total, this being significantly higher than the 5.7% of full-time officers (ONS, 2015). The most recent accurate figure regarding ethnic minority populations in the United Kingdom come from the 2011 national census, which showed that in England and Wales 14% of the population was made up of members from a background other than "white" (ONS, 2012).

The Special Constabulary across the United Kingdom is currently undergoing wide and deep-rooted changes at a time when policing in general has faced financial constraints and restructuring and subsequent upheaval. For example, in 2005, Barry Loveday argued against the amalgamation of the 43 force areas into 17 larger ones (Loveday, 2005). Eleven years on, although there has been some amalgamation of certain specialist services, the 43 regional police forces continue to exist.

18.7 Deploying Special Constables

Although special constables have traditionally been used as a support mechanism for their full-time colleagues (College of Policing, 2013), some

---

[*] For further details of the case, see Foster, Newburn, and Souhami (2005).

constabularies have recognized in recent years that their expertise and experience in their work and/or leisure can be utilized to address local law enforcement challenges.

For example, in one region, the nighttime economy is policed solely by SCs during the busiest nights of the week. They are overseen by a "regular" police inspector but generally take full patrol responsibility for the location, the center of a small but busy university town. In utilizing SCs in this manner, the SCs collectively feel neither "secondary to" nor "under the scrutiny of" regular officers. In taking "ownership" of the policing of the nighttime economy, the SCs make the decisions regarding the deployment of their officers and the responses to issues as they arise. According to the command staff, such hegemony provides the SCs with a sense of purpose and job satisfaction.

In a second example, specialists in IT and cyber matters are currently being recruited as SCs in a pilot role, which will see them working voluntarily within two constabularies to tackle cyber crime. In the future, it is anticipated that appropriate individuals with such expertise will be taken on as either police support volunteers (PSV) or SCs, dependent upon the perimeters of their role.

It is acknowledged that the role of volunteers in policing has much to offer under the umbrella of the United Kingdom's "Citizens in Policing," which includes not only SCs, but also police support volunteers, "Watches," and cadets.* The SC is the only volunteer with full enforcement powers, but in contemporary society, there are people who want to volunteer their time, expertise, or just support without wishing to become an SC. Historically, management departments in the police have been both uncomfortable and risk averse, and although some constabularies are recognizing the need to embrace their volunteers at all levels, SCs have, according to a number of such officers, been treated as additional personnel without recognizing that they are also volunteers. On the other hand, there are still many career police officials who do not view SCs with the same level of appreciation. For example, one new SC, who had been on duty with an experienced sergeant, was shocked to hear her companion tell her that she needed to "stay out of any confrontations because you can't arrest anyone." Although probationers cannot patrol without a mentor until all appropriate training is completed, they do have full powers of arrest. Ultimately, it appears that the respect for and utility of volunteers in policing across the United Kingdom may be on the rise as government officials have recognized the impressive contribution that the Special Constabulary and SCs have made to maintaining peace and tranquility within their communities.

* http://www.college.police.uk/What-we-do/Support/Citizens/Pages/default.aspx

References

Allen, G., & Dempsey, N. (2016). *Police Service Strength,* Briefing paper No.00634, House of Commons Library.

Boyle, D. (2015). *Let me through, I'm a cop! Dozens of police officers disciplined for abusing their warrant cards to get into bars and football matches and blag free train travel,* Mail Online at http://www.dailymail.co.uk/news/article-3060513 /Let-m-cop-Dozens-police-officers-discplined-abusing-warrant-cards-bars -blag-free-train-travel.html.

College of Policing. (2013). *Becoming a Special Constable, Workforce Policy and Strategy* at specialsteam@college.pnn.police.uk

College of Policing. (2015). *FAQs (powers, time commitment, training, promotion)* at http://recruit.college.police.uk/Special/Pages/faqs.aspx.

Donnelly, D., & Scott, K. (2010). *Policing Scotland,* 2nd ed., Abingdon, Willan.

Farrell, M. (1983). *Arming the Protestants,* London, Pluto Press.

Foster, J., Newburn, T., & Souhami, A. (2005). *Assessing the impact of the Stephen Lawrence Inquiry,* London, Home Office.

Gill, M., & Mawby, R. I. (1990). *A Special Constable: A study of the police reserve,* Aldershot, Avebury.

Home Office. (2016). *Police use of firearms statistics, England and Wales: Financial year ending 31 March 2015* at https://www.gov.uk/government/statistics/police -use-of-firearms-statistics-england-and-wales-financial-year-ending-31-march -2015.

Loveday, B. (2005). Police reform: Problems of governance and accountability; management challenges surrounding current proposals for police restructuring. *Police Journal,* 78 (4), 339–350.

Neuberger, J. (2009). *Volunteering across the criminal justice system: Baroness Neuberger's review as the Government's Volunteering Champion,* http://www .oneeastmidlands.org.uk/sites/default/files/library/volunteers%20in%20cjs.pdf.

Office of National Statistics. (2012). *Ethnicity and national identity in England and Wales 2011, 11th December 2012,* London, Home Office.

Office of National Statistics. (2015). *Police Workforce England and Wales, March 31, 2015,* London, Home Office.

Reay, W. T. (2012). *The Specials, How They Served London; The Story of the Metropolitan Special Constabulary,* London, Ulan Press.

Reith, C. (1956). *A New Study on Police History,* London, Oliver and Boyd.

Seth, R. (2006). *The Specials,* Trowbridge, The Cromwell Press.

Police Volunteers and Other Deployment Options

IV

Police Community Support Officers in the United Kingdom

19

A Midpoint between Career and Volunteer Officers

ANNETTE CRISP

Contents

19.1 Introduction

This chapter provides some context to the current state of community policing in England and Wales and explores some of the factors that led to the development of the police community support officer (PCSO), one of the newer members of the wider police family in the United Kingdom.

In the United Kingdom, it seems that the police service is constantly in a state of flux, apparently caught between community expectation and political necessity on one level and, on a more *practical* note, caught between the officers' perceptions of "*real policing*" (Bryant et al., 1985) and "*rubbish jobs*" (Bowling, 1999, p. 256; Waddington, 1999; Walklate, 1996, p. 197) on another. Very few newly attested police officers, if asked, would see their career extending before them with the sole focus of policing the more mundane local community problems, and yet this task is one that is fundamental to policing by consent as it reinforces the bonds that members of local communities have with their "peacekeepers." Indeed, the role and behavior of the *Beat Bobby* or community police officer has been subject of much *civic mythology* with an older generation of the British public reminiscing fondly about a time (which seemingly didn't exist) when you could leave your back door unlocked without any unfortunate consequences, would always see a policeman when you needed him, and a kindly word or a *clip around the ear* would be meted out equally by the police to ensure that crime was addressed or prevented. This myth appears to have successfully been reinforced by the media who talk about a return to the good old days of George Dixon (a fictional TV police officer from the 1950s) and appears to be the fallback position of politicians and senior officers alike when defending community policing initiatives.

Although recent history might subscribe to alternative descriptions about the development of the role of the community police officer, the concept of the *Beat Bobby* is one that has, in contrast, been for a number of years devalued by serving officers and denigrated within the police culture. This is essentially because the role is perceived to encompass duties that fall within the *rubbish work* category, the antithesis of the crime-fighting character of *true policing*, and, as such, is associated with officers who are perceived to be *sick, lame, lazy*, and not fit to do the proper job of policing,* which is, of course, to catch villains.

The police culture is strongly resistant to change, which is why changes to policing tend to be motivated by *error, revolt*, and subsequent *imposition* as opposed to evolution. Some changes are strongly associated with societal tensions, which, when exacerbated by the police persona's psychological detachment from community-based policing (reinforced by the police culture), have resulted in poor police practice. Such events, as are discussed, are core to the development of the role of the PCSO.

19.2 History and Overview

In 1983, the Home Office, the government department responsible for the police, proposed in *Circular 114* that public sector organizations should be working toward "*economy, efficiency, and effectiveness*" (Home Office, 1983); this meant that they should be focusing on outputs toward a measurable conclusion (or product) rather than inputs. The ultimate but silent aim of this proposed efficient practice undoubtedly was the amalgamation of the police forces within England and Wales. This political challenge to the structure of policing was calmed by the robust defense of their independently controlled

---

* Other roles that fall into this category and that are similarly denigrated are those associated with back room, desk-bound policing, such as professional standards and police training.

force areas by the chief constables, who, at the time, were able to put this particular sleeping tiger to rest with an effective dose of their own politicking and influence.

The conservative government had, contemporaneously, already used their power to politicize the police in that they were being used more readily to subdue political protest, such as those that arose as a consequence of the miners' strike (1984), and subdue community unrest, of which the Brixton riots of 1981 is an example. The resulting community–police friction was widely debated with calls for changes to the organization, role, and responsibility (Johnston, 2003; Manning, 1977; Shearing & Wood, 2003; Wood, 2004) and led to changes to the legislation that directly affected police procedures in the case of the Brixton riots, The Police and Criminal Evidence Act of 1984.

The police themselves were finding that controls over their roles and their autonomy as public servants to local communities was under further threat from legislation, such as that included in the Police and Magistrates Courts Act of 1994, which effectively moved their responsibilities to local communities and provided for greater government control. This caused the then chair of The Association of Chief Police Officers (ACPO), Sir John Smith, to state, "I am inclined to the view that we are witnessing a move, perhaps unintended, for national control of the police by central government."

Policing began to be looked at through a microscope by the politician and commentator alike with the publication of a variety of reports that considered police responsibilities and rewards (i.e., Sheehy Report, 1993) and core and ancillary tasks (i.e., Posen Inquiry by the Home Office, 1995) and looked to develop a policing culture based upon performance that was detached from the idea of policing being a secure *job for life*.

Although the conservative government of the early 1990s focused upon the crime-fighting role of the police (which included the suppression of possible civil unrest) by the late 1990s with the impact of the new Labour government "reforms" came the idea of being "tough on crime and tough on the causes of crime" (Manifesto of the British Labour Party, 1977). This directed the police to consider a wider role, which included public reassurance and reintroduced the concept of a more community-engaged service. The "New Labour" government, driven by the contemporary market-led economy, consolidated the performance requirements for the police, which led to the "Best Value Framework" (Home Office, 1999) being applied to the work of police authorities who had already seen their responsibility and influence reduced in favor of auxiliary government control.

Services, which at one time were perceived as core to "the business," such as prison escort duties and general patrolling, became the subject of what some commentators have dubbed the pluralization of policing

(Coxhead, 2009); this assumed that personnel working in areas not formerly associated with the formal policing manifest, which included the civilian nonwarranted members of the newly regulated security industry, could be called upon to work in policing roles when deemed appropriate. This provided *consumers* with alternatives to formal policing processes if they felt that they would get a "value for money" service elsewhere. This refocus not only impacted upon the police but, by this time, all public agencies.

The principles of business reinforced by the processes involved in the theories of *New Public Management* were adopted by all public agencies as the government continued the political trend to cut costs and provide a more efficient service to the public. Maguire (2002) indicates that government set organizational goals and employed internal (to each organization) change drivers that linked to improving efficiency and service for *consumers* as opposed to *citizens*. This linked to compulsive competitive tendering to cut costs, performance targets, and public service agreements. The responsibility to meet the requirements set by public policy was delegated to a number of organizations, which set groups against one another as competitors, to gain funding via the process of public tendering. Nationally, agency heads were provided with significant freedom as to how to implement changes. This, in some cases, meant that aspects of work expected to sit within an agency remit were sold off to private business. Organizations thus refocused upon "core" and "ancillary" functions, which, in some cases, led to fragmentation.

19.3 Civilianization

The need to release more frontline officers to undertake the task of policing rather than engaging in back room bureaucratic processes had been identified by the government as a significant problem (PA Consulting Group, 2001). It was therefore unsurprising that the idea of the more formal integration of civilians as frontline members of the police family was introduced in the government white paper "Policing a New Century, A Blue Print for Reform" (Home Office, 2001). This document also explained the potential deployment duties of these new civilian staff members as relieving frontline officers of the more routine policing responsibilities.

Having highlighted the possible roles of new members of the wider police family, government continued a process of contracting out policing roles, which was consolidated within the Police Reform Act (Parliament of the United Kingdom, 2002).

19.4 Historical Role of Civilians in Policing

Civilians have been involved in the peripheries of policing for some time. These functions provide a mixed economy (Crawford et al., 2005) of staff employed generally in public reassurance roles by local authorities (as neighborhood or street wardens) or businesses, mainly working within the security industry (Button, 2002). In more formal policing, the Taverne Report of 1966 identified and facilitated the arrival of specialist posts whose technical contributions to policing are generally unseen by the public, such as crime scene photography, the taking and reviewing of fingerprints, or working as scenes of crimes officers (Highmore, 1993). Loveday (2004) notes, however, that historically the independent contribution of civilian staff to the work of the police has been neglected by police reviews such as those undertaken by Her Majesty's Inspectorate of Constabulary (HMIC), which served as a reminder of the apparent high status of the work of sworn staff and, in contrast, the low status of the civilian contribution. He cites Parrett (1998) in recognizing that as a result of the relatively menial tasks they were asked to perform that civilians were perceived as cheap substitutes to enable the police to undertake the *real job* at hand. This appears to be reflected in the lack of any distinctive career pathways by civilians either in specialist or other roles within the police service and was reinforced by the Operational Policing Review of 1990, which meant that even more senior posts within the police service, such as those that focused on specialisms such as finance IT or human resources and that might more appropriately be held by experienced civilian staff, *could* be held by serving officers. The logic of this proposal was that they would be in the best position to command and more fully appreciate the duties of a regulated organization. The reality, however, in terms of the service utilizing the most qualified or effective personnel in a post may be quite different. The idea of the police service offering a job for life *literally*, for some officers, meant that on retirement as a uniformed officer they would continue to work for the police service in a civilian post. This concept is associated with Howgrave-Graham's (1947) "anticivilian position," which considered that the best training for work as a police civilian was to have experienced firsthand the role of a police officer.

19.5 Impact of Police Culture on Police/Civilian Working Relationships

Research in the 1990s by Highmore (1993) into police–civilian integration observed a number of issues within police–civilian working relationships, which became manifest in apparent feelings of self-importance and disdain toward civilian staff by serving officers.*

This high-handed attitude toward civilian staff, who may have been technologists or hold expertise in supporting forensic roles, was identified by Williams (2004) and others as part of a process of undermining nonpolice expertise, which was acknowledged by the officers themselves in Highmore's research. The poor state of the police–civilian relationship was further exemplified by Cope (2004), who found that the product of analytical work undertaken by specialist crime analyst roles was used reactively to justify preplanned police initiatives as opposed to proactively seeking out opportunities within intelligence-led policing, thus undermining its worth as an important policing tool.

Undoubtedly, differences in working conditions and pay have reinforced the perceptions of a two-tier organization; however, the police culture has also impacted on behaviors, which, for some, have been experienced as workplace bullying (Highmore, 1993, p. 47; Parrett, 1998, p. 97).

Largely as a result of the hierarchical operational structures within policing, police officers tend to find themselves in positions in which they will be responsible for the management of civilian staff, which has, again, caused, in some areas, significant difficulties. Not only do civilian staff have different terms and conditions from those of police officers, but few police managers, according to a survey by ACPO in 1990, had received any management training to enable them to understand the differences and outline subsequent expected responses (Parrett, 1998, p. 153). The results of the Neyroud Review of 2011 and the later Windsor Review (2012) found that little had changed since the ACPO survey and repeated the need for the police to develop a more professionally qualified management structure.

Poor management practices may ultimately lead to bullying and harassment, which may be associated with accusations of inappropriate behavior and possible legal action. This appears to be the case in the police service as research by the public service union UNISON (2000, 2009) revealed that 21% of their civilian staff respondents stated that they were being bullied by police officers. Thirty-nine percent of all respondents felt that this behavior was associated with the police culture:

> In UNISON's view the results show that bullying has become part of the management culture of many police forces, and it is often being allowed to happen and carry on unchecked. The survey clearly demonstrates that bullies can get away with it and that this goes unchecked because workers are scared to report it. (Rayner, 2000, p. 5)

---

* This behavior has also been reflected in the attitudes of some officers toward members of the Special Constabulary, volunteer attested officers with the same powers, obligations, and responsibilities as regular officers. These volunteers have consequently experienced difficulties integrating into the service (Berry et al., 1998).

The uneasy relationship already identified between officers and civilian staff appears to be one that might have left PCSO recruits to the service feeling uneasy about their future; the next section, however, considers how they have become assimilated into the police family to become useful partners in frontline community policing.

19.6 PCSO in England and Wales

The introduction of the role of PCSO in 2002 was initially observed as another facet of a continuing political trend, as part of the wider workforce modernization agenda, which, at the time, developed support structures for workers employed in the public services in order to maximize limited resources. This arguably provided an opportunity to displace the less complex tasks associated with any specific role in, for example, offender management, nursing, or teaching to ensure that key personnel were free to undertake the more rigorous professional requirements of their job.

The role of the PCSO, defined within the Police Reform Act (2002), provided an opportunity for chief constables to appoint frontline uniformed staff to provide a visible presence in the community with powers *they* deemed to be sufficient to deal with minor issues and combat low-level disorder. This would consequently release police officers from the perceived "rubbish" jobs in order that they might focus on more complex policing tasks. To ensure flexibility, chief constables were provided with a set of standards and a choice of discretionary policing powers for their local PCSOs. These were subsequently updated by The Police Reform Act of 2002 (Standard Powers and Duties of Community Support Officers) Order 2007.

To further encourage the uptake of the new role, chief constables were granted additional ring-fenced government funds from which the new frontline resources might initially be supported. *At the time, the general perception of the more cynical rank and file police to this new post was that that the job would disappear when the funding ran out.*

Instead of the anticipated positive response by local communities to the introduction of this new frontline post, there was much confusion with community leaders asking why this new role should be created at all when there appeared to be a need to recruit additional police officers? This concern was fueled by adverse media coverage, which highlighted the potential negative impact of the role and referred to PCSOs as plastic police, monkeys and 4.95s.* One of the many complications at this time was caused by

* This is taken from the phrase "I'm not dealing with the monkey; where is the organ grinder?" and from modern police slang that means not quite Five-O, after *Hawaii Five-O*, the U.S. police TV program.

the different expectations of the role. This was further muddled by the differences in policing powers adopted by chief officers for local needs, which meant that PCSOs in one shire force would have different powers associated with their duty from another PCSO stationed a couple of miles down a road in another force area. In addition to the confusion about the post, the police–cultural devaluation of the new position began almost immediately with the Police Federation opposing the creation of what they perceived would be an "ill equipped and ill trained second layer of law enforcers" (Berry, 2007).

To a certain extent, the concerns expressed by the Police Federation were primarily correct in that newly appointed PCSOs were provided locally with haphazard, cut-down versions of "in house" training courses. As a result, the training was basic and provided for the minimum level of skill and operational proficiency. Cooper et al. (2006) noted the lack of time provided to develop appropriate training packages for PCSOs, which meant that each force area had to develop its own packages, the content and quality of which varied from force to force. For the majority of PCSOs at this time, training lasted one week (Unwin, 2006), after which they were expected to be in a position to work closely with troubled communities on issues associated with quality of life and with any number of other complex problems. The early PCSOs consequently either continued to do what they had always done (i.e., the recycled ex-traffic warden recruits focused on parking offenses) or endeavored to undertake independent learning (some with the support of local beat officers) and gain supplementary experience, making themselves useful in other ways. Unfortunately for some, the lack of direction and understanding of policing powers and role meant that hiding in plain sight seemed the best option, which fueled police gossip about lazy or incapable PCSOs.

In a 2014 review of the role in Cambridge, the following statement, which was taken from a reflective staff survey based on police managers' experiences, sums up a common national occurrence: "We were given these staff and had literally no idea what we were supposed to do with them" (Sutherland, 2014).

This was not subsequently helped in the wider community by continued negative press, which highlighted incompetence or laziness or that suggested, more seriously (and incorrectly), gross neglect of duty (BBC, 2007).

A television documentary sponsored by the then Labour government, *Beat: Life on the Street*, broadcast on the ITV channel in 2006, which, it was hoped, would redress levels of satisfaction as a result of the bad press, was relatively successful, changing public opinion about PCSOs from 28% of the public stating that they had satisfaction and confidence in the role to 62% in 2006 (Sutherland, 2014). This success was sadly undermined by a report that consequently stated that, in breach of OFCOM rules, the Home Office had paid the broadcaster (ITV) a considerable sum of money (£400,000) to promote the cause.

In addition to the development of the PCSO, the year 2002 also saw the introduction by the government of a more formal framework by which crimes should be recorded by the police (National Crime Recording Standards) and APACS* indicators, which, together, standardized crime reporting and police performance specifications. The effect on policing was unfortunate in that, at a local level, BCU commanders were provided with targets for activity, such as arrests or detected crime, which would indicate the apparent efficiency of their officers. The result was that the more confrontational processes, such as "stop and search," were overly relied upon to meet targets, and officers were expected to spend little time on community reassurance procedures (which were not evaluated by the performance criteria). Although such processes might help, in some cases, to reduce crime, they may also damage community relations (Joyce, 2006). In contrast, the role of PCSO was developed as a nonconfrontational, reassuring police presence and was *not*, at that time, associated with performance targets, which meant that "their relationship with communities began as a less retributive one" (Crisp, 2013). Although many police officers began to become more detached from the community-engagement side of community policing in order to meet government targets by focusing on *"response duties,"* the role of PCSO was apparently expected by government to fill the gaps. The ACPO later noted their role as the following:

> ...contributing to the policing of neighbourhoods, primarily through highly visible patrol with the purpose of reassuring the public, increasing orderliness in public places and being accessible to communities and partner agencies working at local level. The emphasis of this role, and the powers required to fulfil it, will vary from neighbourhood to neighbourhood and force to force. (ACPO, 2005, p. 6)

Although the role of PCSO might have originally been interpreted by some as an imposition by government on the police service in order to "police on the cheap" (Evans cited by Broster, 2007), their deployment had a distinct focus, along with community policing initiatives, in providing a visible presence in high crime areas in order to reduce crime (Paskell, 2007). As a consequence, these officers are still more generally associated with policing poorer communities that are unable to independently finance crime reduction strategies in order to protect their homes or personal property. As the role was developed as a civilian post, it also opened up opportunities to diverse groups of people who formerly would not have been in a position to be associated with the wider police family because they did not fit into the archetypal profile of a police officer (Cooper et al., 2006; Francis, 2003; Johnston, 2005). This made it possible for individuals with a whole new set of skills and experiences to be introduced into policing. As a result, the role nationally has provided an opportunity for individuals to *test the water first*

---

* Assessments of Policing and Community Safety.

as PCSOs before applying to become police officers, thus supporting government recruitment initiatives for diverse groups (Home Office, 2010, p. 14). Not all recruits, however, saw the PCSO role as a stepping-stone to becoming a police officer, and those have endeavored in the main to develop the role as a focus of support for local people with an almost evangelical zeal. Many have been able to utilize their unique skills to the benefit of particular community groups.

In the Norfolk Constabulary, for example, there is currently a Portuguese-speaking PCSO who not only patrols in districts where Portuguese is spoken in Norfolk, but who has also been able to teach police officers about the Portuguese language and culture to develop more meaningful relationships with local communities. Similar examples of PCSO-led initiatives within community settings can be found in a number of police forces around the country.

Although the role and powers had been clearly defined within the Police Reform Act, the practical application of both powers and duties expected by colleagues of assorted ranks of the police service meant that although some of the PCSOs were absolutely focused on what they *could or couldn't* do, the perceptions of managers and colleagues were on what they *should* or *shouldn't* do. When this cloudy interpretation of duties was mixed with the ambitions of PCSOs who wanted to become more involved in the policing role or the fears of others who did not wish to be perceived as insubordinate, the result was potentially disastrous as some were sent to emergency calls in potentially dangerous circumstances and others were expected to deal with matters that were beyond their remit, such as cutting down the bodies of suicide cases as part of a sudden death investigation (Crisp, 2008, unpublished).

The influence and behaviors associated with the police crime-fighting culture identified by Reiner (2000) were subsequently identified in the actions of some PCSOs, who, in spite of the key expectation of the role to provide a visible presence, were required while on duty to undertake plainclothes surveillance—the sort of role that would have previously been undertaken by qualified detective constables.

It seemed that, as a resource, the willing or coerced PCSO could be used in all manner of ways, and in spite of ACPO guidance about those tasks that were within the remit of the job, a review of the National Police Improvement Agency (NPIA) noted that "this local flexibility has resulted in PCSOs performing certain roles which are not closely aligned to those set out in the guidance" (NPIA, 2008, p. 8). By August 2007, PCSOs were beginning to make an impact fiscally if not physically, which caused the *Daily Mail* newspaper to complain that the Labour government were replacing full-time police with "plastic bobbies" (Leake, 2007), and Jan Berry, the then chair of the Police Federation, to express concerns that instead of being the eyes and ears of the police their increasing presence motivated by cost would result in the deskilling of police and additional policing powers to be necessarily granted to PCSOs.

Notwithstanding, the role has demonstrated its worth to the communities it serves, being identified as partially responsible for the reduction in crime and the increase in public confidence and awareness of community safety (Casey, 2008; Francis, 2003, p. 18; HMIC, 2004a,b; Johnston, 2005). Despite some initial apprehension, the benefit of the civilian–police partnership working has also been seen as valuable by their police partners on the front line (Cooper et al., 2006; Lund, 2004; Wilson, 2004). In September 2007, five years after the introduction of the PCSO role, the NPIA assembled a more nationally applicable list of training requisites, formally introducing the *Wider Police Learning and Development Programme* (WPLDP). These skills were finally recommended as core to PCSO training in the PCSO Review (2008) and subsequently integrated into local training pathways, which provided links to the *Initial Police Learning and Development Programme* (IPLDP). In 2012, in spite of fears that the function of the PCSO could still disappear, there is an acceptance by the police service nationally that the recruitment and training route of the PCSO or Special Constable will facilitate the recruitment of direct entrants to police officer IPLDP training programs.

19.7 The Future

The publication by HMIC of *Policing in Austerity: One Year On* (HMIC, 2012) provides a gloomy forecast of policing in times of global recession and looks at a future in which there will be necessary reductions in staff levels and changes to police structures. In spite of this, the role of the PCSO survives as the report indicates that police forces are beginning to move PCSOs into nonvisible roles that support "areas of greatest harm and risk" (HMIC, 2012, p. 37). Although these changes withdraw them from their original brief of providing a visible uniformed presence in the community, it certainly appears that the police service might now be reluctant to lose this resource. This may, of course, change again if police posts are continued to be at risk. Experienced officers have already been *dispatched* from service by means of Police Regulation 19 and, according to a statement by the Shadow Home Secretary Yvette Cooper, there has been an average of a 6% reduction of frontline policing posts since 2010 (Travis, 2012).

In a recent review of PCSO resources, Cambridgeshire Constabulary note that, in spite of a lack of academic fieldwork into the impact of the PCSO in recent times, they believe that there is no substantive evidence that PCSOs have a positive impact on reducing crime and antisocial behavior (Sutherland, 2014). Their review, however, continues by highlighting the non-measurable benefits of the role, which are still aligned with the core requirement of the post, identifying, in addition to basic policing support, their assistance to vulnerable victims of crime and in outreach activities within local communities, as positive benefits of the job. This research also makes links between public satisfaction and the role, finding an increased level of satisfaction associated with policing overall, which is linked to contact with PCSOs. As the review notes, "any sizeable reduction in PCSO numbers could have a considerable negative impact on overall public satisfaction with the constabulary" (Sutherland, 2014, p. 28).

So what now? Could we now be about to see a radical change to the role and responsibilities of PCSOs? Their success in local communities has been based on their willingness to act in a supporting role for the police and provide a visible reassuring presence with few policing powers. As a result, the competent officers have learned to use their powers of communication and discretion to keep order in a similar way to that found in early policing strategies. There are certainly savings to be made in employing more PCSOs than police officers to police our streets. A ratio of 12 PCSOs could be trained against one police officer according to data gained from a Freedom of Information request (FOI ref 0322/2009 2009). The PCSOs themselves are keen, according to research undertaken by UNISON (UNISON, 2009), to be granted additional policing powers and take on board additional responsibility. They were also successfully deployed in recent civil unrest to calm and reassure areas close to rioting.

Like the review for the Cambridgeshire Constabulary formerly noted, the result of a recent review of the role of the PCSO by Leeds City Council suggests that, although in Leeds the PCSOs community based role is changing, broadening the duties, policing-based powers, and geographical patrol area of the PCSOs, there is no intention to reduce numbers as the role is identified as being valuable to the continuation of community-based policing (Brogden, 2014). In Cambridge, the value of PCSO staff, both within the organization and as ambassadors of the police to other partner agencies and community projects, is seen as inestimable.

In a scenario-based question, set as part of the Cambridgeshire review, police managers were asked about a choice between the recruitment of more PCSOs or fewer police officers. Some managers agreed that it might be better to use PCSO resources as they were less likely to be moved or abstracted to other duties.

From this evidence, it seems inevitable that change will happen, but it is disappointing to think the changes that may be already in the pipeline will necessarily remove the very positive contribution to community policing that PCSOs have already made. There is a difference between PCSOs and police officers, which has made them more valuable to local communities in that their visibility has made a positive impact on reassuring communities about crime without concerns about the force and tensions associated with fighting crime—a role that the police successfully undertakes.

References

ACPO. (2005). *Guidance on Police Community Support Workers.* London: ACPO.

BBC News online. (Sept. 21, 2007). Police defend drowning death case http://news .bbc.co.uk/1/hi/7006412.stm (accessed 1/7/2012).

Berry, G., Izat, J., Mawby, R. C., Walley, L., & Wright, A. (1998). *Practical Police Management* (2nd edn). London: Police Review Publishing.

Berry, J. (2007). Police Federation Community Support Officers. http://www.polfed .org/federationpolicy/CSO.asp (accessed 11/9/12).

Bowling, B. (1999). *Violent Racism: Victimisation, Policing and Social Context.* Oxford: Oxford University Press.

Brogden, A. (2014). Scrutiny Board (Safer and Stronger Communities) Review of the role, number and allocation of PCSOs in Leeds February 2014. http:// www.leeds.gov.uk/docs/Scrutiny%20report-%20review%20of%20PCSOs%20 in%20Leeds.pdf (accessed 5/5/15).

Broster, P. (Sept. 20, 2007). Force hires more plastic police than real bobbies. http:// www.express.co.uk/posts/view/19606/Force-hires-more-plastic-policemen -than-real-bobbies (accessed 6/7/12).

Bryant, L., Dunkerley, D., & Kelland, G. (1985). One of the Boys, *Policing, 1*(4), 236–244.

Button, M. (2002). *Private Policing.* Willan: Exeter.

Casey, L. (2008). *Engaging Communities in Fighting Crime.* London: Cabinet Office of the United Kingdom.

Cooper, C., Anscombe, J., Avenell, J., McLean, F., & Morris, J. (2006). A National Evaluation of Community Support Officers Home Office Research Study No. 297, Home Office.

Cope, N. (2004). Intelligence led policing or policing led intelligence? Integrating volume crime analysis into policing. *British Journal of Criminology, 44*(2).

Coxhead, J. (2009). *The pluralisation of policing: The police private security and public consent.* Lambert Academic Publishing.

Crawford, A., Lister, S., Blackburn, S., & Burnett, J. (2005). *Plural Policing: The Mixed Economy of Visible Patrols in England and Wales.* Bristol: Polity Press.

Crisp, A. (2008). The training needs and requirements of the PCSO. unpublished.

Crisp, A. (2013). The Training and Education of Police Community Support Officers and the Future of British Policing. In P. Stanislas, ed., *International Perspectives of Police Training and Education*, pp. 237–253. Routledge, London.

Francis, I. (2003). Quality Street. Community Support Officers. *Police Review* 30/5/03.

Highmore, S. (1993). *The Integration of Police Officers and Civilian Staff: A Study of Internal Service Quality.* Police Research group. Home Office.

HMIC. (2004a). *Modernising the Police Service: A Thematic Inspection of Workforce Modernisation—The Role, Management and Deployment of Police Staff in the Police Service of England and Wales.* London: Home Office.

HMIC. (2004b). *Workforce Modernisation in Europe Survey.* Home Office: London.

HMIC. (2012). *Policing in Austerity: One Year On*. London: Home Office.

Home Office. (1983). Circular 114.

Home Office. (1995). *Review of Police Core and Ancillary Tasks*. London: Home Office.

Home Office. (1999). *Best Value: Briefing Notes for the Police Service Audit and Inspection*. London: Home Office.

Home Office. (2001). *Policing a New Century, A Blue Print for Reform*. London: Home Office.

Home Office. (2010). *Policing in the 21st Century: Reconnecting Police and the People*. London: TSO.

Howgrave-Graham, H. M. (1947). *Light and Shade at Scotland Yard*. John Murray.

Johnston, L. (2003). From "pluralisation" to the "police extended family": Discourses on the governance of community policing in Britain. *International Journal of the Sociology of Law, 31*, 185–204.

Johnston, L. (2005). From Community to Neighbourhood Policing: Police Community Support Officers and the Police Extended Family. *London Journal of Community and Applied Social Psychology, 15*, 241–254. Wiley.

Joyce, P. (2006). *Criminal Justice*. Cullompton, Willan Publishers.

Leake, C. (2007). Labours 'plastic bobbies' to replace full time police. *Daily Mail* http://www.dailymail.co.uk/news/article-473229/Labours-plastic-bobbies-replace-time-police.html#ixzz0ZrEYklt2 (accessed 1/5/12).

Loveday, B. (2004). Literature Review for HMIC Thematic Inspection on Civilianisation.

Lund, S. (2004). Forces are choosing to pay for CSOs. *Police Review*, Vol. 12, March.

Maguire, M. (2002). Crime statistics: The 'data explosion' and its implications. In M. Maguire et al. (Eds.), *The Oxford Handbook of Criminology: 3rd Edition*. Oxford: OUP.

Manifesto of the British Labour Party. (1977). http://www.labour-party.org.uk/manifestos/1997/1997-labour-manifesto.shtml/ (accessed 5/7/12).

Manning, P. (1977). *Police Work: The Social Organization of Policing*. Cambridge, MA: MIT Press.

Neyroud, P. (2011). *Review of Police Leadership and Training*. Home Office.

NPIA. (2008). Neighbourhood policing programme. *PCSO Review* July 2008, NPIA.

PA Consulting Group. (2001). Diary of a Police Officer. Police Research series Paper 149. London: Home Office.

Parliament of the United Kingdom. (2002). *Police Reform Act 2002*. London: Parliament of the United Kingdom.

Parrett, L. (1998). *Past, present and future role of civilian personnel in the police service of England and Wales*. University of East Anglia.

Paskell, C. (2007). Plastic police or community support? The role of police community support officers within low-income neighbourhoods. *European Urban and Regional Studies, 14*, 349–361.

Rayner, C. (2000). Bullying at work in the Police Section membership of UNISON. London: UNISON.

Reiner, R. (2000). *The Politics of the Police. Third Edition*. Oxford: Oxford University Press.

Shearing & Wood. (2003). Governing security for common goods. *International Journal of the Sociology of Law, 31*(3), 205–225.

Sheehy Report. (1993). *Inquiry into Police Responsibilities and Rewards*, Cm 2280.I, II, London: HMSO.

Sutherland, J. (2014). The PCSO Review—An Evaluation of the Role, Value and Establishment of Police Community Support Officers within Cambridgeshire Constabulary. http://www.cambs.police.uk/about/foi/policies/The%20PCSO%20Review%20Redacted%20Version.pdf (accessed 5/5/15).

Taverne Report. (1966). *Police Manpower, Equipment and Efficiency*. Home Office, London.

Travis, A. (2012). Police jobs: Nearly 6,800 frontline posts have been cut since general election. *The Guardian*. http://www.guardian.co.uk/uk/2012/sep/10/frontline-police-jobs-cut-election (accessed 13/9/12).

UNISON. (2000). Police staff bullying. Report no. 1777, London.

UNISON. (2009). Survey of PCSO opinions for channel 4 dispatches programme. Sunday, September 20, 2009. Cops on the Cheap Channel 4 Dispatches. http://www.channel4.com/programmes/dispatches/articles/cops-on-the-cheap-survey-results (accessed 6/7/12).

Unwin, S. (2006). Community Support officers: A force for the futures. A study into the training and employment of Police Community Support Officers http://www.national-pcsos.co.uk/JOSSMAN2.pdf (accessed 6/7/12).

Waddington, P. A. J. (1999). Police (Canteen) Sub-Culture. *British Journal of Criminology, 39*(2).

Walklate, S. (1996). Equal opportunities and the future of policing, in F. Leishman, B. Loveday & S. Savage (Eds.), *Core Issues in Policing*. London: Longmans.

Williams, R. (2004). The Management of crime scene examination in relation to the investigation of burglary and vehicle crime. Home Office online report 24/04 http://library.npia.police.uk/docs/hordsolr/rdsolr2404.pdf (accessed 6/7/12).

Wilson, J. (2004). Training Support. What training are forces giving to community support officers across the country? *Police Review* 23/4/04.

Windsor, T. P. (2012). Independent Review of Police Officer and Staff Remuneration and Conditions Final Report.

Wood, J. (2004, March). Cultural change in the governance of security, *Policing and Society, 1*, 31–48.

Part-Time and Reserve Law Enforcement
The Texas Experience

20

NATHAN R. MORAN
ROBERT D. HANSER

Contents

20.1 Introduction

This chapter assesses reserve and part-time law enforcement agencies within the state of Texas and their role in corresponding state, county, and municipal agencies. State and local laws are reviewed that affect the use and function of these reserve and part-time law enforcement individuals.

Part-time law enforcement personnel appear to be no different than their full-time counterparts; however, there are some minor differences that separate the two employment distinctions. These primarily consist of certain restrictions that Texas places on reserve and part-time law enforcement regarding their status and the number of hours they work monthly.

The importance of having law enforcement was evident following the state's inception. Throughout the times of the Wild West, there was a plethora of significant criminal activity, such as bank robberies, stagecoach heists, and shootouts. The only law enforcement bodies to speak of were comprised of ex-cons and gunmen themselves. During this time, government regulations overseeing the installation and maintenance of police agencies were nonexistent. The current criminal justice system has evolved considerably since those times. Modern law enforcement has been professionalized by maintaining a governing body in charge of creating laws and standards controlling the accreditation of licensing and commissioning. This chapter begins with the history of the Texas Commission on Law Enforcement Officers Education and Standards (TCLEOSE).

20.2 History of TCLEOSE

TCLEOSE was created on August 30, 1965, when Senate Bill 236, of the 59th legislative session, passed Article 4413. However, there were no appropriations for funding at this time. During the 60th legislative session, on September 1, 1967, Wallace D. Beasley was appointed director, and there was the addition of four employees. The addition of employees brought funding for the commission. Glenn H. McLaughlin served as the first chairman of the commission, and there was the addition of three levels of peace officers: beginner, intermediate, and advanced. By September 20, 1968, the commission had awarded its first certificates to peace officers. During the 61st legislation, on September 1, 1969, the commission amended the original act so that all peace officers appointed on or after September 1, 1970, must meet certain employment and certification standards set by the commission. Peace officers who were active prior to this date were grandfathered in by this commission. This time period also saw numerous police academies being established (Texas State Senate, 1965).

By January 1, 1973, the basic peace officer course increased its requirements to 240 hours, and the basic reserve peace officer course was created with a 70-hour requirement. House Bill 1203 was passed on September 1, 1975, during the 64th legislation. The bill required the reporting of appointments in training. Additionally, House Bill 1205 established disqualification for felony conviction. By January 1, 1976, it was required that peace and reserve officers have medical examinations prior to licensure, and the commission recommended psychological examinations as well. House Bill 1396 was established on September 1, 1977, and changed the probationary period from one year to six months for peace and reserve officer training. On December 11, 1979, there was a rule put in place that prohibited peace and reserve officers from being appointed if convicted of driving while intoxicated (DWI) or driving while under the influence of drugs (DUID) within 10 years of conviction.

By January 1, 1981, requirements for the basic peace officer course had increased from 240 to 320 hours. On September 1, 1984, the commission stated that grandfathered licenses had expired if the officer left the agency on or before this date. The commission also declared that reserve officers with degrees were required to test for compliance through training. On August 25, 1985, the commission passed a measure stating basic peace officer certificates, basic reserve certificates, and permanent licenses were to be issued if an officer's training and exam were passed and he or she had an L-1 on file. September 1, 1985, brought on several changes to the licensing process. For instance, after this date, there were no more temporary licenses for peace officers, and there were requirements stating that licensees must be drug free. Additionally, the minimum age was increased to 21 for peace and reserve officers, and the basic peace officer course increased from 320 to 400 training hours. Reserve officers who had been trained as such were grandfathered in to intermediate reserve status; also, reserves who completed the basic peace officer course and passed the licensing exam were issued basic peace officer certificates and issued permanent peace officer licenses. By November 12, 1985, reserve training became credible toward peace officer certification. On February 1, 1987, the commission passed a rule that required out-of-state reserve training for licensing if the other state had a certification or licensing requirement. On September 15, 1989, the commission passed a measure that called for holders of an inactive peace officer license to reactivate their license before working as a reserve officer.

The decade of the 1990s brought even more changes to the commission's licensing procedures. On September 1, 1993, agencies that appoint reserve officers, county jailers, or public security officers may provide training and education in civil rights, racial sensitivity, and cultural diversity within 24 months. On December 1, 1994, requirements for reserve officer certificates increased to 228 hours for basic peace officers, 190 hours for intermediate peace officers, and 142 hours for advanced peace officers.

On January 1, 2002, the basic reserve peace officer course was discontinued. The intermediate and advanced reserve courses were cut next on January 1, 2004. In September 2004, crisis intervention training (CIT) and standardized field sobriety testing (SFST) increased the basic peace officer certification training to 618 hours. House Bill 1438 was passed in 2005 giving continuing education credit to peace officers who served at least 12 months on active military duty within a 24-month cycle. Additionally, House Bill 2677 required the terminating agency to identify the reason for terminating a police officer. On June 15, 2007, House Bill 486 was passed, and it allowed the commission to establish uniform, continuing education for police chiefs. House Bill 2580 was passed in September of 2009 establishing a police officer employment opportunity website by the Texas Workforce Commission. Additionally, House Bill 2068 required retired police officers to obtain an identification card.

20.3 Licensing Requirements for Police in Texas

In 1969, the 61st legislature required that all peace officers be certified by the commission prior to appointment. This took effect beginning on September 1, 1970. The amendment also authorized the commission to establish minimum requirements for certification. However, law enforcement officers elected under the Texas Constitution are exempt from these minimum requirements.

In 1979, the 66th legislature required the commission to certify county jailers. The statute provided one year for county jailers to acquire the necessary basic jail training.

In 1983, the 68th legislature enacted SB 155, requiring the commission to prescribe the content of examinations and conduct examinations for each license issued by the commission.

In 1987, the 70th legislature enacted authority for the appointment of public security officers. These consisted of persons employed or appointed as armed security officers by the state or by a political subdivision of the state but not security officers employed by private security companies that contract with the state or a political subdivision.

In 1987, the 70th legislature required the commission to adopt rules providing for the accreditation of telecommunicator training programs and acknowledgement or certification of telecommunication operators (1701.405). This also required that a telecommunicator complete the required training, the basic telecommunications certification course, within one year of the date of appointment. Agencies with 20 or fewer employees or agencies that do not perform 24-hour law enforcement services were exempted. Telecommunicators are not issued a license, but they do receive an acknowledgement letter from the commission.

In 1997, the 75th legislature amended Section 511.0092(f)(2) of the government code, requiring that employees of counties, municipalities, and private vendors have a formal contract with the respective jurisdiction in order to hold federal prisoners and prisoners from jurisdictions other than Texas must be licensed by the commission. These jailers must meet the same requirements as county jailers.

20.4 Texas Local Government Code 341.012
Police Reserve Force

In 2005, the Texas State Senate revised the Texas Occupations Code Title 10 Chapter 1701 to comprehensively outline the general provisions for all law enforcement officers working within the State of Texas (Texas State Senate, 2005a).

Texas Local Government Code 341.012 regulates the creation of reserve law enforcement personnel. It reads as follows:

> The governing body of a municipality may provide for the establishment of a police reserve force. The governing body may also establish guidelines, qualifications and standards of training for members of the reserve force. The members of the reserve force shall be appointed by the Police Chief and serve at their

discretion. The reserve force may be called into duty by the Police Chief when deemed necessary to preserve the peace and enforce the law. A member of the reserve force that was not a peace officer described in the Code of Criminal Procedure article 2.12 may only do so during the discharge of official duties. An appointment to the reserve force must be approved by the governing body before that said person may carry a weapon or conduct themselves as a peace officer. A reserve peace officer may only act as a supplemental entity to an active full-time peace officer. A reserve peace officer isn't eligible for participation in any program provided by the governing body that is considered a financial benefit of full-time employment benefit even if a reserve peace officer is considered a peace officer under Criminal Procedure 2.12. Additionally, they aren't eligible to participate in any pension fund created for the benefit of full-time peace officers. A reserve peace officer also isn't exempt from chapter 1702 occupations code where the authority is given to the Mayor of a type A general law municipality to summon a special police force under section 341.011. (Texas State Senate, 2005b)

20.5 How to Become a Reserve Peace Officer

To become a reserve peace officer, one must be very direct and specific in search of a sponsoring agency. Because not all police agencies utilize a reserve police force, the first thing a prospective reserve officer must do is find an agency that utilizes reserve peace officers and research what the organization's requirements are to become a reserve officer. The first step in finding reserve police work would be to contact smaller agencies within a prospective officer's jurisdiction and inquire if they are hiring reserve officers because larger municipalities rarely utilize reserve police officers. However, there are several different avenues to find reserve work. These include county sheriff departments, the constable's office, and school district police agencies.

The next step in becoming a reserve officer is to obtain the proper training. This can prove to be difficult in some cases because reserve officer training is scarce. However, a prospective candidate can obtain training from a full-time police academy at a local college and apply for reserve positions after becoming licensed. After completion of the academy, one must take the TCLEOSE state peace officer licensing examination. The exam normally consists of a 200-question test that covers many different areas, such as the Texas State Penal Code, Texas Traffic Code, Family Code, and additional topics deemed important by TCLEOSE. A score of 70% is required to pass the exam. Prospective reserve officers can take the exam without being employed with a police agency, but they are responsible for locating an agency to hold their license to maintain a commission. In the meantime, TCLEOSE will keep the prospect's license in an inactive status until a suitable police commission can be found to sponsor their commission. However, a prospective reserve officer is required to maintain 20 hours of continuing education a year. Once a suitable police agency is found, the prospective reserve officer will apply and submit to an interview; a polygraph; and physical agility, psychological, and drug tests just like a full-time officer would.

After being hired by an agency, it may require the reserve officer to enter into a training program for the position he or she will be placed in. An entry-level position for any police officer will typically be in the patrol division. However, if the applicant has specialized skills or training, he or she can be placed in a different division, such as the forensic or investigative division. Initially, reserve officers are assigned to a full-time officer during their training and monthly work assignment, especially if the reserve officer is assigned to patrol duties. In this case, the full-time officer will accompany the reserve officer and assist with traffic stops, report writing, and the filing of charges. In the case of an officer having a specialized skill, the reserve officer may find him- or herself working independently under the supervision of a full-time sergeant or lieutenant.

The annual continuing education requirements of a reserve police officer are the same as a full-time police officer. Every year, officers need to obtain 20 continuing education hours per year or 40 continuing education hours per two-year period. The reserve officer may opt to take in-service training at his or her local agency, in-service courses at the local college, or online and correspondence training from an independent authorized training center.

20.6 Duty Requirements for Reserve Officers

Most agencies that utilize reserve officers require a minimum of 16 hours of work per month. However, most reserve officers work 40 or more hours a month. Most reserve officers receive the majority of their hours on weekend shifts similar to the National Guard and reserve military units. Having said this, there are certain occasions when a reserve officer may work during the week. The majority of reserves are utilized to augment the presence of officers during the busiest times of the week although reserve officers who are working under a specialized detail or investigative unit can be called to service at any point during the week. Reserve officers working these specialized jobs typically log the most hours. Usually, reserve officers aren't paid for the minimum 16 hours they are required to work per month because the constable or chief typically uses these hours in exchange for holding the reserve's peace officer commission. Furthermore, the agency that sponsors the officer may require the reserve to be on call for special assignments.

20.7 Difference between a Reserve and Full-Time Officer

Although the license and qualifications of reserve and full-time officers are exactly the same, there is a significant difference in how an agency views the two different distinctions. Duty assignments are one of the biggest differences between the two distinctions. In most agencies, reserve officers are prohibited from working alone, and full-time officers frequently work independently. Additionally, reserves aren't normally assigned to specialized divisions that require extensive training or long-term investigations because of obvious time constraints. However, there are rare cases in which a reserve officer is a retired homicide or forensic specialist who could be enlisted for these specialized skills. Furthermore, a full-time officer is considered to be on duty 24 hours a day, and a reserve is only on duty during his or her assigned monthly hours.

Although full-time officers receive a salary, medical insurance, and a retirement plan, reserve officers usually don't receive any compensation or employee benefits. Reserve and full-time officers are also promoted on a different scale. However, if a reserve is promoted to supervisor, he or she will still have authority over full-time officers under his or her command. Usually an agency will not allow a reserve officer to supervise a full-time officer unless there are extenuating circumstances.

Some may ask why reserve officers would submit themselves to all of the risks and dangers associated with police work if they don't receive compensation and benefits. The answer is a simple one. Those who register and pay for police academy training out of pocket need to be sponsored by an agency so their license doesn't expire. Additionally, being a reserve officer is a way to gain important experience before obtaining full-time employment. For instance, many smaller agencies require the officer to have two or more years of experience in the field before they will hire someone on full time. They do this because small agencies lack the funding to provide adequate training to new officers. After gaining valuable reserve experience, a reserve officer can gain full-time employment without putting the small agency in a financial bind. Retired, full-time officers are also motivated by becoming a reserve officer because they want to retain their peace officer license. Furthermore, many retired officers have a void left by the absence of police work, camaraderie, and brotherhood. This can be marginally filled by working the minimum 16 monthly hours required by a reserve officer.

20.8 Extra Employment

Extra employment is an area of great debate throughout law enforcement. Many agencies attempt to regulate the number of hours that an officer can work while off duty. The majority of agencies limit the amount of time that can be worked while off duty to 40 hours of extra employment a week. This is done for obvious safety reasons. Officers who overexert themselves are at an elevated risk of mistakes and erroneous judgment, putting themselves and their fellow officers at risk. Having said this, there is a large number of reserve officers who take advantage of having their peace officer license and seek out additional employment, sometimes even working 40-plus hours extra. In many cases, it is a necessity because they're essentially working 16 unpaid hours for the agency holding their license.

There are a few counties that prohibit reserve officers from working off-duty, police-related jobs within their jurisdiction. Harris County is one of these counties. Harris County is the fourth largest county in the United States and is home to the fourth largest city in the United States: Houston. The district judge within Harris County declared that it was illegal for reserve officers to work off-duty assignments because of lobbying from full-time officers. These full-time officers feel that they should only be considered for additional, lucrative, off-duty work because they are out in the field enduring the risks of police work at a much higher rate than reserve officers. However, surrounding counties outside Harris County allow reserve officers to work extra police-related jobs. If their agency will allow it, these are the only extra employment opportunities for reserve officers in Harris County.

Certain agencies require that an officer obtain a generic peace officer uniform before working extra employment opportunities. This is done to eliminate representation of the agency while the officer is working these off-duty jobs. The topic of extra employment can be a hot-button issue because of the lucrative nature of these jobs. Officers can normally receive anywhere from $25 to $50 an hour to work these extra employment opportunities. Critics of this type of employment believe that officers shouldn't be paid extra money for a job that they were sworn to do. On the other hand, supporters feel that officers are vastly underpaid for the service they provide to the public, and the additional compensation is justified because of the dangerous nature of police work.

Most opponents of reserves working extra jobs insist that the lack of experience by the reserves puts everyone at an elevated risk of negative incidents occurring. Skeptics feel that full-time officers have the day-to-day experience, which has equipped them with the proper tools to deal with a multitude of different situations, and reserve officers lack these qualities. But this argument weakens when police retirees are introduced into the extra employment equation. This is a topic of debate, and there are reserve peace officer associations lobbying on behalf of reserve officers. However, their effectiveness has been called into question.

Aside from the addition of extra pay, there are some intangible benefits for police officers working extra employment opportunities. In some cases, officers will accrue retirement benefits and social security points by working these part-time jobs. Although in jurisdictions that don't allow reserve officers to work extra employment, these benefits don't apply. There are also other extra employment opportunities that are not police related, such as airport ramp agents, real estate agents, and other various jobs, based on their skills and education. It is important to consider that even though an officer may be working outside law enforcement, officers must respond to crime in their presence.

20.9 Model Deputy Program

The Model Deputy Program was devised by Harris Constable Office Precinct 9. This program is designed to employ reserve deputies on an as-needed, "fill in" basis. Precinct 6 employs reserve deputies with an hourly wage to work special assignments within the agency. Typical assignments include DWI task force roundup or any special event at which a large crowd is anticipated. The program was designed to augment the full-time deputy force and to prevent reassigning patrol staff to special events. This helps provide an adequate special event officer presence without weakening officer patrols and beat assignments (Harris County Constable Precinct 6, 2016).

As with many government programs, there is opposition to this measure. Full-time officers are at the forefront of opposition to this measure. The full-time officers in Precinct 6 feel that special event employment should be allocated to off-duty, full-time deputies as overtime. However, this is a less financially feasible argument because overtime would be paid at time and a half, and reserves would be working at a base hourly wage. It is mandatory that all special event positions be filled because they are funded by a federal government grant. Additionally, it is beneficial for Precinct 6 to maximize grant money efficiently to continue federal funding of police initiatives in the future.

References

Harris County Constable Precinct 6. (2016). *Reserve Deputy Program*. Houston: Harris County Constable Precinct 6.

Texas State Senate. (1965). *Senate Bill 236: The Texas Commission on Law Enforcement*. Austin: Texas State Senate.

Texas State Senate. (2005a). *Texas Occupations Code Title 10 Chapter 1701 Law Enforcement Officers*. Austin: Texas State Senate.

Texas State Senate. (2005b). *Texas Local Government Code Title 11A Chapter 341 Municipal Law Enforcement*. Austin: Texas State Senate.

NYPD's Retiree Mobilization Plan
Keeping Retired Officers Active

21

THERESA C. TOBIN

Contents

21.1 Introduction

After the tragic events of the terrorist attacks on September 11, 2001, people's altruism hit a peak. After witnessing two hijacked planes crash into New York City's Twin Towers, accounting for the death of 2,753 people at the World Trade Center site, many people volunteered and offered a multitude of services and goods across New York City.* Police, fire, and emergency medical service departments from across the nation, and some from around the globe, sent resources, including their personnel, to help first with rescue operations and later with recovery operations. Out of the 36,000 units of blood donated to the New York Blood Center on September 11 and the days immediately thereafter, only 258 units were actually used.† The death toll for first responders on that day stands at 343 firefighters and paramedics, 37 Port Authority police officers, and 23 New York City Police Department (NYPD) officers, not including the hundreds of first responders who have died as a direct result of World Trade Center health-related illness.

Although volunteers came from every walk of life and every ethnic group, religious denomination, and nationality, the impetus of the NYPD's efforts in the aftermath of September 11 to develop a program to utilize retired sworn

---

* http://nymag.com/news/articles/wtc/1year/numbers.htm
† http://www.cnn.com/2013/07/27/us/september-11-anniversary-fast-facts

members of the NYPD in the aftereffects of a human-made tragedy or natural disaster are thoroughly explained and examined. Manpower levels in the NYPD over the past two decades has fluctuated between 34,000 and 42,000 uniformed members. Given that NYPD officers can retire after 20 years of service, the number of retirees is far greater than those on active status. During the first quarter of 2016, there were more than 43,000 retired NYPD officers living in the New York City region and around the country. This pool of people is probably one of the most highly trained, talented, and skilled groups available for possible deployment during a critical incident. It is also true that the vast majority of retired members of police departments nationwide enjoy maintaining a connection with both active and retired members of the law enforcement community.

Many retired NYPD members arrived at the World Trade Center site to help and utilize their skills, accumulated after many years as active officers with the NYPD, only to be turned away. This was, in part, because there was no formal way of identifying retired members and their skills and in what capacity they could be most helpful. As a result, planning to create and institutionalize a program was initiated, whereby the NYPD could reach out and activate a response plan in which retirees could be a part of the NYPD's response to critical incidents.

The NYPD eventually established this program and called it the Retiree Mobilization Plan (RMP).* Using the retired members' monthly pension statements, the NYPD wrote to all retired members, explaining to them that they could elect to volunteer their services during critical incidents once they officially registered with the department. Additionally, existing police fraternal organizations and retiree clubs were contacted and requested to inform their members. A portal on the NYPD's website, titled "Actively Retired," was created specifically for retired members. Via this portal, a retired member, once logged in and authenticated, can register for the RMP and identify skills he or she possesses for inclusion in the database. The Actively Retired website is a secure website, viewable only by RMP volunteers, not all retired members. The website is used to disseminate information and procedures for activation. Once retired members are registered on the website, they are given an RMP identification card, which features the retired officer's name, employee identification number, and a bar code. This card, along with their NYPD identification card, must be presented at all volunteer mobilizations. An NYPD duffle bag, which includes a size-specific RMP shirt, fluorescent traffic vest, baseball cap, whistle, and flashlight, is given to each NYPD RMP volunteer.

The activation of the RMP is directed by the police commissioner. Once it is activated, a series of procedural steps is set in motion. The chief of personnel, who oversees the coordination of the RMP, confers with the chief of

---

* Operations Order 16, 3/14/06, New York City Police Department.

department (the highest ranking member of the NYPD) to determine the number of retirees, any specific skills required, and duration of the retiree mobilization. Also determined at this time are the report locations, any duties and specific responsibilities to be assigned to the retirees, and any pertinent instruction to be given to them at the staging area. The identities of qualified registered volunteers that meet specific skills are obtained by utilizing the actively retired website database.

The locations of the primary staging areas for responding RMP volunteers to report to are based on several factors. Three locations within New York City were selected as primary staging locations for retirees. These areas were based on the capacity and convenience of responding retirees. Those retirees who lived in the Bronx and north of New York City were asked to respond to the NYPD's outdoor shooting range in the Bronx. For those RMP members who live in Brooklyn or Queens or on Long Island, they are asked to report to Floyd Bennett Field in Brooklyn, where the NYPD's special operations division (i.e., the aviation unit, harbor unit, and other highly specialized units) and driver training school are located. Last, those retirees who lived in Manhattan, Staten Island, or south of New York City were asked to report to NYPD headquarters, located in downtown Manhattan.

When retired members of the service are requested to volunteer and are flying into an area airport, the location of the airport determines the staging area the volunteer reports to; for example, if a volunteer is responding from Florida but arriving at JFK International Airport, that volunteer reports to the Brooklyn staging location site. Although it is generally envisioned that one or two primary staging areas would be activated based on the size and the scope of the mobilization, the chief of personnel may also designate other staging areas as needed and as the situation dictates.

21.2 Notification of RMP Volunteers

The primary notification mechanism is to notify RMP members via phone and e-mail, and if these services are disrupted or disabled, retired volunteers are notified via radio and televised broadcasts. A telephone blast is sent to the selected RMP volunteers as well as to their e-mail addresses, including the date, time, and location of the staging area. The notification also requests the retired volunteers to call a designated RMP hotline or e-mail the Actively Retired website, indicating whether they are able to respond.

As part of the NYPD's emergency incident response (i.e., NIMS) protocol, it is the NYPD's responsibility to provide adequate staffing to each of the activated staging areas to verify the identity, skills, and licenses of all responding volunteers upon their arrival as well as transporting the retired volunteers between the staging areas and the deployment locations.

The responding RMP volunteer must be registered on the Actively Retired website and must possess both the RMP identification card and the official NYPD retiree identification card in order to participate in RMP activities. A list of all responding volunteers is maintained, including the names, addresses, cell phone numbers, and emergency contact numbers. If a volunteer is from out of state, his or her temporary lodging location is obtained.

21.3 Deploying RMP Personnel

Once all properly identified RMP members are placed on an assignment sheet, which indicates their deployment locations and assignments, RMP volunteers are sent out to the locations as directed by the NYPD's chief of department, the highest ranking uniformed officer in the agency. Each retired volunteer is required to wear the appropriate volunteer shirt as well as any equipment deemed necessary and to carry their required identification. The staging area remains activated throughout the operational period.

The incident command staff is responsible for the appropriate utilization and assignment of all RMP volunteers. Their primary functions are in support positions and under no circumstances are the volunteers placed into assignments requiring enforcement action.

At the conclusion of the operational period and upon determination by the incident command staff, RMP volunteers who are no longer needed or whose tour of duty has been satisfied are transported back to the staging area. The general rule is that the tour of duty for an RMP volunteer is not to exceed eight hours unless the police commissioner directs it and if it is agreed upon with the volunteer. There is not a minimum amount of tour expectation for retired volunteers; a volunteer may choose to dismiss him- or herself from an assignment at any time after a notification to a ranking officer on the scene, who will ensure the proper notifications are made. It is the duty of the staff of the NYPD personnel bureau to ensure and verify that all deployed volunteers have returned and are accounted for based on the original roster sheets. After this verification, volunteers are dismissed. It is the responsibility of the incident command post to account for RMP volunteers at all times.

Assigned staff from the NYPD personnel bureau is responsible, upon conclusion of the operational period, to prepare a detailed report containing the following information:

1. The number of notifications sent to registered volunteers
2. The number of volunteers who indicated they would respond, but did not report for duty
3. The total number of actual volunteers who responded and are deployed

To acknowledge the participation of the volunteers during a critical incident, certificates of appreciation, signed by the NYPD police commissioner, are prepared for all RMP volunteers.

21.4 Issues for Consideration

Several issues of concern have been raised by RMP volunteers. The focus of these concerns involved injury or death occurring as a result of participating in a mobilization resulting from a response to a critical incident or large-scale emergency. It was eventually determined that Section 23(5) of the New York State Defense Emergency Act authorizes the police commissioner to organize, recruit, and train individuals to act as volunteers in matters of civil defense, including critical incidents, large-scale events, and natural or manmade disasters.* And if a volunteer is injured or dies while acting as an agent for the NYPD, medical coverage and other benefits are provided[†] under the same law that covers the NYPD's auxiliary police officers, a volunteer reserve police force within the NYPD Patrol Services Bureau. Volunteers or their beneficiaries are eligible to apply for benefits, including hospitalization and medical coverage, lost wages, and funeral and survivor benefits should death result in the course of the volunteer service. In addition, New York City General Municipal Law section 50-k includes as an "employee" a volunteer expressly authorized to participate in a city-sponsored volunteer program.[‡] This effectively extends the representation and indemnification of retirees should they be identified in any subsequent civil action so long as the individuals are acting within the scope of the volunteer program and not engaged in any action that involves intentional wrongdoing or reckless conduct. This provision applies to claims for property damage or personal injury involving NYPD vehicles that a volunteer has been authorized to operate.

21.5 RMP Exercises and Drills

After the initial orientation seminar at police headquarters, the personnel bureau holds several seminars to certify retired members in the Citywide Incident Management System (CIMS) based on the National Incident Command model. CIMS was created post–9/11 under federal mandate and

---

* 2006 New York Code - Defense Emergency Act 1951 784/51
† New York New York City Administrative Code (new) - Chapter 1 - § 14-147 Workers' Compensation for Members of Auxiliary Police
‡ www.nyc.gov/html/doh/downloads/pdf/em/mrc-liability-info.pdf

establishes command and control of critical incidents involving terrorism, weapons of mass destruction, and natural disasters.

A number of other exercises have been held for RMP volunteers. One exercise was a mock mobilization, which tested the RMP notification system as well as the check-in procedures and staging areas. The training, conducted by the NYPD's Emergency Service Unit (ESU), focused on procedures utilized by the Federal Emergency Management Agency (FEMA) and the Urban Search and Rescue (US&R) teams that conduct searches at scenes of disasters. Part of the training was to show retirees the search techniques and the markings that are used by the US&R teams should the retirees respond during an emergency for which US&R teams are deployed. "Structural triage" is used to identify, assess, and mark buildings in the area of the incident and serve to inform members of the status of each location. The markings inform US&R responders of the presence of hazardous materials, dead human remains, live victims being extricated, and the results of searches of the location. The Search Assessment Marking System was also explained and illustrated as it identifies the teams conducting the search, time of search, and the final status painted on the location. The training also reviewed the proper equipment and procedures for decontamination at disaster scenes.

On another occasion, a different training exercise was held at the NYPD's firearms and tactics section located in the Bronx, another predesignated mobilization point. RMP volunteers received training on FEMA procedures in the organization, site layout, resource accountability, safety, and demobilization of points of distribution (POD). A more recent RMP drill was conducted at a New York City community college to illustrate the latest techniques of cardiopulmonary resuscitation and other medical first aid measures.

21.6 RMP Mobilizations

In October 2013, Hurricane Sandy, which made landfall as a Category 2 storm, forced the closure of all three New York City area airports and the subway and commuter transit network, caused more than 110 homes to burn to the ground in Queens, and resulted in the flooding of midtown and lower Manhattan and most coastal neighborhoods. On November 1, 2012, 4.8 million customers remained without power in 15 states and the District of Columbia.* This situation caused the first activation of the

* www.cnn.com/2013/07/13world/americas/hurricane-sandy-fast-facts/

RMP program on November 2, 2012. The NYPD sent out the following e-mail blast:

> Dear Retirees:
> Due to the aftermath of Hurricane Sandy, the Police Commissioner has ACTIVATED the Department's Retiree Mobilization Plan effective immediately. This disaster has affected the whole tri-state area, and if you are able to assist in any way please contact the Personnel Bureau... The e-mail should contain a good contact number and location/Patrol Bureau you can assist in.
> Respectfully,
> Personnel Bureau*

Members reported to Miller Field on Staten Island and met personnel from the mayor's office. A temporary headquarters was established for members of the RMP to check in, and detail rosters were prepared and forwarded to police headquarters. RMP volunteers were also sent to two other locations in Brooklyn and Queens. The mobilization remained active for two weeks.

21.7 Conclusion

The NYPD's RMP has proven to be a successful program that has been effectively implemented for engaging retired members in the event of a critical incident. The talent, skills, and abilities of this cohort of professionals has resulted in the development of a highly professional cadre. The experience each retiree volunteer brings to a situation is immense given the multitude of practical experiences and qualifications. In the beginning of 2016, the NYPD RMP program had approximately 3,000 volunteers. Both the RMP program and the large complement of NYPD auxiliary police officers provide an invaluable set of resources to the NYPD should tragedy or crisis impact New York City in the future.

* RMP e-mail message sent to RMP volunteers, November 2, 2012.

Personal Reflection and Insight

V

An Enchanting and Captivating Story of an Essex (United Kingdom) Special Constable

22

GEORGE W. COOK

Contents

Name: George Cook, MBE
Joined Volunteer Police: December 1963
Retired: October 2010
Police Agency: Essex (United Kingdom) Police

22.1 This Is My Story: George Cook

My two elder brothers became regular police officers, a career that I had intended to follow. Sadly, when I applied to join, I did not pass the very strict eyesight test. I was devastated by this and was advised by the recruiting sergeant to apply to join the Special Constabulary with the hope that my eyesight might improve over time.

I applied and was successful in becoming a probationer special constable in the Southend-on-Sea Borough Police Force in December 1963. This was an independent police force in the County of Essex that had been established in 1914. In the 1960s, the Southend-on-Sea Borough Police was the envy of most other UK police forces because the local council made sufficient finances available to the police to ensure that they had excellent equipment. For example, the Southend Police had tailor-made uniforms—unheard of in most other British police forces—and they also had Jaguar cars as patrol vehicles. There was a waiting list to join the Southend Borough Police with applicants coming from all over the country. The Southend Police merged with the Essex Police in 1969 to become the Essex and Southend-on-Sea

Joint Constabulary. This name was changed to the Essex Police in 1974. I was proud to have marched alongside regular colleagues during the final parade of the Southend-on-Sea Constabulary prior to its amalgamation with Essex Police.

When I initially joined the Special Constabulary, our uniforms and equipment—that is, whistle, truncheon, and handcuffs—were identical to those of our regular colleagues. The primary difference was that special constables had shoulder flashes (i.e., patches) stating "Special Constabulary." Some members of the public rather foolishly called us "hobby bobbies" and thought we could not arrest them; they soon learned that we had the same powers as our regular colleagues. These flashes were removed a few years later. Today, both regular and special officers wear the same uniforms and receive identical defensive skills training and pertinent equipment. The majority of police officers in the United Kingdom are unarmed. I support this view. We have armed officers deployed in high-powered vehicles available 24/7 if we need them.

One of my brothers was a regular (i.e., full-time) police officer based at police headquarters in Southend, so I had to serve at another police station in the borough, that is, Westcliff-on-Sea. My other brother was a regular London Metropolitan Police Officer. In those days, "initial" training for probationer members of the Special Constabulary consisted of 10 lectures delivered by a regular sergeant. I, like most special constables, gained knowledge and skills by going on duty with experienced regular and special colleagues.

On my first duty, I was introduced to the special inspector who advised what was expected of me. He then introduced me to a special sergeant who became my mentor for the next year. In those days, when on patrol, we did not have radios, and our only communication with police headquarters was conducted via telephones in static police posts or through scheduled meetings with regular or special supervising officers. If you did not appear at the appointed time, either at the police post or agreed upon meeting place, you were in serious trouble. After a few months of going on duty in the company of experienced colleagues, I was allowed to patrol on my own. Having said that, at night we patrolled in pairs.

Special constables were not generally liked by regular police officers in the early 1960s because the regulars were not well paid and special officers were seen by some as a form of cheap labor. This view among many regular officers prevailed until their pay was substantially increased several years later. During this period, I persevered; went on duty at least three or four times per week, including most Friday and Saturday evenings when the police were at their busiest due to public order situations; and was eventually accepted by the majority of regular officers at Westcliff Police Station as a colleague. I still had hoped to become a regular officer in due course.

During my first three years, all duties were carried out on foot, which included many traffic control duties, that is, standing in the middle of busy junctions controlling the traffic by well-practiced hand signals. This could be quite exciting if an emergency vehicle with its bell ringing was on a call and traveling on the wrong side of the road. One soon learned how to deal with such situations, albeit sometimes I had to explain to irate drivers why I had waved vehicles forward from two different directions nearly causing them to crash into each other.

Southend-on-Sea is a seaside resort about 40 miles from London, and in the 1960s, 1970s, and early 1980s, it was a gathering spot for large numbers of people—often up to 600 bus loads—who descended on the town to get drunk, which usually resulted in numerous fights. I think it was in these situations that I became accepted by regular colleagues because I always stood shoulder to shoulder with them in public order situations.

During the Easter and summer bank holidays, the police had to mount sizeable operations to deal with the large number of youths ("mods" on scooters and "rockers" on motorcycles) who descended upon the town to fight each other. In those days, we did not have human rights legislation to worry about, and we would stop these groups at the borough boundary and railway stations and either prevent them from entering the town or remove their belts and suspenders, which meant they had to walk around with their hands in their pockets, thus not able to fight. We also had told shops not to sell them string. Obviously, we could not do that today, but it worked well then, and we had the full support of the local population.

On most bank holiday Mondays in the 1960s, 1970s, and 1980s, the police would organize special trains to take the large number of troublemakers back to London. I was always on duty during bank holidays. It was busy, and one got "thumped" on occasions but we—the police—always won the day. As you may know, the vast majority of British police officers are unarmed, and from the date I joined to nearly 2000, our only source of protection was a wooden truncheon, which we rarely used. There was too much paperwork to complete if we used it!

Approximately three years after joining, I asked the regular patrol sergeant one night if I could go on duty in a police car. He looked me up and down but ultimately did agree. Afterward, motor patrols became a regular duty for me from then on. I loved the thrill of going on a "shout on blues and twos"—flashing blue lights and sirens—and normally managed to get on motor patrols when on duty. Volunteer officers were not allowed to drive police cars, but nevertheless, we could become the "observer" to the experienced full-time officer.

Over the years, I made numerous friends in the regular police, and this allowed me to team up for a period of about six years as a "regular observer" on traffic enforcement patrol. Their primary duties involved the control of traffic, catching speeding and drunken drivers, and dealing with road accidents, many of which resulted in serious injury or death. I never got used to death, but over a period of time, I learned to handle the situation far better. There was not any counseling in those days, just a cigarette and a cup of tea back at the police station. We also attended the majority of day-to-day incidents requiring police attendance, for example, domestic violence, burglaries, and fires, to name but a few. I also responded to the scene of some suicides, which were never very pleasant, especially those on the railways, which were called "one unders."

I was considered a "rebel" by some of my volunteer supervising officers because I was always going on duty with regular colleagues instead of working with my special supervisors. I knew I was a rebel, but I learned far more about policing skills this way and continued my quest to become a regular officer. This enabled me to become accepted by regular colleagues, who I also did most of my socializing with off duty.

Other common duties included raids on premises for drugs and underage drinking and policing a wide variety of festivals, carnivals, parties, and football matches, at which, on occasion, there were serious public order problems. I recall one challenging day when we had to call in reinforcements from adjacent county police forces and the London Metropolitan Police. In addition, I often carried out plainclothes duties in an effort to catch burglars, deal with prostitutes, and other criminal behavior. I also attended two aircraft crashes at the local airport. Fortunately, no one was seriously injured in either crash.

In the mid-1970s, I decided not to consider applying to become a regular police officer because I was well established in my civilian job in merchant banking. Eventually, I was promoted to special sergeant and moved to Leigh Police Station. After a few years, I was transferred to Shoebury Police Station and then, on promotion to special inspector, moved to police headquarters in Southend. All three posts involved operational policing responsibilities. After several years, I was promoted to special superintendent with a much larger span of responsibility for supervising volunteer officers, and more and more of my time was spent on management issues as opposed to operational policing duties. However, I took every opportunity to go out on patrol, so I could "keep my feet on the ground."

In 1998, I was promoted to deputy commandant of the Essex Police Special Constabulary working from the police headquarters in Chelmsford. For the next six years, I worked with the commandant managing the volunteer officers within the Essex Police, which numbered approximately 400 officers. During this time, there was much more interaction and communication with other police forces in England and Wales and increasing liaison with the central government and the Association of Chief Police Officers (ACPO) over the future strategic direction of the Special Constabulary.

In 2004, I was promoted to chief officer of the Essex Police Special Constabulary, a post that I thoroughly enjoyed until my retirement in 2010. Although I loved operational policing (e.g., my last major participation in a serious public order situation being in 2005 at the age of 60 when I realized that I was not as young as I used to be for fighting and rolling around on the ground), this role gave me the opportunity along with other colleagues in England and Wales to influence the future strategic direction of volunteer police officers in England and Wales. The police in Scotland is a separate entity. During this time, I was tasked by the chief constable to embark on a major recruiting campaign to increase volunteer numbers to 600. With the stalwart support of colleagues, this was successful. Along with colleagues nationally, I was also actively involved in national campaigns to promote the value and need for volunteer police officers and the enhancement of their training.

In my roles as deputy commandant and later chief officer, I and many of my volunteer colleagues in Essex had important roles in antiterrorist hijacking exercises. In fact, we were involved in the response to an actual hijacked aircraft at Stansted Airport, which is the designated UK airport for hijacking incidents. I gained a great deal of knowledge about Essex Police and national procedures for dealing with these major incidents. This was to prove extremely useful because when Her Majesty the Queen presented me with my MBE (i.e., Member of the Order of the British Empire) at Buckingham Palace, she actually asked me how the police dealt with hijackings at Stansted Airport. I was able to provide a professional answer.

Having a full-time, paid job and also a demanding role within the Special Constabulary often meant that my social life suffered. I was also fortunate to have understanding girlfriends and employers, the latter allowing me time off from my paid job in order to carry out my police responsibilities. With the current economic challenges in the United Kingdom and indeed worldwide, this is not as easy to achieve today because employers quite rightly expect "their pound of flesh."

In 2005, at the age of 60, I decided to take early retirement from my paid job—which reduced my future income considerably—in order to devote my time to the increasing demands of directing the Special Constabulary in Essex, whose numbers were approaching 600, and to commit to my important role as chair of the Association of Special Constabulary Chief Officers (ASCCO). This decision took into account that I was also responsible for caring for an increasingly frail elderly mother.

I strongly believe that managing volunteers requires far more skills, diplomacy, and business expertise than managing paid staff. Unless volunteers are handled in a professional and understanding manner, they can "vote with their feet." I sat on many major policy-making panels in the Essex Police, and I often had to have robust debates with senior regular chief officers when they tried to introduce policies that had not taken into account the ethos and needs of volunteer police officers. I was usually successful in convincing them to amend proposals to cater to the unique needs of volunteers.

I relished the challenges that my roles presented, including the establishment of ASCCO, which I founded and served as the first elected chair in 2008. Volunteer policing, at long last, had "seats within the corridors of power" in central government and also within the highest echelons of British policing. I was often the only chief officer representing volunteer officers at some of these meetings, but I was a tenacious character. I like to think that regular chief officers and representatives from regular staff associations started to listen to the views of volunteer police officers via my robust debates. This national role necessitated regular meetings with government ministers, police authorities, and staff associations on the future strategic direction of the Special Constabulary nationally. I continue to believe that ASCCO has enabled the views of the Special Constabulary to be heard and acted upon nationally.

For the last two years of my service, I spent the majority of my time on national issues in my role as chair of ASCCO with the day-to-day management of the Special Constabulary in Essex delegated to my deputy chief officer.

In 2006, the Suffolk Police, an adjacent police force to Essex, experienced a major incident with the murders of several prostitutes. This incident received worldwide coverage, and being a smaller force, Suffolk requested aid from many other police departments across England. For the first time in modern history, this included the deployment of many volunteer police officers from across eastern England. The Essex Special Constabulary provided considerable support to the Suffolk Police. I and several of my senior colleagues visited Suffolk on several occasions looking after the welfare of our officers who were working 12-hour shifts until the murderer was apprehended. I am happy to report that the majority of employers willingly allowed the members of staff who were special constables sufficient time off to assist their regular colleagues. It was as a result of this specific series of incidents that legislation was amended to allow special officers to operate in England and Wales with full police powers. Prior to this, special officers could only operate in adjacent jurisdictions with police authority. Special constables now regularly support colleagues in other agencies across Britain when necessary.

Today, the Special Constabulary, whose numbers are nearly 20,000 nationally, is an integral and valued resource within policing in the United Kingdom. It is not a no-cost option but rather a low-cost alternative, and police volunteers are a significant asset in community engagement.

22.2 "The Police Are the Public and the Public Are the Police"

The United Kingdom has a long and proud tradition of volunteering, and special constables are an excellent example of people from across the diverse communities contributing many hours of duty per month helping their regular colleagues to maintain not only law and order, but a peaceful way of life. The volunteers involved in policing across the United Kingdom are clear examples of how Sir Robert Peel's key principle—"the police are the public and the public are the police"—has been and will continue to be attained.

22.3 End of an Exceptional and Enjoyable Career

My retirement party was a splendid affair attended by numerous colleagues and friends from Essex and across the country. Several chief constables from other police forces attended, and among many gifts and accolades was a personal letter from the home secretary acknowledging my significant contribution to volunteer policing over the course of 47 years.

Some would say that my greatest achievements within volunteer policing were receiving an MBE from Her Majesty the Queen for my long service to policing and the founding of ASCCO. Yes, of course, I was tremendously proud of these achievements, but for me, being involved and accepted as part of the policing arena across the United Kingdom by numerous regular and special colleagues, together with helping the public and making numerous lifelong friends, were the major rewards.

And yes, I would do it all over again.

Using Volunteers in Other Government Organizations

VI

Using Volunteers in the Correctional System 23

FRANCIS G. OLIVE III
MELISSA M. MIELE

Contents

23.1 Introduction

When thinking about volunteering in corrections, one may initially think that they are limited to helping offenders in a jail or prison. However, volunteers can also assist staff in parole, probation, and other community correctional settings. Understanding the motivations of individuals who choose to volunteer in these types of settings and then placing volunteers in positions that complement their interests will help to retain volunteers. The process for becoming a volunteer in a correctional setting is multifaceted and is unlike other opportunities due to strict policies and procedures. Once appointed as a volunteer in one of these correctional settings, effective volunteers appear to share similar characteristics that are outlined below. This chapter concludes with a number of success stories describing how two individuals (i.e., the chapter authors) were able to transform their volunteer experiences into successful careers and how they benefited from an effective supervisor–volunteer relationship within a correctional facility.

23.2 Historical Context

According to Kratcoski (1982), "the earliest criminal justice and social control elements in American society relied upon volunteers" (p. 30). In addition, Kratcoski further contends "early parole programs depended upon volunteers until they became part of the formal justice system" (p. 30). As the early correctional services began to develop, they began hiring professionals and paid personnel, and there was a decreased use of volunteers. However, in the 1950s and 1960s, there was a rise in crime and social concern, which led to an increase in volunteerism that is still obvious today (Kratcoski, 1982).

Starting in the 1970s, there has been an increase in the number of federal, state, county, and local correctional facilities. Shields, Chapman, and Wingard (1983) contend, "the fiscal crisis of the 1970s and 1980s has led governments to increase their use of volunteers" (p. 57). In addition, as the use of probation and parole has recently increased, there has also been an increased need for the use of volunteers in community corrections. Volunteers have been and continue to be integral parts of correctional agencies and have helped with providing different types of treatment, religious services, educational programming, and vocational programming and have additionally assisted correctional staff in their day-to-day duties (Bayse, 1993).

23.3 Characteristics and Motivations

In order to utilize volunteers as a dependable resource, it is important to understand the characteristics and motivations of volunteers to better recruit, deploy, and support these individuals so that they may continue to work within these facilities and departments.

Correctional volunteers were found to be a highly educated group in comparison to the general population (Tewksbury & Dabney, 2004). They also appeared to practice openness, indicating the importance of being honest, sensitive, flexible, steady, and dependable while engaging in their work with offenders (Kort-Butler & Malone, 2015). These volunteers identified various motivations for working with the offender population, most commonly a religious calling, but also a desire to help others, being asked to volunteer, knowing a family member or friend who is or has been incarcerated, or having formally been incarcerated themselves (Tewksbury & Dabney, 2004). Others described their own past experiences and the realization that they could have been incarcerated due to bad decisions as a primary motivation to volunteer in the correctional setting (Kort-Butler & Malone, 2015). Understanding the motives for why an individual chooses to volunteer can provide important information on how to recruit additional volunteers and as to where volunteers might be most appropriately utilized based on their qualifications and individual reason for donating their time.

Placing volunteers in positions that are consistent with their motivations may also help encourage them to continue their work. It is important for administration to identify positions that are appropriate for volunteers and then provide training associated with these positions so that this cadre feels prepared to provide services in the correctional environment (Tewksbury & Dabney, 2004). According to Kort-Butler and Malone's (2015) findings, volunteers were more likely to remain in volunteer service when they felt that they were "providing support to offenders, such as offering encouragement in times of crisis [and] making a difference by demonstrating compassion for offenders and building relationships with them." In addition to providing free services, volunteers can serve as role models to the offenders because they are not employed by the criminal justice system (Bayse, 1993).

It appears there are also personal benefits that motivated individuals to continue to volunteer within the correctional system, including feeling that the work they were doing was rewarding, fulfilling, uplifting, and worthwhile (Kort-Butler & Malone, 2015). All in all, it seems that when volunteers are provided the opportunity for the above personal benefits, along with feeling that the offenders were appreciating their service, volunteers felt more satisfied with their work and held positive perceptions of not only the facilities they volunteered in, but also the staff and offenders they worked with (Tewksbury & Dabney, 2004). Supporting volunteers both through training and continued supervision to ensure they feel as if they are making a difference in the lives of offenders seems to be the best method to maintain volunteers long term.

23.4 Getting Started as a Correctional Volunteer

Most volunteers in correctional settings, which include service in jails, prisons, and community corrections, are required to undergo a background screening prior to becoming a volunteer. Some agencies, such as the U.S. Probation Department, many local jails, and the state department of corrections, require that volunteers complete an application, fingerprinting, and a background investigation that examines past employment, criminal records, motor vehicle records, credit reports, and may also ask if they know an individual (i.e., a close friend or family member) who is currently incarcerated. Once an individual passes the background investigation and is appointed as a volunteer, he or she will have to complete an orientation that will review the rules and regulations of the respective correctional agency. After completing their orientation, the new volunteers usually will work with a volunteer coordinator who will deploy them in a specific unit, review their responsibilities, and introduce them to their direct supervisor.

23.5 Contemporary Overview: Jails and Prisons

Volunteers are being increasingly relied upon throughout the criminal justice system due to expectations that facilities will provide more with decreasing budgets. According to the Federal Bureau of Prisons (2009), when depending on staff alone, correctional administrators are unable to meet all offender needs and therefore must utilize volunteers to provide the services necessary for the care and treatment of offenders. More than 10,000 individuals volunteered in federal facilities in fiscal year 2009 while providing various services (Federal Bureau of Prisons, 2009). Prisons and jails offer many opportunities for individuals to volunteer.

The areas within the correctional system in which volunteers can be utilized are vast. The Federal Bureau of Prisons reports that volunteers provide religious, counseling, parenting, recreational, educational, vocational, and release preparation services as well as mentor offenders both while incarcerated and after release (2009). The Massachusetts Department of Corrections (MA DOC) indicates that they are currently utilizing approximately 1,500 volunteers in very similar capacities outlined by the Federal Bureau of Prisons (Turco, 2016). MA DOC identified the following areas in which volunteers can work:

- Religious services, including regular services, religious education, pastoral counseling, bible studies, prayer groups, fellowship groups, and observance of religious holidays
- Recreation activities, including fitness and yoga
- Self-improvement groups, which are described as "structured offender coordinated groups designed to reduce offender idleness and enhance reentry by providing offenders with a forum to develop interpersonal communication, problem solving, and basic life skills"
- Substance abuse education and treatment that focuses on education and raising awareness about the consequences of substance abuse
- Education, including basic adult education, English as a second language, tutoring, preparation for achieving a high school equivalency degree, transition to college, and college classes
- Vocational training, including auto body, automotive, cosmetology, carpentry, culinary arts, graphic arts, welding, computer skills, IT, serve safe, OSHA, and horticulture

The use of volunteers in these identified areas at both the federal and state levels can serve to "enhance programming and the process of reintegration by disrupting the delinquency network and providing offenders with a network of pro-social community members and activities" (Turco, 2016). Without the dedication of volunteers, it would not be possible to continue to provide all of these services at the level at which they are currently being provided.

Although the use of volunteers in corrections can provide multiple benefits, there are also some issues that may arise. Tewksbury and Dabney (2004) caution that utilizing volunteers can raise issues regarding the quality of services provided and matters involving safety of both the volunteers and offenders. Ensuring volunteers complete orientation and training prior to working within the facility could help to decrease challenges and problems encountered when later working with the offender population. Rules, such as not bringing contraband items into the facility, not taking items out of the facility, and not doing favors for offenders, such as making phone calls or delivering mail or letters, are commonly discussed in both federal and state facilities. However, despite the multiple rules regarding volunteer–offender interactions, there have been instances in which these rules have not been followed (Kort-Butler & Malone, 2015). Long-time volunteers discussed the importance of following the rules, maintaining good boundaries, and avoiding favoritism to prevent being manipulated by the offender population. Volunteers also discussed the importance of setting personal boundaries and maintaining a relationship, rather than a friendship, because "offenders did not need another friend, but they did need support and encouragement from a 'straight' person" (Kort-Butler & Malone, 2015). Therefore, aside from initial training, it seems continued supervision within the facility should be implemented so that volunteers feel they have adequate support when dealing with difficult situations that may arise with the offender population.

23.6 Contemporary Overview: Parole, Probation, and Community Corrections

The opportunities for volunteers in community corrections are very similar to those experienced in prisons and jails. Basic duties can include maintaining contact with offenders at the office and in the community, helping conduct investigations on offenders, maintaining records, helping to prepare reports, and attending court proceedings (United States Probation Department, n.d.). In addition to these basic duties, volunteers also may have the opportunity to work with specialized units or departments that provide specific services. Volunteers interested in casework and counseling are often able to assist officers and counselors. If a volunteer is interested in education, there are opportunities to tutor the offenders, teach classes, and help them prepare to take their exams and to earn a high school equivalency degree. Even though most reentry services happen while the offender is still incarcerated, volunteers can also help in assisting the offenders get involved with services in the community. In addition, volunteers can work with crime victims as liaisons to ensure they are supported and their needs are properly addressed. Some community correctional agencies also have various boards and panels that volunteers can assist with, including restorative justice panels, victim impact panels, and reparative boards (Vermont Department of Corrections, 2016).

23.7 Some Impressive Success Stories

As has been outlined, there are many benefits to prison and correctional administrators in utilizing volunteers. There are also additional rewards for the volunteers themselves that have not yet been considered.

Francis Olive III began his career in corrections as a volunteer. At the age of 19, he was an undeclared major in college, and he was advised to complete an internship with a local jail and house of corrections. He had the opportunity to work with the gang task force and learn about gangs and their impact on security in the facility. At this time, Francis decided that he would major in social work (the college did not have a criminal justice major at the time) because he could work in a correctional setting with a social work degree. For his senior practicum, he was required to complete 400 hours of fieldwork and had the opportunity to work with the After Incarceration Support System (AISS) Program, which helped offenders to prepare for their release back into the community. Francis completed needs assessments, release plans, and referred the offenders to community agencies that could serve their needs. He was able to work with individuals and also facilitated psycho-educational groups with offenders. After he completed his 400 hours, he remained as a volunteer for the following semester due to the positive relationship he had with his supervisor and the importance of the work he was doing.

After receiving his bachelor's degree, Francis began working on his master's degree in social work and was required to complete another practicum; this time he volunteered at the U.S. Department of Probation and Pre-trial Services in New York City. He was required to provide substance abuse treatment to groups and also meet with participants individually on a weekly basis. In addition, he assisted probation staff in their duties, graded substance abuse assessments, and also helped with release planning. Last, he also was trained in neurolinguistic programming and was able to assist staff in facilitating these groups.

Unfortunately, at the time Francis completed his internship with federal probation and graduated with his master's degree, there were no full-time positions due to budget cuts. As a result, he initially faced challenges with obtaining employment. Several years later, Francis contacted his internship supervisor at the local jail and house of corrections where he began volunteering, and he was informed that there was an upcoming correctional officer's test and was advised to take it. After taking the test and going through the hiring process, Francis was hired as a correctional officer and completed the seven-week, boot camp-style academy training. After completing the academy, he began his career as a correctional officer working in the special operation unit that provided both inner and outer perimeter security. He was then promoted to correctional counselor and worked with high-risk offenders who had been recently sentenced. He was responsible for a caseload of 35 to 40 inmates and conducted assessments and program referrals, helped to create an anger management program, facilitated anger management classes, sat on various committees and boards, and assisted the correctional officers he worked alongside. Due to his education and experience, Francis was eventually assigned an intern, Melissa Miele.

As a senior undergraduate student at a university, double majoring in both criminal justice and psychology, it was expected that Melissa would complete an internship to successfully graduate with her bachelor's degree. It is one thing to learn about corrections through textbooks, class discussions, and assignments; it is very different to learn about the correctional arena through hands-on experience. Therefore, an internship allows one to gain experience through volunteering in the field and may be one of the most important parts of your education in which you begin to prepare to enter the workforce.

Through her university, Melissa had the opportunity to volunteer as an intern at a county correctional facility as a correctional counselor. The internship occurred over a three-month period; during this time, there were expectations to be met for both the university and the correctional facility. Throughout the experience, Melissa was able to attend numerous training courses in which she expanded her knowledge of policy and procedure, facility operations, and services provided both within the jail and in the community. Melissa was assigned a caseload and met with offenders one-on-one to complete both counseling and casework duties. She was able to network with staff in all different departments and learn about their roles in the facility. All in all, Melissa was able to deeply immerse herself into the correctional environment and gain a clearer understanding of what it is like to work in the correctional profession.

Following the experience Melissa gained during her internship, she knew that the correctional setting was the field she wanted to pursue. The next step toward this goal was to further her education, so she completed her master's degree and a more in-depth externship and then felt that she was ready to begin her career in corrections. Due to the great experience Melissa had during her initial internship, it was clear to her that she wanted to work for the correctional facility she had initially volunteered in. Following graduation, she contacted Francis about possible employment, and he was glad to refer her to the appropriate human resources personnel and give her a recommendation. In his recommendation, Francis described his experience supervising Melissa. He described her enthusiasm and commitment and that she was a very quick learner. After being trained, she had a solid understanding of her responsibilities and was able to work very well with the offender population. Francis described Melissa as a consummate team player, very professional, and indicated she was highly respected by both staff and offenders.

When a position as a mental health clinician became available, Melissa applied. During the four interviews that followed, she was able to use her experience during her internship to highlight why she would be a good fit in the facility. Having volunteered also meant that the correctional facility had the opportunity to look back and review the performance evaluation of her internship. This experience, along with her education, led to Melissa being hired. She began her career in the very department she gained her first experience working in the field. After working as a mental health clinician for almost two years, Melissa was given the opportunity to be promoted to correctional counselor after successfully graduating a seven-week academy and passing multiple physical fitness tests. She now gets to work in a competitive, fast-paced environment doing the work she is passionate about, and it all started with an internship that paved the way for her career.

23.8 Conclusion

The use of volunteers throughout the plethora of correctional settings is not only beneficial, but likely a necessary element for providing a high level of care to offenders, support staff, and in maintaining public safety. It is interesting to examine how historically the correctional field originally placed a heavy reliance on volunteers, moved away from this practice, and now has returned to depending on volunteers to support and often provide necessary services. It is evident that effective correctional volunteers share certain characteristics and motivations to work with this challenging population. And there are sufficient opportunities for these volunteers to assist offenders and staff, including site security, casework, individual and group counseling, treatment, education, religious services, vocational trades, and reentry services. Although the field of corrections benefits from the use of volunteers, the individuals who volunteer also have the opportunity to experience both personal growth and professional development.

References

Bayse, D. J. (1993). *Helping Hands.* Arlington, VA: American Correctional Association.

Federal Bureau of Prisons. (2009). *State of the Bureau.* Washington DC: US Department of Justice.

Kort-Butler, L. A., & Malone, S. E. (2015). Citizen volunteers in prison: Bringing the outside in, take the inside out. *Journal of Crime and Justice, 38*(4), 508–521.

Kratcoski, P. C. (1982). Volunteers in corrections: Do they make a meaningful contribution? *Federal Probation, 46,* 30–35.

Shields, P. M., Chapman, C. W., & Wingard, D. R. (1983). Using volunteers in adult probation. *Federal Probation, 47,* 57–64.

Tewskbury, R., & Dabney, D. (2004). Prison volunteers: Profiles, motivations, satisfaction. *Journal of Offender Rehabilitation, 40*(1/2), 173–1813.

Turco, T. A., III. (2016). Program Description Booklet. *Massachusetts Department of Corrections,* 1–59.

United States Probation Department. (n.d.). Student internship opportunity. Retrieved from http://www.ctd.uscourts.gov/ctp/Employment/intern%20announcement.pdf

Vermont Department of Corrections. (2016). Volunteer opportunities. Retrieved from http://www.doc.state.vt.us/volunteer/volunteer

Federal Government Volunteers
The United States Coast Guard Auxiliary

24

THERESA C. TOBIN

Contents

24.1 Introduction: The United States Coast Guard

"Semper Fi," an abbreviated version of "Semper Fidelis," Latin for "always faithful," has been the official motto of the United States Marine Corps since 1883; it advocates loyalty and commitment to their Marine comrades-in-arms. "Semper Paratus," Latin for "always ready" is the motto of the United States Coast Guard Auxiliary.

The United States Coast Guard was established in the early years of this country when congress passed a bill authorizing the construction of 10 boats. Known as the "Revenue Marine" and then as the "Revenue Cutter Service" established on August 4, 1790, their mission was to guard against smugglers along the country's coastline. On January 28, 1915, President Woodrow Wilson merged the Revenue Cutter Service and the U.S. Lifesaving Service, both tasked with protecting life and property from the ravages of the sea, into the United States Coast Guard. The Coast Guard, as a military service in times of war or whenever directed by the president, operates as a separate service under the Department of the Navy, defending the nation against terrorism and foreign threats. During peacetime, the Coast Guard, operating as a federal law enforcement agency, enforces maritime law and performs lifesaving missions at sea, guarding more than 12,000 miles of the nation's coastline* and multiple ports.

There are 11 official missions of the Coast Guard: port and waterway security, drug interdiction, aids to navigation, search and rescue, living

* http://www.infoplease.com/ipa/A0001801.html

marine resources, marine safety, defense readiness, migrant interdiction, marine environmental protection, ice operations, and law enforcement. According to the Coast Guard, in 2012, the Coast Guard responded to 20,512 search and rescue cases and saved more than 3,800 lives, conducted nearly 17,000 security boardings on suspicious vessels bound for the United States, conducted more than 46,000 recreational vessel boardings, issued more than 8,000 citations, visited 1,150 recreational boat manufacturers in conjunction with state efforts to provide education and ensure compliance with federal regulations, investigated and responded to more than 3,000 pollution incidents, and removed more than 166,000 pounds of illegal cocaine bound for the U.S. mainland.*

The primary homeland security mission is port and waterway security. Not only are the people who use, live, and work on the water protected, but so are marine resources and maritime commerce. In a post–9/11 world, the U.S.' waterways and ports are considered a prime target; therefore, the Coast Guard's ability to respond to a terrorist attack as well as training in counterterrorism and having a designated response plan are of key importance. The Coast Guard's initiatives, whether it's detecting weapons of mass destruction, boarding vessels, or conducting checks and securing waterfront facilities, all accomplish this purpose. Members of the Coast Guard have been trained to deter and combat terrorism in U.S. waters. Officially, the four major national defense missions of the Coast Guard are maritime intercept operations, deployed port operations/security and defense, peacetime engagement, and environmental defense operations.

Drug interdiction, in particular cocaine, accounts for most of the Coast Guard's drug seizures; in fact, it accounts for more than half of all the U.S. government seizures of cocaine each year. Using the waterways, because they are so voluminous along the American coastlines, drug, human, and contraband smugglers make attempts to enter the mainland. The Coast Guard works closely with other federal agencies, including the Drug Enforcement Agency; the Federal Bureau of Investigation; and the Bureau of Alcohol, Tobacco and Firearms.

The Coast Guard also enforces immigration laws at sea. It is estimated that thousands of people attempt to enter the United States illegally every year by sea. When discovered, the Coast Guard, working with foreign countries and other federal agencies, detain undocumented migrants at sea, allowing them to be safely returned to their country of origin without the costly processes required if they had successfully entered the United States. The majority of vessels that the Coast Guard encounters with migrants aboard are dangerously weighed down, unseaworthy, or otherwise unsafe. The Coast

* http://www.gocoastguard.com/about-the-coast-guard/learn-the-history

Guard also enforces laws regarding the Exclusive Economic Zone (EEZ), which is the area surrounding the U.S.' coastal waters and seabed, which the United States claims exclusively for fishing, drilling, and other economic activities. This is essential for American fisheries, and the Coast Guard also assists on the international front, enforcing international agreements to suppress illegal, unreported, and unregulated fishing activities in international waters.

Although the Coast Guard is the military branch of the armed forces responsible for many enforcement functions, their oldest mission is search and rescue. The U.S. Coast Guard and their Aviation Survival Technician (AST) program coordinate response to maritime distress calls from boaters, whether it involves imminent loss of life, personal injury, or property damage to their boat. There is no other agency as adequately prepared for search and rescue on the water as the Coast Guard, and they are proud of their long tradition of immediate response, routinely resulting in saved lives.

The Coast Guard has search and rescue facilities on the East, West, and Gulf coasts as well as in Alaska, Hawaii, Guam, and Puerto Rico and on the Great Lakes and many inland waterways. With more than 76 million recreational boaters in American waters, the Coast Guard additionally relies heavily on the U.S. Coast Guard Auxiliary, their volunteer complement, for promoting recreational boating safety.

Although search and rescue is a well-known function of the Coast Guard, boating safety and accident prevention are important components of their work. Boating safety is crucial in preventing an incident at sea. However, when a maritime accident occurs, the Coast Guard is responsible for conducting the investigation, often involving merchant vessels, offshore drilling units, and marine facilities. Other functions of the Coast Guard include maintaining maritime aids for waterway navigation, such as buoys, signs, markers, and lighthouses, which ensure boaters have nautical guideposts to assist them on the water. The Coast Guard also conducts ice-breaking operations in the Great Lakes and Northeast regions. These areas often experience subzero temperatures, which create icy and treacherous conditions for maritime commerce. The Coast Guard is capable of providing year-round access to the polar regions and operate the International Ice Patrol to protect ships transiting the North Atlantic shipping lanes.

Protecting marine life, whether plants or animals, is also a function of the Coast Guard. It is the federal agency tasked with protecting the U.S. Exclusive Economic Zone (EEZ), which is the world's largest, comprising 3.4 million square miles of ocean and more than 90,000 miles of coastline. The focus is keeping American waters clean and safe as well as protecting the ecosystem of our oceans and ensuring the livelihood of endangered marine species.

The Coast Guard has been under the jurisdiction of many federal departments throughout American history. Originally falling under the auspices of the Treasury Department and remaining there for 177 years, the Coast Guard was transferred to the Department of Transportation in 1967. In 2003, the Coast Guard was transferred again, to its current home, the newly established Department of Homeland Security with nearly 42,000 men and women actively serving in the Coast Guard.

24.2 United States Coast Guard Auxiliary

In 1939, Congress established a "United States Coast Guard Reserve" under the Commandant of the Coast Guard, which was granted four specific responsibilities: (a) the advancement of safety to life at sea and upon navigable waters; (b) the promotion of efficiency in the operation of motorboats and yachts; (c) the expansion of the knowledge and compliance of the laws, rules, and regulations governing the operation and navigation of motorboats and yachts; and (d) the supplementation of operations of the Coast Guard. The United States Coast Guard Reserve is composed of Americans who are owners of motorboats or yachts.*

Congress passed the Auxiliary and Reserve Act of 1941, which renamed the volunteer section of the U.S. Coast Guard Reserve the "U.S. Coast Guard Auxiliary." Today, the U.S. Coast Guard Auxiliary has units in all 50 states, Puerto Rico, American Samoa, Guam, and the Virgin Islands. There are four levels in the U.S. Coast Guard Auxiliary: flotilla, division, district, and national. The national staff officers are responsible, along with the commandant, for the administration and policy-making for the entire U.S. Coast Guard Auxiliary. The district provides administrative and supervisory support to divisions and promotes policies of both the district commander and national committee. The flotillas in the same general geographic area are grouped into divisions. The division provides administrative, training, and supervisory support to flotillas and promotes district and national policy.

The U.S. Coast Guard Auxiliary continues to work diligently to promote safe boating. And in the summer of 2015, the U.S. Coast Guard Auxiliary effectively utilized social media to provide a boating safety app, which allowed individuals to file a float plan, report suspicious activity or pollution, and learn about safe boating on a mobile device. The Auxiliary's tasks include maintaining a database of all boating safety classes, searchable by zip code; the development of a brochure that lists the federal safety equipment requirements for boats and safety tips; the promotion of a boater "Float Plan," which

* https://www.uscg.mil/auxiliary/administration/aux-history.asp

is a form the U.S. Coast Guard Auxiliary recommends be completed prior to a person going boating and maintained by a reliable person; distributing information for the safe disposal of flares and the proper use of VHF radios, codes, and protocol; developing recommendations involving digital selective calling (DSC) for recreational boats and an automated calling system, a part of the Global Maritime Distress and Safety System (GMDSS); and advertising the online link to the Recreational Boating Accident Report, which is required when a person dies, has been seriously injured in a maritime accident, has disappeared, or a boat has been damaged in excess of $2,000.

Today, the U.S. Coast Guard Auxiliary has more than 30,000 members serving in more than 1,000 local units. The U.S. Coast Guard Auxiliary plays an essential role in boater safety endeavors. The Coast Guard Auxiliary contributes more than 2 million hours per year in the classroom and at the ramp and pier and operates 2,250 vessels, 180 aircraft, and 1,700 radio facilities on U.S. waterways.* In addition, the Coast Guard Auxiliary courses provide instruction to boaters at all levels, from beginners to advanced. The purpose is to minimize the loss of life, personal injury, property damage, and environmental harm associated with recreational boating. The courses range from sailing skills and seamanship to navigating with GPS to lines and knots. The courses vary in the length of time and are geared toward various audiences.

The U.S. Coast Guard compiles statistics each year on reported recreational boating accidents. According to the 2015 Recreational Boating Statistics, there were 4,158 boating accidents, resulting in 626 deaths and 2,613 injuries.† In cases in which there was a fatality and the cause of death was known, approximately 76% were due to drowning. Most disturbing was that approximately 85% of the drowning victims were not wearing a life jacket even though life jacket usage is highly recommended.‡ The Coast Guard Auxiliary is very proactive in ensuring recreational boaters are wearing a life jacket when on the water, and this is listed as part of their vessel safety checklist.

The Coast Guard Auxiliary also performs, free of charge, vessel safety checks. Vessels that do pass the safety checks are those that are in full compliance with all federal and state boating laws. This allows boat owners to have peace of mind knowing that not only does their boat meet the federal safety standards, but also that in an emergency they will have the necessary equipment to save lives and summon assistance. The items that are checked include life jackets, registration and numbering, navigation lights,

---

* http://www.cgaux.org/
† http://www.uscgboating.org/library/accident-statistics/Recreational-Boating-Statistics
   -2015.pdf
‡ http://www.uscgboating.org/library/accident-statistics/Recreational-Boating-Statistics
   -2015.pdf

ventilation, fire extinguishers, distress signals (flares, horn, etc.), and battery cover and connections. These items are all required by state and federal laws, and if they are missing or defective, the boat owner can receive a citation during the course of a Coast Guard inspection.

24.3 Service in the United States Coast Guard Auxiliary

Retired NYPD Sergeant Ron Doda, a New York-based vice flotilla commander in the U.S. Coast Guard Auxiliary, was asked why he joined the auxiliary. He recalled very vividly, having just retired in August 2001, the evacuation of lower Manhattan on September 11, 2001. Members of the Coast Guard, having seen the first plane crash into the World Trade Center's North Tower, put a call out for all boats to respond to lower Manhattan and watched hundreds of merchant mariners piloting tugboats, ferries, and other types of watercraft form a boat lift that safely evacuated 500,000 people in just nine hours from the southern tip of the island of Manhattan.* Ron, an avid boater himself, felt compelled to join the ranks of the Coast Guard Auxiliary, and he continues to serve today. After becoming a member of the Coast Guard Auxiliary, Ron is now a maritime captain, which means he is licensed to operate a 25-ton maritime vessel. "The education provided by the Coast Guard is unsurpassed," he says. Whether playing the role of a communications officer, which he is, or educating the public, it is clear that thousands of lives are being saved. The Coast Guard's Recreational Boating Safety Education Program is second to none!

24.4 Conclusion

The ability to do the things one enjoys as well as have the chance to impact people's lives in a positive and caring way is one of the reasons so many people find joining the U.S. Coast Guard Auxiliary attractive. It allows its members to be on the open water and perform public service by enhancing boater safety. Given the functions and responsibilities of the Coast Guard, it is no wonder that the volunteers of the U.S. Coast Guard Auxiliary are so highly respected and appreciated.

---

* http://coastguard.dodlive.mil/2011/09/remembering-911-a-decade-later/

Volunteers in American Firefighting

25

CHARLES R. JENNINGS

Contents

25.1 Introduction: The History of Volunteers in Fire Services

The origins of the volunteer firefighter in the United States extend to the founding of the 13 colonies. This illustrious history will assist in properly understanding the traditions and need for services fulfilled by volunteers in public service agencies. And how such needs continue to be filled across the country.

25.2 Origins of the Volunteers

The use of volunteers for public safety and security dates to the earliest years of the nation's founding. The origins of America's first volunteer fire company is contentious, but authors attribute this honor to Boston, Massachusetts, where an engine was imported from England in 1679. Other cities followed suit and acquired hand-powered pumps and related equipment to suppress fires. Many cities during this era enacted various combinations of building regulations, requirements for safe construction of chimneys, mandates for the provision of fire buckets and tools, and fire patrols to detect fires during evening and night hours when they could grow undetected and threaten entire neighborhoods or communities (Earnest, 1979).

Even with the purchase of equipment, firefighting remained haphazard, and results were decidedly mixed in many communities. Tired of the ineffectiveness of the ad hoc firefighting, cities began to move to more formally organized firefighting. This effort would evolve into the formation of the Boston Fire Society in 1717, a proper "fire company" as commonly defined. Philadelphia's Union Fire Company, cofounded by Benjamin Franklin, began operation in 1736, taking control of a fire engine purchased by the city some years earlier.

These early fire companies were exclusively volunteer affairs, often staffed by citizens selected for their civic prominence or capabilities. Service was regarded as an honor. The rise of volunteer fire companies with a defined chain of command began to provide order and regulation. Similar fire companies took root across the country, and their membership often reflected the varying makeup of their communities—with some companies being staffed by recent immigrant tradesmen and laborers and others by property owners, businessmen, and political figures (Greenberg, 1998).

Service occupied a central place in the lives of members of fire company members. The associated contingent pride was thought to contribute to competition among fire companies, leading to fire control that was more effective than during the days when all citizens bore the responsibility for firefighting. The companies were credited with increased efficiency and efficacy in a period that lasted for several decades. Such organization was necessary as firefighting moved from buckets to hand-powered engines. The rise of steam-powered fire engines, occurring at the same time as cities were continuing to urbanize and develop improved means for water supply, introduced a technological threat to the big city volunteers. The steamers, as they were called, could produce superior pumping with a minimal crew. As such, the days of the labor-intensive, neighborhood fire company were soon in decline (Earnest, 1979).

By the last quarter of the 19th century, the big cities were adopting steamers and hiring paid firefighters to staff them. Although many cities continued to rely on volunteers, the era of the big city firefighting volunteer ended by the turn of the 20th century.

25.3 Current Volunteer Statistics

According to the U.S. Fire Administration, there are more than 1.1 million firefighters in the United States, of whom 786,000 are volunteers (nearly 69%). Similarly, of the 30,052 fire departments in the United States, only 8% are fully paid (career), 26% use some combination of career and volunteer personnel, and almost 20,000 departments (66%) are exclusively volunteer (U.S. Fire Administration).

Figure 25.1 shows that the majority of the U.S. population is protected by career firefighters, and the vast majority of fire departments are staffed by volunteers or some combination of personnel (Haynes & Stein, 2016). The implication is that many volunteer fire departments serve relatively small populations. This small population being served has important implications for connections with the communities they serve and the challenges they face.

The number of volunteer firefighters is decreasing on a per capita rate, and this trend has been apparent for decades. At the same time, the number of career firefighters has been increasing slightly in absolute terms but declining on a per capita basis (Haynes & Stein, 2016). The meaning of this

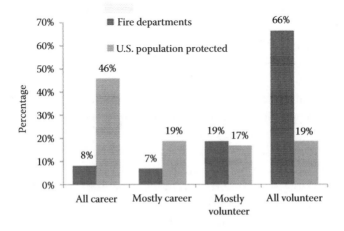

Figure 25.1 Fire departments by population protected and composition. (From Haynes, H. J. G. & Stein G. P., *U.S. Fire Department Profile – 2014*, National Fire Protection Association, January 2016.)

trend is not entirely clear, but the balance between career and volunteer fire-fighters appears to be slightly declining for volunteers.

25.4 Qualitative Stories of Volunteers

Volunteers have a large role in service delivery. They enable communities to benefit from an array of services that would otherwise be unavailable due to funding and limited staffing of most governmental organizations. Volunteer fire departments can assume multiple legal organizational forms, depending on state or provincial laws and local customs.

25.5 Services Delivered

Volunteers fulfill all roles in fire service delivery in many communities. This includes response to all sorts of emergencies. Volunteer departments in suburban areas often provide specialized services, such as vehicle accident response and extrication, hazardous materials inspection, and the operation of specialized equipment, such as aerial apparatus. The training requirements for these special operations can be extensive, and such services may be subject to oversight by higher levels of government or judged against industry standards.

Services provided by modern fire departments include the following:

- *Fire suppression*: Firefighting is the basic task that unifies fire departments of all types. Depending on the local hazards present in a community, the fire department may be required to be proficient in industrial fires, tall buildings, stores and warehouses, and natural hazards, such as wildfires. Depending on the local communities, some departments develop considerable expertise in fighting fires in their predominant building type.
- *Fire prevention*: Most fire departments engage in some basic fire prevention tasks. Fire prevention is commonly divided into three elements: public fire education, fire prevention inspections, and review of new building construction for code compliance. In many communities, the task of public fire education is often left to volunteers although it is not uncommon that a paid code enforcer or plan reviewer may be a volunteer firefighter as well, thereby bringing that expertise to their job. In the past, public fire education was really an exercise in public relations. The trend is toward more serious public fire education efforts targeting specific fire scenarios and measuring results. Often, outside support from an academic institution can facilitate such efforts.

- *Emergency medical services*: The provision of emergency medical services (EMS) can take many forms, ranging from providing assistance at auto accidents, support with transporting patients, and providing basic or advanced life support paramedic services, including operation of ambulances. EMS calls for service easily outnumber fire calls, particularly among those agencies that operate ambulance services.
- *Technical rescue*: Technical rescue includes specialized equipment and training to deal with challenging rescues from collapsed structures, construction sites, trenches, and complex vehicle accidents. The equipment and training to be proficient in these areas is extensive. These services may be provided at different levels, depending on community needs, often on a regional basis.
- *Hazardous materials*: Dealing with accidental release of chemicals, biologic agents, and radioactive materials is included in hazardous materials response. Hazardous materials response training standards are federally regulated in the United States. Because of the high levels of training, complexity, and cost of equipment, and relatively low number of such events, these services are most commonly provided on a regional basis, such as at the county or multicounty level.
- *Emergency management*: In many communities, the fire chief often serves as a lead official for managing disasters and unplanned events of all types. Some fire chiefs may be formally designated as emergency management directors, and some play a supporting role. In any case, the volunteer fire department is the largest pool of personnel available on a 24-hour basis to perform any number of tasks to support and maintain normalcy in a community. Fire departments may be primary responders to hazards, such as flooding, earthquakes, tornados, hurricanes, and other threats.
- *Community Emergency Response Team (CERT)*: CERTs are a formalized volunteer disaster response group composed of local residents. Their skill sets and duties are often complementary to the fire service mission although they may be affiliated with other agencies in the community. (For more information on CERTs, please refer to the Federal Emergency Management Agency's website, i.e., http://www .fema.gov/community-emergency-response-teams/.)
- *Law enforcement support*: Although largely a regional phenomenon, some departments operate "fire police" who can provide traffic control and scene security tasks at incidents, such as vehicle accidents and crowd control at emergency scenes. These personnel, who may or may not also perform firefighting duties, serve as a supplement to local law enforcement. In many small communities, the local sheriff's deputy may be a volunteer firefighter as well.

Volunteer fire departments in many cases can provide service comparable to career fire services, boasting short response times and adequate staffing. Even in cases in which response times are longer, the larger numbers of volunteers available can provide some advantages and contribute to community resiliency in times of disaster.

25.6 Tax Avoidance

One of the most evident advantages of volunteer fire and emergency services provision is the reduced costs borne by the community. A study by the National Fire Protection Association estimated the cost to replace the services of volunteer firefighters in the United States would be $139 billion in 2011. This figure compares to the costs of governmental outlays on local fire protection of some $40 billion annually (Hall, 2014). Volunteers often engage in extensive fundraising, which can further reduce reliance on tax revenues. The importance of this "willing donation" versus reliance solely on government revenues suggests the strong support for volunteer fire departments among the public they serve.

25.7 Community Pride and Engagement

Volunteer fire stations often have "social halls," which can range from small meeting rooms to elaborate ballrooms that can seat hundreds. These facilities, regardless of how modest or opulent, are often the primary gathering places for community events. Rental fees for these halls serve as a source of revenue to support the fire services and a reasonably priced venue for special events. Weddings, graduation parties, anniversaries, and just about any event are commonly held in these facilities by members of the community. Perkins and Metz (1988), in their research on volunteer firefighters, confirmed the strong sense of community pride, commitment, and cohesion among volunteer fire departments. These benefits are real and can be a critical element of civic life in those communities.

25.8 Future Challenges

Amid this benign and overwhelmingly positive assessment of the volunteer fire services falls a series of real challenges facing these organizations. Although these threats are significant, the volunteer fire services have managed to adapt and continue to protect life and property in their communities. A number of future challenges are outlined below.

25.8.1 Population Change

The change in population demographics can be both positive and negative. In communities, particularly isolated rural areas, population loss reduces the pool of residents to serve as volunteers. Circumstances of economic decline that often accompany population loss may actually exacerbate demand for services. On the contrary, growing communities often see increasing numbers of calls for service. New residents, particularly when they relocate from urban areas served by career fire departments, may have little interest or even awareness of the need to support their volunteer fire department and may expect the same variety of services they had while living in the city.

25.8.2 Rising Training Standards and Expectations

Volunteer fire departments were once afforded tremendous deference from public scrutiny. As training requirements are developed at the national level, even those departments that do not require them for their members are judged according to whether they may meet them in the event of an adverse outcome. Increased hostility to taxes and antigovernment sentiment have led to public funding for volunteer fire services being questioned. Of course, high profile cases of excessive or reckless spending and the lack of clear financial controls in many public service organizations and government agencies have often received wide exposure in the media (Moore, 2015).

25.8.3 New Needs

Adapting to new community challenges and needs is a hallmark of volunteer fire and emergency services. However, the decline in fires nationally and rise of emergency medical and other services are forcing departments to demand more time and training of their members and the purchase of specialized equipment that may be more expensive or require more frequent replacement. Older members who joined when an initial period of training was followed by sometimes decades of amiable participation in weekly drills, followed by shared refreshments with their peers, may bristle at the new demands and expectations. This is particularly the case for emergency medical services, which do not receive the same public regard and do not share the drama and visibility of firefighting in the community.

25.8.4 Fewer Volunteers

The number of volunteers has generally been declining on a national basis. Organizations that once were primarily fraternal and social have become increasingly professionalized. Where waiting lists to join were once common, departments are now competing for members by using advertising, public events, and incentives to recruit and retain members (Peetz, 2014; Hajishengallis, 2013).

25.8.5 Other Attractions

Fire services once served a preeminent role in the public's eye. Years of effort devoted to training and gaining the respect of one's peers was a long-term undertaking. Increased residential mobility, the rise of myriad competing ways to engage with the community, and time commitments of the fire service all work against attracting and retaining volunteers.

25.8.6 Demise of the "Local Economy"

Many volunteer fire services drew on local workforces, working in small or locally owned businesses. These businesses often released employees to answer fire alarms, and their proximity to the community made response times feasibly short. As economies changed, employment moved out of smaller communities, and some employers did not release their employees, particularly as alarms became more frequent. The pace of economic activity is such that even the local attorney, auto repair station proprietor, or tradesman cannot afford to be absent from work.

25.8.7 Diversity

As communities become more diverse, volunteer fire services must reach beyond their traditional demographic groups to attract new members. This is important to both provide staffing and maintain legitimacy within their communities. Some fire companies, originally staffed by residents of ethnic enclaves, have often struggled to attract a diverse community when compared to more homogeneous neighborhoods.

25.8.8 Physical Fitness and Medical Standards

Volunteer firefighters suffer from many of the same health risks as their career counterparts. Although improvements have been made in safety, medical standards and physical fitness continue to be major challenges (National Volunteer Fire Council). Some departments may not implement proper screening for lack of funds or fear that they would disqualify their members from service. Volunteers often serve in active roles well beyond the retirement age of their career departments.

Numerous studies have shown that volunteer firefighters have significant numbers of members who are plagued with excess weight, high blood pressure, coronary disease, or other ailments that heighten their risk of cardiovascular accident, which is the leading cause of firefighter fatality (Hammer & Heath, 2013).

25.9 Economies of Scale and Organization

One major area that has not received sustained attention is the issue of scale in delivery of volunteer services. With the trends stated earlier, the historic patterns of fire departments, stations, and administrative organization have been slow to adapt. Community pride, history, and loss of prestige tend to maintain fire departments even when population or developmental changes or loss of membership make service provision ineffective (Fuoco, 2016).

When such conditions exist, fewer members try to sustain "too many" fire stations or equipment, leading to longer response times, shortages of personnel willing to assume leadership roles, and unsustainable financial demands on local tax bases and capacity to donate.

Volunteers are not cost-free. Training, administrative support, medical clearance and maintenance, and protective equipment have continued to become more costly. As these costs are applied across numerous small departments, the costs can begin to approach the costs of a career department, especially when volunteers begin to hire career staff to supplement their services. In suburban areas, it is not uncommon that neighboring fire departments may employ a single employee, but those employees could be pooled to provide more effective services.

Experience has shown that resistance to consolidation or regional provision of services is strong—both from volunteers who fear loss of control or autonomy and local communities that fear loss of identity as their local fire department may change their name or even the color of fire apparatus. Volunteers routinely lobby elected officials and the public quite effectively to protect their resources (Mikulan, 2014).

25.10 Future Opportunities

The future also holds promise for the volunteer provision of fire and emergency services and this large pool of engaged citizens. Some opportunities for growth and enhanced service are suggested below.

25.10.1 Emerging Roles

There are many duties outside of the traditional fire service mission being demanded of volunteer organizations. Volunteer departments often take in members who only wish to serve in delivery of emergency medical services. Similarly, important preventive functions, such as public fire education, installation of smoke detectors in dwellings, and administrative tasks, can be done by members who may be unable to meet the requirements for delivering emergency services.

Such roles provide a way to productively utilize senior members and engage nontraditional cohorts within the community who may be motivated to serve. Even some career fire departments have embraced this use of "administrative" volunteers for the same reasons.

25.10.2 "Modern Volunteer"

Social media and its deep adoption by young people have changed the way that people define and get involved in community service. Fueled by appeals on social media and a desire to help, emergent groups "pop up" rapidly following disasters or other community threats. Hurricane/Tropical Storm Sandy saw the emergence of a host of emergency volunteer-led initiatives (Fink, 2012; McKay, 2013).

Such developments suggest that the volunteer spirit is alive and well, but fire services need to learn how to engage with these well-intended and often very competent efforts. Tapping into social media and effectively utilizing emergent volunteers are key strategies for success.

25.10.3 Credentialing Volunteers

Preregistration and credentialing are two key challenges that could enable greater utilization of these "modern volunteers." One of the key barriers to utilizing these community-based resources has been their apparent mismatch with the paramilitary, command-and-control culture of fire services. Fire chiefs need to be able to know that the person presenting themselves as willing and capable of providing assistance during an emergency is indeed trained, reliable, and not a threat to emergency workers or the public.

Credentialing is the process of vetting someone's affiliation and their competence, usually demonstrated by training or certification. For example, a nurse may arrive at a scene to volunteer, but without credentialing, the incident commander would have no way to know the person's identity, what type of nurse he or she is, or whether his or her certification was current. The same scenario could be imagined for even mental health counselors, structural engineers, cooks, or even delivery drivers.

25.11 Summary

Fire services are caught in a trend toward more community-based delivery of services (Thiel, 2012). Their organization and membership make them examples of public engagement. Merely having an unpaid workforce is not enough, however, to escape scrutiny. Volunteer fire services are not immune to financial abuses, insularity, and difficulty adapting to changing communities. By embracing engagement with community groups and political entities, volunteer fire services can help ensure that they remain responsive to local needs and can continue to receive the support they need.

The volunteer provision of fire and emergency services continues to evolve. In spite of the real challenges facing this profession, the large numbers of departments and the reliance of so many communities on their services suggest a long, if not unclear, future. The volunteer services bring important benefits in terms of community cohesion, tax avoidance, and provision of quality services.

Public expectations continue to rise, and new demands for service are pushing fire departments to consider providing new services, such as emergency medical services, broader missions of injury prevention, and public fire education. Ironically, the demands on volunteer fire chiefs may grow as they balance service provision while recruiting and retaining firefighters in a more difficult climate.

The greatest challenges facing the volunteer fire service are managerial, that is, the demand for regional consolidation, fiscal transparency, public accountability for effective performance, and increasing regulation and industry norms.

References

Earnest, E. (1979). *The Volunteer Fire Company: Past and Present.* Briarcliff Manor, NY: Stein and Day Publishers.

Fink, S. (2012). A Queens High-Rise Where Fear, Death, and Myth Collided. *The New York Times*, December 19.

Fuoco, L. W. (2016). Ingram volunteer fire company disbanded as borough opts for Pittsburgh services. *Pittsburgh Post-Gazette.* April 11. http://www.post-gazette.com/local/west/2016/04/11/Ingram-fire-company-disbanded-as-council-opts-for-Pitstburgh-services/stories/201604120110

Greenberg, A. (1998). *Cause for Alarm: The Volunteer Fire Department in the Nineteenth Century City.* Princeton, NJ: Princeton University Press.

Hajishengallis, O. (2013). Fire Departments Try to Extinguish Staffing Crisis. *USA Today.* September 30, p. 03a.

Hall, J. (2014, March). *The Cost of Fire in the United States*, Quincy, MA: National Fire Protection Association, p. 29.

Hammer, R. L., & Heath, E. M. (2013). Comparison of Aerobic Capacity in Annually Certified and Uncertified Volunteer Firefighters. *Journal of Strength and Conditioning Research, 27*(5), 1435–1440.

Haynes, H. J. G., & Stein, G. P. (2016, January). *U.S. Fire Department Profile—2014.* National Fire Protection Association.

McKay, J. (2013). Sandy Created a Black Hole of Communication. *Emergency Management*, January 28.

Mikulan, V. (2014, July). Volunteer Fire Department Consolidation in Pennsylvania. *Fire Engineering*, pp. 14–21.

Moore, E. (2015). Fire Alarm. *Newsday* November 6–10. http://www.newsday.com/long-island/complete-coverage-fire-alarm-1.1532062

National Volunteer Fire Council. NVFC Heart Healthy Firefighter website. www.healthy-firefighter.org/fitness

Peetz, B. (2014). Battling Brain Drain. *Fire Engineering.* February 12, pp. 12–18.

Perkins, K., & Metz, C. (1988). Note on Commitment and Community Among Volunteer Firefighters. *Sociological Inquiry, 58*(1).

Thiel, A. (2012). Contemporary Fire and Emergency Services. In A. Thiel & C. R. Jennings (Eds.), *Managing Fire and Emergency Services.* Washington, DC: International City/County Management Association.

United States Fire Administration. Firefighters and Fire Departments. http://www.usfa.fema.gov/data/statistics/

Volunteers in Emergency Medical Service in the United States

26

JOHN S. YOUNG

Contents

26.1 Introduction

Volunteer participation in emergency medical services (EMS) in the United States is a very widespread phenomenon. VolunteerEMS.Org* (an organization dedicated to matching individual volunteers to local organizations) currently lists 511 agencies in 41 states, and the Virginia Association of Volunteer Rescue Squads includes 329 volunteer EMS agencies, rescue squads, fire departments, and specialty related agencies in the commonwealth with more than 18,000 members.† A report by the Institute of Medicine (2007), citing an earlier study by the Congressional Office of Technology Assessment and the Minnesota Department of Health, noted that three quarters of EMS personnel in rural areas were volunteers, and similar figures have been found in studies by individual states.

---

* http://www.volunteerEMS.org
† http://www.vavrs.com

It is difficult to characterize volunteer EMS activity as it reflects a wide variety of local initiatives. Just as in the case of professional services, volunteer EMS organizations have a diverse set of relationships with fire/rescue organizations in those communities. Equally diverse is the pattern of interactions among paid staff and volunteers when both exist in a jurisdiction. Some volunteer services focus nearly exclusively on ambulance and basic life support (EMT-B, BLS) services, and others extend to advanced life support (EMT-P, paramedic, ALS) service. Still other agencies (as in the case of Virginia Beach) include specialized squads, such as search and rescue and marine rescue.

The ongoing operation of the Virginia Beach EMS Marine Rescue Team (MRT) reflects the fact that the city has responsibility for 36 miles of Atlantic Ocean and Chesapeake Bay coastline, 14 miles of the Intracoastal Waterway (ICW), and 8,000 acres in the Back Bay National Wildlife Refuge. Fully half of the city's area (248 of the 497 square miles within the city limits) is covered by water.

26.2 History of Volunteer EMS in the United States

The history of volunteer EMS squads is as varied as is their structure. The earliest volunteer rescue squads were established in the 1920s.* There are vying claims of precedence from New Jersey, Virginia, and Texas. The Roanoke, Virginia, squad is claimed variously to have been founded in 1922 and 1928, its founder having been inspired by witnessing a drowning in 1909. The Belmar, New Jersey, squad was founded in November 1927[†] in a community that already had fire companies but not rescue or first aid. The Harris County Emergency Corps (HCEC) was founded in 1927 as a volunteer rescue and first aid group with the support of the existing Houston Fire Department and the Houston Police Department. The Spring Lake, New Jersey, squad was formed in 1928 and subsequently incorporated 1930. It is notable that three of these four initial squads had a particular interest in water rescue. In 1929, they were training for water rescue in Roanoke, and the Belmar and Spring Lake departments in 1934 were rescuing survivors of the Morro Castle fire and beaching.

A common element of volunteer EMS is that many volunteer organizations were founded due to either the absence of or a breakdown in the delivery of EMS services by local government. For example, the Virginia Beach

---

* http://www.emsmuseum.org
† http://www.belmarhistoricalsociety.org

Volunteer Rescue Squad (Rescue 14/Rescue 8 in the current Virginia Beach EMS structure) was founded in response to a lack of service:*

> One cold December afternoon in 1951, a local woman was struck by a car near the corner of 24th Street and Atlantic Avenue. Attorney J. Peter Holland III found himself at the scene and called for an ambulance. Unfortunately, the Fire Department's ambulance was disabled and couldn't help. With nowhere to turn, Holland called the nearby Fort Story Army installation, but the dispensary was hesitant to send help since the person injured was not in the military. Holland persisted, and nearly an hour after his initial call, an ambulance from Fort Story responded to take the woman to Virginia Beach General Hospital, just three blocks away.

In response to the situation, Mr. Holland and friends founded the Princess Anne–Virginia Beach Rescue Squad, Inc., on May 1, 1952.

A similar situation led to the founding of the Bravo Volunteer Ambulance Service (Bay Ridge Ambulance Volunteer Organization),† which is currently the largest volunteer ambulance service in New York State. In 1974, New York City ambulance response times in the neighborhoods in southwest Brooklyn near the Verrazano Narrows Bridge could be in excess of one hour. The volunteer squad was able to cut response times to five minutes.

Many current volunteer EMS organizations have their origins in volunteer fire departments, established in areas where sparse populations mitigated against the formation or effective use of municipal departments. Despite the fact that Virginia Beach is the most populous city in the Commonwealth of Virginia, many of its rescue squads began as small community volunteer fire departments prior to the incorporation of the much larger and largely rural–suburban Princess Anne County into the city in 1963. Thus, of the current constituent squads in the Virginia Beach City Department of EMS, almost all began as volunteer fire departments:

- Ocean Park (Rescue 1/22) was founded in 1944 as a volunteer fire department.
- Davis Corner (Rescue 2) began in 1943 as an auxiliary fire department (its rescue component added around 1955).
- Chesapeake Beach (Rescue 4) was chartered in 1942 (incorporated in 1948) as a volunteer fire department (rescue/EMS component added in 1962).
- Princess Anne Courthouse (Rescue 5/21) was established in 1947 as a volunteer fire and rescue.

---

* https://www.vbvrs.org/about/history
† http://www.bravoambulance.org

- Creeds (Rescue 6) was established in 1952 as a volunteer fire and rescue.
- Kempsville (Rescue 9/19) was founded in 1950 as a volunteer fire department (ambulance service was added in 1953; the fire component was dropped in 1997).
- Blackwater (Rescue 13) was founded in 1958 as a volunteer fire and rescue.
- Plaza (Rescue 16/18) was founded as the Lynnhaven Volunteer Fire Department in 1962 (in 1965, it got its first ambulance).
- Sandbridge (Rescue 17) was founded in 1974 as a volunteer fire and rescue. Since 1977, professional firefighters have taken over fire operations at the station.

26.3 Virginia Beach Department of EMS

The current organization of the Virginia Beach Department of EMS (VBEMS) reflects the relatively recent formation of this large city from a series of small towns located in a relatively rural setting. This distinguishes it from many urban areas in which a true city structure existed in the 19th or even 18th century. Thus, although Virginia Beach is the most populous city in Virginia, it is also the largest, such that its population density remains relatively low, and development is concentrated so that it still reflects the towns of the 19th, 18th, and even 17th centuries. Virginia Beach has a population density of only 1,759 persons per square mile, roughly half that of Richmond (3,415), one fifth that of Alexandria (9,314), and less than one 15th that of New York City.

It is intriguing to note the very different patterns of development of fire and EMS services following the merger of Virginia Beach and Princess Anne County to form a city in 1963. The VB Fire Department, previously largely a collection of volunteer squads, became almost exclusively professional, and EMS services remained overwhelmingly volunteer. At present, the Fire Department has 434 career members, 42 civilian support staff, and 60 volunteers. Volunteers are recruited only for support roles at present, not as firefighters.

In contrast, the Department of Emergency Medical Services has 56 career staff and more than 1,100 volunteers ranging from EMT-Bs to advanced paramedics as well as specially trained squads, such as MRT. It is tempting to speculate regarding how much the drive to replace volunteer firefighters with paid professionals provided an impetus to the development of a robust volunteer EMS system by displacing volunteers already trained in EMS procedures and accustomed to donating significant time to community service.

Although lifesaving efforts have a long history in Virginia Beach, pre-dating the establishment of the first U.S. Lifesaving Service station in the area in 1874, the Marine Rescue Team of VBEMS is a comparative new-comer. Originally founded as the EMS Dive Team in 1991, it was incorpo-rated in 2002 as a 501(c)(3) nonprofit, the Virginia Beach Volunteer Water Rescue Team, Inc., mirroring the structure of the other constituent squads in VBEMS. Since its founding, it has developed capabilities in beach patrol and shore-based rescue in addition to water-based rescue, using both boats and personal watercraft (Jet Skis). Like all of the squads, it is fully integrated into the EMS command structure, relying on central dispatch and reporting to the VBEMS shift supervisor.

26.4 Overview of the Virginia Beach Marine Rescue/EMT Unit

The current organization and capabilities of the VBEMS MRT reflect several factors:

- The integration of several different necessary capabilities within a single organization
- The broad support of VBEMS in terms of city funding, community support, and local expectations
- The complexities of integrating police, fire, and EMS departments as well as private lifeguards in a unified, citywide Emergency Management Program

Internally, EMS MRT has grown from the initial dive team to include programs based on rescue boats and personal watercraft, rescue swimmers, and close coordination with the city's lifeguard service, responsible for the beaches outside of the resort/hotel area, such as Sandbridge.* MRT is staffed 24/7 with divers, boat coxswains and crews, and rescue swimmers available at all times. Divers, dive tenders, and dive boat operators are Emergency Response Diving International (ERDI) certified, and rescue swimmers are all certified by StarGuard, the Red Cross, or a comparable agency. All boat crews have training by the Virginia Department of Game and Inland Fisheries, and many have supplemented this with the more extensive training provided by the U.S. Coast Guard Auxiliary. Coxswains are internally qualified in addi-tion to ERDI certification and must maintain quarterly currency on all MRT vessels. MRT is progressing toward a requirement that all coxswains have

---

* Lifeguards in the resort area are contracted by the City from Virginia Beach Lifesaving Service, a private company.

a USCG captain's license for uninspected passenger vessels. As a result of its focus on training and certification, MRT is one of only seven teams in the United States certified by the U.S. Lifesaving Association (USLA) as an aquatic rescue response team.

MRT currently operates three rescue trucks, an ATV, and two personal watercraft (the latter only in warm months), in addition to its rescue boats:

- 15.5-foot wing inflatable (kept with the primary duty truck for small water bodies)
- 16-foot Mercury rigid-hulled inflatable boat (RHIB) for the ICW and Back Bay
- 20-foot Sea Ark metal boat (primarily for shallow-water rescues in the Back Bay)
- 24-foot Northwind RHIB (outboard, for Chesapeake Bay and Atlantic Ocean rescues)
- 24-foot Willard RHIB (inboard diesel, primarily for ocean rescues)
- 24-foot safe boat (dual outboard, enclosed cabin)

Both divers and boat crews are equipped with appropriate personal protective equipment, enabling operation year-round, and the team also maintains a capability in side-scan sonar (boat-mounted and Towfish) as well as night-vision equipment.

The MRT's equipment represents a mix of city property and equipment acquired via grants and donations to the team's nonprofit organization. Operating and maintenance costs are underwritten by the city. All of the team's members are volunteers with a typical commitment of four 12-hour duty shifts per month, plus a six-hour training day monthly. The overwhelming majority of calls include both the current duty crew and half a dozen or so off-duty members.

As might be expected in a city with as much waterfront as Virginia Beach, not only EMS, but also police and fire departments have marine assets. With a centralized EMS dispatching system, participation by all three agencies in the Hampton Roads Marine Incident Response Team, and a degree of overlap in capabilities, the deployment of marine resources in Virginia Beach is often a complex ballet. One example is the deployment of divers. In the first hour following submergence of a potential victim (a very short window considering travel and diver dress-out times), a dive is considered a rescue with primary EMS responsibility. After that, it is a recovery dive with primary responsibility going to the police and a different set of needs. In practice, EMS and police divers routinely support one another on dive calls.

Ensuring the most appropriate use of equipment and personnel with adequate depth but avoiding redundancy requires constant effort. Interagency cooperation has been continually improving in recent years. Internally, there is an ongoing need to ensure that field supervisors, who primarily have EMT–paramedic rather than marine rescue backgrounds, understand the capabilities of MRT and are neither overly cautious nor unjustifiably optimistic.

As with all volunteer organizations, recruiting and retention are an ongoing challenge, particularly in light of the significant time commitments and training requirements of the various jobs on the team. MRT has been blessed with regards to recruiting by the large presence of the U.S. military in the area. Well-trained, active-duty and retired volunteers have significantly boosted the team's capabilities. Unfortunately, the demands of federal service have sometimes adversely affected retention. Active team members have been called to overseas deployment, ordered to new duty stations, or given mandatory overtime by employers with consequent loss to the team.

26.5 Present State of Affairs

Three very different pictures emerge when one considers the state of affairs of volunteer EMS services. At the national level, there are multiple indications of an ongoing or accelerating crisis, particularly in rural areas. In the Virginia Beach Department of EMS, there appears to be long-term stability with some changes "around the edges." For the Marine Rescue Team, there is a recent history of positive change.

26.6 Volunteer EMS Services in the United States

As noted earlier, a major fraction of EMS nationwide is provided by volunteers, particularly in rural areas. This assessment is confirmed by the massive statistical compilation on EMS prepared by NHTSA in 2011 (NHTSA, 2011). Regarding agencies with on-scene response and ground transport capabilities, data were collected from 48 states. In approximately one third of the United States (i.e., 16 states), more than 50% of the agencies were comprised of volunteers, and in another third of the states (i.e., 16 states), between 11% and 50% of the agencies were made up of volunteers. The remaining third of the states were evenly split between those states with few (1%–10%) volunteer agencies and those with no volunteer agencies. The role of volunteers is even more striking when considered in terms of individuals rather than agencies. In the 30 states out of 46 providing data, more than half of the first responders were volunteers. In 22 (nearly 50%), more than half of the basic EMTs (EMT-B) were volunteers, and in two states, more than half of the paramedics (EMT-P) were volunteers.

A series of studies over the past decade presents a fairly consistent outlook for the future, indicating serious problems looming for EMS, in large
part reflecting the reliance of rural systems upon a decreasing pool of volunteers. In 2006, the Health Resources Services Administration (HRSA, 2006)
published a study addressing EMS services in the smallest, most isolated
rural communities in the United States ("frontier communities"), basing
their data on an expert panel and information from state EMS agencies. The
report noted significant difficulties faced by these primarily volunteer systems. Demographic changes were reducing the already small populations of
potential volunteers with adequate free time, aging volunteers were leaving
and not being replaced, and increasing professional standards were leading others either to resign or not to volunteer. Moreover, employers were
reported as less willing to support their workers' participation as EMS providers during work hours than in the past.

A review published in 2006 by the National Academy of Medicine (2006)
addressed much broader issues within the national EMS system (including
issues of finance, regional coordination, communication, training, and medical supervision) and also noted the same problems of decreasing volunteer
availability and increasing demand (including that imposed by the closure or
restructuring of rural hospitals) on a largely volunteer workforce.

An NHTSA (2008) report on the EMS workforce goes into significant
detail on the difficulties involved in accurately estimating the participation
of volunteers as well as cross-trained firefighters in delivering EMS services.
It noted the earlier estimations of declining volunteer availability and also
that for volunteer firefighters (a presumptively similar group for which better
data were available); the number of volunteers per 100,000 population had
decreased by 28% between 1984 and 2003.

A 2010 study from the University of North Carolina (Rural Health
Research and Policy Analysis Center, 2010) was based on interviews with the
directors of 49 all-volunteer EMS agencies in 23 states. Sixty-nine percent of
the respondents of these predominantly small agencies indicated that they
had problems recruiting and retaining volunteers (recruiting being the larger
problem), and many more stated that this problem was constant or likely
worse than reported and in need of improvement. Interestingly, the problem
was less acute for those agencies that combined fire and EMS services.

Individual states have similarly noted problems facing their volunteer-
based rural EMS systems. A 2011 study for the North Dakota Rural EMS
Improvement Project (SafeTech Solutions, 2011) noted many of the problems
reported above with a great deal more specific data for the state, in which
86% of EMS personnel are volunteers. They characterized the problem as
the expected continued decrease of the "subsidy" provided by volunteers that
had sustained rural EMS services for the preceding 40 years. Among the
more salient findings, beyond difficulties in recruiting younger volunteers to

replace aging ones, were the high proportion of current volunteers who were inactive (46%) or only partially active (16%), leaving 38% of the existing volunteer roster to respond regularly to calls. Also, about 35% of the ambulance services reported difficulty filling schedules for certain times or days. An even more recent report by the Montana Department of Public Health and Human Services, EMS and Trauma Systems Section, to the relevant committee of the state legislature (Montana Emergency Medical Services, 2016) noted the same pattern of problems with the three fourths of Montana that is covered by voluntary EMS systems.

26.7 Volunteer EMS in Virginia Beach

As noted earlier, the Virginia Beach EMS is overwhelmingly staffed by volunteers although there is a significant number of paid professionals. Given reasonable assumptions about time commitments required of the two staff types, one can classify as roughly 85% volunteer in terms of duties run. It is interesting to note that in 2004, when the service ceased to be entirely volunteer, there were claims that a volunteer EMS could not continue to function effectively. The intervening decade has clearly disproved this prediction. A stable balance between paid senior staff and volunteers ranging from new EMT-Bs to senior paramedics appears to have been achieved.

As the largest volunteer-based (if no longer all-volunteer) EMS agency in the country, VBEMS responds to more than 40,000 calls each year with more than 30,000 patients transported with no charge to any patient. The large volunteer labor force reduces EMS expenses by more than eight million dollars annually, and the active participation of the nonprofit organizations associated with the rescue squads results in roughly twice that amount in donated equipment.

26.8 Virginia Beach MRT

The Virginia Beach MRT has, over the past two years, been actively building. Although the overall roster has remained relatively constant at about three dozen individuals, there has been significant turnover. Some of this has reflected the competing demands of members' careers (deployments, as noted above, or incompatible scheduling demands of police and fire department employment). A comparable number, however, reflects the retirement of volunteers unable or unwilling to meet increasingly stringent training and certification requirements and their replacement with more highly trained volunteers.

In 2015, team members provided 11,424 person-hours, running duties, as well as 1,241 person-hours spent on training days and 655 person-hours at special events throughout the year. Team coxswains logged more than 1,000 hours underway. The team responded to a total of 197 calls and, in 131 cases, actively participated in rescue efforts. (In the other cases, incident command had the team and often all responders stand down when it was clarified that no one was actually in distress or that fewer resources were needed.) Of the 131 active calls, 86 were boats in distress, 40 potential drownings, 4 cars in the water, and 1 missing aircraft.

26.9 Two Success Stories

In general, the success of volunteer participation in EMS is hard to depict by specific cases. In many cases, particularly in rural areas, the success of volunteer participation is the existence of any EMS service at all. In most cases, there is little or no difference between the rescue actions of volunteer and professional EMS with comparable levels of training; the difference is in the cost of ensuring that such service is available. One area of particular contribution is in the availability of specially trained squads. Professional EMS and cross-trained firefighters must, out of necessity, focus on the types of cases that generate the most call volume. For less routine cases (i.e. search and rescue, water rescue, etc.), volunteers can supply uniquely concentrated expertise. Volunteers can also supply "surge" capacity for dealing with disasters. The following individual cases are intended to illustrate these capabilities.

26.9.1 Virginia Beach MRT

At approximately 1230 hours on Sunday, September 27, 2015, a marine incident response was sent out for a possible drowning at Sandbridge. A 42-year-old civilian who had entered the water in an attempt to rescue a 17-year-old (who, in the event, was able to self-rescue) was missing. The MRT duty crew left a dive training exercise to respond to the scene, and a second crew manned the nearest rescue boat. Arriving at the scene approximately 10 minutes after receiving the call, the first duty crew determined that two initial responders (firefighters) had entered the water without tending lines and were themselves in trouble in the strong rip current. One crew member entered the water wearing water rescue personal flotation device (PFD) and a tether tended by the other crew member, and in cooperation with a member of the Sandbridge Rescue Squad (and former lifeguard), was able to assist the underequipped firefighters and a police officer to safety. Although the primary victim, unfortunately, could not be saved, rapid and appropriate response by MRT personnel prevented the loss of first responders in these very challenging conditions.

26.9.2 Regional EMS

On July 10, 2014, South Hampton Roads was struck by a severe thunderstorm, causing widespread flooding and downed power lines and causing severe traffic tie-ups throughout the region. The storm also caused a tornado touchdown at the Virginia Beach Oceanfront.* In addition to severe structural damage to buildings and vehicles, a flood of calls for EMS were received by 911 dispatch. At the same time, many regularly staffed units were severely hampered in their ability to reach the affected area.

By instituting an "EMS-ALL call," the department was able to mobilize dozens of volunteers to staff surge ambulances, zone cars (specially equipped vehicles that allow paramedics greater mobility in assisting BLS-staffed ambulances), and squad trucks (with tools for vehicle extrication and other specialty rescues), and senior staff established a triage station at the nearest rescue squad (Rescue 14) so that patients could be evaluated and prepared for transportation to the hospital by a mass-casualty bus. This citywide surge capacity is an inherent advantage of a system in which a large number of part-time volunteers is used. Had the same number of routine duties been filled by full-time employees, there would not have been a similar surge response capability for a disaster.

26.10 Summary/Conclusion/Recommendations

To a significantly greater extent than in the case of police and fire departments, volunteers appear to remain a central component of EMS. There does appear to be an ongoing problem of maintaining this model in small rural communities given the demographic and economic changes in the country over the past few decades. To some extent, this may reflect that the provision of EMS services has not received the support from state governments that police and fire services have. It may equally be the case that these other essential services are being comparably stressed by the changes impacting rural communities.

In this regard, it should be noted that fire and EMS departments share a handicap regarding surge capability in that although they do have mutual assistance agreements with neighboring jurisdictions, they lack the "defense in depth" available to police from higher levels of government. In Virginia, for example, local police and sheriff's deputies can be augmented not only by trained state police (including those provided by specialized agencies, such as the Marine Police or the Department of Game and Inland Fisheries), but also

* http://www.vbrescuefoundation.org/wp-content/uploads/2014/09/RescueLines_Fall2014
  -FINAL-1-4.pdf

by troops of the National Guard and State Guard (Virginia Defense Force), many of whom are explicitly trained in police duties (such as traffic management and crowd control) appropriate to dealing with natural disasters. This backup is not present for fire or rescue personnel and cannot be solved by cross-training. In the case of a tornado, for example, fire department personnel will often have to deal with gas leaks and electrical faults and may be hard pressed to divert staff to the concomitant surge in EMS calls.

As shown by the example of the BRAVO Volunteer Ambulance Service, however, even large cities with professional EMS organizations can see benefits from the addition of volunteer EMS providers to the system. In Virginia Beach, the large volunteer EMS, directed and supplemented by paid professionals in senior positions (technical and training as well as managerial) has not only enabled significant cost savings, but has also provided for a surge capacity that would be simply impossible with a fully professionalized department. Moreover, it has supported the development of highly trained specialty response teams that could not be accommodated in any reasonable budget for a professional department.

References

Committee on the Future of Emergency Care in the United States, Health System, Board on Health Care Services, Institute of Medicine, *Emergency Medical Services at the Crossroads*, Washington, DC: National Academies Press, 2007.

HRSA, US Department of Health and Human Services, *Emergency Medical Services in Frontier Areas: Volunteer Community Organizations*, April 2006.

Montana Emergency Medical Services, *Report to Education and Local Government Interim Committee*, January 2016.

National Academy of Medicine, *Emergency Medical Services: At the Crossroads*, June 2006.

National Highway Traffic Safety Administration, *EMS Workforce for the 21st Century: A National Assessment*, Final Report, June 2008.

National Highway Traffic Safety Administration, *National EMS Assessment*, Final Draft 2011. Available from the National Association of State EMS Officials (https://www.nasemso.org/documents/National_EMS_Assessment_Final_Draft_12202011.pdf).

Rural Health Research and Policy Analysis Center of the University of North Carolina, *Rural Volunteer EMS: Reports from the Field*, Final Report No. 99, August 2010.

SafeTech Solutions, LLP, *A Crisis and Crossroad in Rural North Dakota Emergency Medical Services*, June 2011.

Conclusion VII

Using Volunteers in Policing
Final Thoughts and Recommendations

27

JAMES F. ALBRECHT

Contents

27.1 Considerations for a Police Volunteer Program

The chapters within this book have likely developed convincing support for the implementation and utilization of a volunteer program within a police organization. There are a variety of potential implementation options for using volunteers in the policing arena. These range from administrative assistance in a police facility to citizen neighborhood patrol to armed police reserves with full law enforcement authority. In addition, this book has highlighted the plethora of policies and practices in place, varying from the national guidelines in place in the United Kingdom (e.g., Special Constables) and Singapore to the state legislation that regulates police reserves in California (e.g., Los Angeles Police Department) to the local models observed in many counties and cities (e.g., New York City Police Department) across the United States.

Some critical issues have been raised as they relate to the use of volunteers by police administrators. Two primary issues are whether police volunteers should be armed and if they should be permitted to make lawful arrests in line with career police personnel. Considering either or both of these alternatives clearly places a large burden on local government and law enforcement leadership as neither option can be contemplated lightly. The commensurate responsibilities and liabilities are immense.

Although using volunteers to address certain agency tasks may appear to be a "bargain," a police administrator must ensure that the proper investment in time, training, and equipment is made in addition to strong efforts to guarantee that volunteer morale is maintained at an even pace. And in jurisdictions in which unions, police associations, and collective bargaining organizations are present, there may be strong resistance that must be properly addressed.

Two implementation alternatives likely will be looked upon positively by police executives. One involves the development of a reserve cadre of retired law enforcement personnel that could be called upon during crisis and large-scale events (e.g., Florida Highway Patrol Reserves and NYPD Retiree Mobilization Plan program). In most cases, training and equipment costs would be minimized, and the vast experiences and qualifications that these policing veterans have banked could be deployed to the benefit of the agency and the local community. In some states (e.g., Texas), these reserves are called upon on a part-time basis when needed, thereby saving the jurisdiction considerable cost.

A second alternative that many police leaders have instituted over the last few decades has been a "hybrid" model of law enforcement personnel who are paid employees who are normally unarmed but who have distinct arrest and enforcement authorities (e.g., NYPD School Safety Officers, NYPD Traffic Enforcement Officers, and Community Support Officers in the United Kingdom). Although not volunteers, per se, these resources would be lower cost options for jurisdictions. However, jurisdictions may face preliminary opposition if police unions or similar organizations are present.

Before developing or continuing a police volunteer program, a number of considerations must be evaluated in order to determine if using volunteers would be a good fit for that respective jurisdiction. Many of these issues and concerns are outlined below.

27.2 Police Volunteer Program Benefits and Goals

A police volunteer program can clearly achieve a number of benefits for the police agency, and these should be specifically delineated as goals for any of these initiatives. These benefits and goals include the following:

1. Community involvement in the law enforcement scheme
2. Enhanced information and intelligence gathering
3. Better community understanding of policing challenges
4. Increased crime prevention presence
5. Trial period for those interested in police employment

6. Improved community trust and agency transparency
7. Cost-efficient crime prevention
8. Specialized capabilities available when needed

Sir Robert Peel's original principles of policing (Lee, 1901), although developed in the 1820s, continue to provide the foundation for modern law enforcement practices. In particular, one tenet stands out as critical in today's world:

> To maintain at all times a relationship with the public that gives reality to the historic tradition that *the police are the public and that the public are the police,* the police being only members of the public who are paid to give full-time attention to duties which are incumbent on every citizen in the interests of community welfare and existence. (Lee, 1901)

As such, a police administrator must be guided by the input and demands of the community when contemplating management and deployment options. It is imperative that members of the neighborhoods being served play instrumental roles in organizational priorities. A number of volunteer program options would allow that possibility.

By enhancing public trust, it is expected that community members would come forward with critical information and criminal intelligence that would improve agency efficacy. And direct involvement and engagement would increase public understanding of the challenges that police administrators and frontline personnel routinely encounter. It is clear that any and all efforts that improve agency transparency and sincerity be strongly considered.

Using volunteers in neighborhood patrols, whether uniformed or not, should increase organizational omnipresence, if not only as extra eyes in the field, and should enhance crime prevention efforts at reduced cost if properly deployed. Extensive research has revealed that deploying volunteers in the field has resulted in notable declines in crime, and this impact has been found to be enduring (Wo, Hipp, & Boessen, 2016).

And in the era in which police budgets have been tightening, the use of volunteers in specific positions (e.g., cyber investigations, aviation and marine patrols, forensic accounting, etc.) would enhance agency effectiveness when dealing with seasonal or extraordinary events or investigations for which highly paid full-time staff cannot be financially supported. As many of the chapters have underscored, the tasks and responsibilities of the policing profession are extensive, and no law enforcement administrator should be left ultimately admitting that specific considerations or challenges will not be addressed. It is apparent that using volunteers to fit these unique roles would remedy this dilemma.

27.3 Potential Challenges and Concerns

Before developing or continuing a police volunteer program, a number of issues should be considered. Police administrators must comprehensively answer the following questions:

1. Will the use of police volunteers increase organizational effectiveness?
2. Will the use of police volunteers increase agency efficiency?
3. For which specific tasks could volunteers be used?
4. Are there any state or local laws or regulations that must be considered when contemplating the deployment of volunteers?
5. Can the police volunteer program increase organizational diversity (i.e., age, race, ethnicity, and community representation)?
6. Could there be any potential resistance to the use of volunteers (e.g., from unions, police associations, community groups, political organizations, special interest groups, etc.)?
7. How extensive will the screening process be?
8. How comprehensive will the training program be?
9. What commitment is expected of the volunteers?
10. Will the volunteers be armed?
11. Will the volunteers have enforcement powers?
12. What in-service training will be implemented?
13. What quality assurance and auditing measures will be utilized?
14. Will the volunteers have civil service protections like full-time personnel?
15. Will the volunteers receive any type of insurance, retirement, or service (e.g., decreased tax rate) benefits?
16. What measures will be taken to ensure that volunteer morale and satisfaction will remain elevated?
17. Is there funding available in the agency budget to ensure that a police volunteer program, incorporating all of the above considerations, can be properly developed and maintained?

The rewards of implementing a professional police volunteer program are obvious, but without thoroughly examining these and other important factors, the inherent benefits may never reach fruition.

27.4 Uniform Classification Scheme for Police Volunteers

The absence of uniform national or international definitions for the classification of the different types of police volunteers must be addressed. As has been outlined within the text, the terms "volunteer," "auxiliary," and "reserve" are often used interchangeably. Complicating this issue is that many of these labels have been specifically designated by state or local legislation or police organizational policy. In lieu of creating a standard title for specific roles, Wolf, Albrecht, and Dobrin (2015) have developed a practical typology for classifying police volunteers based on deployment task and law enforcement authority.

The tiered scheme for police volunteers can be divided into five distinct categories (Wolf, Albrecht, & Dobrin, 2015, p. 46):

- *Level 1*: Police agency volunteer (unarmed)/no arrest or law enforcement authority; this would include those with very minimal or no police training who are uniformed or nonuniformed personnel and who assist the agency with administrative duties, public relations events, minor traffic control duties, or other non-law enforcement functions.
- *Level 2*: Community patrol (unarmed)/no arrest or law enforcement authority; this would include those with some level of documented training who are uniformed or nonuniformed personnel who perform patrol activities and act as the "eyes and ears" of their policing agency. This level of personnel would not have any type of law enforcement function or authority granted.
- *Level 3*: Police patrol (unarmed)/some law enforcement powers; this would include those with partial to moderate levels of documented training, who are uniformed or nonuniformed personnel, who perform patrol activities, and who act as the "eyes and ears" of their policing agency, and have some type of law enforcement function or authority. This might include the ability to issue parking citations, write simple police reports, or similar functions.
- *Level 4*: Sworn volunteers (armed)/most law enforcement powers; this would include those with a significant amount of documented training who are uniformed or nonuniformed personnel who provide or can provide a law enforcement function. Their law enforcement authority or functions may be limited. For example, this might include individuals who have no authority to work alone or to take police action while off duty.
- *Level 5*: Sworn volunteers (armed)/all law enforcement powers; this would include uniformed or nonuniformed personnel who serve in a capacity equal to that of a full-time law enforcement officer. These individuals are not limited in their authority or responsibilities and follow the same regulations and have the same training as full-time law enforcement personnel.

Identifying volunteers by specific level as outlined above would eliminate the confusion often encountered when referring to program participants as reserve, auxiliary, or simply volunteer and when engaging in interagency discussions.

27.5 Findings and Recommendations

This book has resulted in significant findings and recommendations. The first is that, even when including the costs of developing and maintaining a police volunteer program (i.e., related to screening, training, equipment, and program maintenance), most jurisdictions have observed a dramatic cost savings, particularly when analyzing the manpower-hour costs that would have been incurred had the agency deployed career police personnel to those tasks. In addition, increasing the visible police presence through the use of identified volunteer patrols should have a positive impact on perceived community and officer safety.

The continuing call for more community involvement in law enforcement activities and operations can be addressed through the use of local volunteers. And implementing a police volunteer program would clearly fulfill many of the recommendations of the President's Task Force on 21st Century Policing. Community engagement would likely work wonders in enhancing citizen perceptions of the police and improving agency transparency. Police volunteer programs also have the potential to increase neighborhood esprit de corps and community cohesion.

In line with Peel's principles of policing (Lee, 1901), community advocates and police leaders should jointly assess the local needs to determine what type of police volunteer program or programs would be most appropriate to address those specific concerns. Once those issues have been identified, this book could be used as a resource to determine suitable deployment options. There is clearly no need to reinvent the wheel as there are many program models that can be borrowed from the many successful endeavors observed nationally and globally. In addition, relying on existing models will allow the program implementation team to examine the challenges and benefits previously observed in other jurisdictions.

As formerly noted, it is imperative that those responsible for developing police volunteer protocol and procedure examine the potential for resistance from certain community groups, political advocates, local unions and professional associations, or other sources. Enhanced neighborhood and officer safety should be highlighted as clear benefits, particularly when police budgets have been directed to do more with less.

The implementation of a tiered police volunteer program using the classification scheme highlighted above, which generally reflects the guidelines outlined within the California POST standards, should provide direction to those tasked with program coordination. For those jurisdictions seeking enhanced uniformed patrol from their police volunteers, it may be best to have at least one more category that permits volunteers to engage in administrative and other nonoperational tasks. And consideration must be made to balance the need for proper screening and training requirements with volunteer recruitment efficacy (i.e., longer mandatory training will result in a higher qualified officer but will limit the number of interested police volunteer applicants).

27.6 Summary

It should now be clear that establishing and maintaining a police volunteer program cannot be taken lightly, and many considerations must be analyzed in order to ensure that organizational efficacy, efficiency, and professionalism will be increased. However, it should also be obvious that making a quality investment into that police volunteer program has the potential to result in a productive and professional outcome, enhanced public safety and organizational transparency, and improved community engagement and involvement.

References

Lee, W. L. M. (1901). *A History of Police in England*. London: Methuan and Company.

Wo, J. C., Hipp, J. R., & Boessen, A. (2016). Volunteer Organizations and Neighborhood Crime: A Dynamic Perspective. *Criminology, 54*(2), 212–241.

Wolf, R., Albrecht, J. F., & Dobrin, A. (2015). Reserve Policing in the United States: Citizens Volunteering for Public Service. *The Police Chief, 82*, 38–47.

Index